D1369531

Private
Label
Strategy

Private Label Strategy

How to Meet the
Store Brand Challenge

Nirmalya Kumar
Jan-Benedict E. M. Steenkamp

HARVARD BUSINESS SCHOOL PRESS
Boston, Massachusetts

Library of Congress Cataloging-in-Publication Data

Kumar, Nirmalya.
   Private label strategy : how to meet the store brand challenge / Nirmalya
Kumar, Jan-Benedict E. M. Steenkamp.
      p. cm.
   ISBN-13: 978-1-4221-0167-4
   ISBN-10: 1-4221-0167-3
   1. Brand name products—Marketing. I. Steenkamp, Jan-Benedict E. M.
II. Title.
   HD69.B7K855 2006
   658.8'27—dc22

                          2006023780

To Pratibha

My mother; successful brand extensions

need strong mother brands

—NK

To Valarie

My soulmate, who shows me each day

what love is all about

—JBS

CONTENTS

BOTH OF US GREW UP in a world dominated by manufacturer brands. Brands were everywhere and defined the lives of people as consumers. However, over time, we started to notice a change in the retailscape. More and more retail stores were carrying products with their own label. At the same time, many mom-and-pop stores disappeared, usually acquired or replaced by large chain stores.

In our student days, spurred by a tight budget constraint, we increasingly turned to private labels to save money. We discovered that the quality of store brands was actually better than we had expected. Since then, we have continued to regularly purchase private labels. Private labels have become a permanent feature in our shopping repertoire, mirroring their growing success in industries ranging from food to tires, from over-the-counter drugs to financial services, from household-care products to do-it-yourself products.

In our subsequent academic career, as marketing professors, who are supposed to systematically examine marketplace behavior, we observed three surprising facts regarding private labels. First, the private label phenomenon had received little attention by marketing scholars. Despite the fact that, in many industries, private labels represent formidable competition to manufacturer brands, most research continues to ignore private labels. Instead, the marketing community focuses predominantly on manufacturer brands.

Second, and even more astonishingly, as consultants to many of the largest and best-run brand manufacturers, we found that these companies tended to systematically underestimate the private label threat. Benchmarking by famous brands was usually against other manufacturer brands. It was as if private labels did not exist. This made it rather difficult, if not impossible, to obtain detailed information on private label performance and quality. The prevailing mind-set at brand manufacturers was that private labels were inferior products that consumers would tire of quickly. They were not worthy competitors.

As we discussed with each other the looming threat and success of private labels, we began to see an opportunity for compiling our experiences and knowledge of store brands into an easily accessible book. This is when we made our third startling discovery. Despite the fact that private labels had become a trillion-dollar industry, there did not exist a single book on private labels published by a major publisher and written by an experienced practitioner or academic. Our book hopes to fill this void.

Drawing on our own and other academic research, trade publications, and our consulting experience, we analyze retailer strategies for private labels and challenge brand manufacturers to develop an effective response. We lay out actionable strategies for competing against, or collaborating with, private label purveyors. Our book contains many detailed international case studies, visuals, and hands-on tools, to enable managers to navigate profitably in this radically altered landscape.

Our insights did not emerge overnight. Rather, they were formed and reshaped over the last ten years, especially based on our consulting work and our teaching in executive seminars around the world. This allowed us to refine our insights into retailer strategies vis-à-vis private labels, and into the effectiveness of various counterstrategies developed by brand manufacturers. But let us caution the reader up front. The sources of private label strengths are many and changing, like the multiheaded Hydra of

Greek mythology. Our years of working with brand manufacturers have taught us that there is no silver bullet.

There is no single answer that will solve the brand manufacturers' problems vis-à-vis private labels. Whatever marketing consultants or gurus may claim, no such magic potion exists. But through hard work and consistent effort, the private label threat can be addressed head-on by pursuing seven strategic thrusts: change the mind-set, partner effectively, innovate brilliantly, fight selectively, price competitively, improve quality constantly, and market creatively. And why not? Today's brand manager is in good company. After all, Hercules did not kill the Hydra with a magic bullet but by changing his mind-set (his initial approach did not work), through hard work, by following a consistent and innovative strategy, in conjunction with a partner.

ACKNOWLEDGMENTS

THIS BOOK is the result of a long odyssey through the volatile waters of retailers, brand manufacturers, and private labels. We had the good fortune of being able to rely on trustworthy beacons on this journey. Many colleagues, companies, and marketing practitioners have made an invaluable contribution in making this book a reality.

We owe much gratitude to the marketing discipline in general for the insights generated on private labels, and to a number of colleagues in particular. The contributions of Kusum Ailawadi (Dartmouth College), Bob Blattberg (Northwestern University), Steve Burgess (University of Cape Town), Pradeep Chintagunta (University of Chicago), Daniel Corsten (London Business School), Barbara Deleersnyder (Erasmus University), Bruce Hardie (London Business School), Jean-Noel Kapferer (HEC Paris), Philip Kotler (Northwestern University), Don Lehmann (Columbia University), Kash Rangan (Harvard University), Lou Stern (Northwestern University), Nader Tavassoli (London Business School), and Naufel Vilcassim (London Business School) were especially helpful.

Special thanks are owed to four colleagues, who have been our intellectual sparring partners over the last ten to fifteen years. Katrijn Gielens' (Erasmus University) knowledge of retailing is phenomenal. She has provided us with many important insights that have significantly influenced this book. Marnik Dekimpe (Tilburg University) and Lisa Scheer (University of Missouri) have been our long-standing collaborators for projects on branding, private labels, and distribution. Their capacity to identify weak spots in our arguments and to come up with sound alternatives is truly astonishing. Last but not least, we have had the privilege to work closely with Inge Geyskens (Tilburg University) on many projects involving marketing channels and private labels. She generously shared her insights with us during the entire span of this project.

This book has benefited greatly from our association with three stellar academic institutions: London Business School, University of North Carolina at Chapel Hill, and Tilburg University. We are grateful to the deans of these schools, Laura Tyson, Steve Jones and Douglas Shackelford, and Theo Verhallen, respectively, for generously providing us with resources to work on this book. We learned a lot by teaching at the executive programs of these schools and by interacting with our faculty colleagues.

This book would not have been possible without the close collaboration with a large number of companies. Over the years, we have worked with numerous companies to test our ideas in the real world. Adidas, Ahold, Akzo Nobel, Auchan, Danone, Dow Chemical, Foodworld, GfK, Goodyear, Holcim, Johnson & Johnson, Kraft, Nestlé, Philip Morris, Procter & Gamble, Reckitt Benckiser, Sara Lee, TetraPak, TNS, and Unilever have been especially supportive.

We are grateful to a number of individual managers who have provided us with specific feedback and information, including Thomas Bachl (GfK), Jerome Boesch (Danone), Ian Crook (Tesco), Richard Herbert (Europanel), Christopher Knee (International Association of Department Stores), Ken Lazarus (Cape Union Mart), Judith Puigbo (Apli), and Karel Smit (IRI). Paul Polman (Nestlé, formerly at P&G) has been a true visionary on private labels, being one of the first top managers to regard them as brands in their own right rather than being cheap knock-offs. The support of Alfred Dijs (GfK) and Dick Valstar (GfK) over the last fifteen years has been invaluable. Without their support, this book would not have been possible.

Kirsten Sandberg and Julia Ely of Harvard Business School Press were wonderful in their continuous and enthusiastic support of this book, right from the beginning. Their "hands-on" attitude was much appreciated. Daisy Hutton, Zeenat Potia, Anand P. Raman, Sarah Weaver, and Leslie Zheutlin of HBSP also played key roles in making this book happen. We thank Sophie Linguri and Akhila Venkitachalam for their superb research assistance. We are grateful for the secretarial support provided by Heidi van de Borne, Jeannette Khalil, Yasmine Redman, Margaret Walls, and Suseela Yesudian-Storfjell.

Finally, we want to acknowledge all those executives who work hard every day of their lives, at either retail or manufacturing organizations, trying to build or beat private labels. If they find this book useful, it will be worth all of our efforts.

— *Nirmalya Kumar*
   Jan-Benedict E. M. Steenkamp

ONE

Brands Under Attack from Private Labels

Worldwide annual private label sales:
One trillion dollars

THE TWENTIETH CENTURY was the century of manufacturer brands. Consumers moved from no-name products of inconsistent quality produced by local factories in the nineteenth century to branded products from global manufacturers led by Coca-Cola, Disney, Johnnie Walker Scotch whiskey, Johnson & Johnson's baby powder, Kraft's Jell-O, Levi's jeans, Procter & Gamble's Ivory soap, Nestlé's infant formula, and Unilever's Sunlight soap. These manufacturer brands used emerging media—first newspapers, billboards, and radio; later television and the Internet—to market their message effectively. The branded message to consumers was one of smart shopping—brands are trustworthy, delivering quality, consistency, and innovation at a fair price. Initially, consumers bought manufacturer-endorsed brands as symbols of quality, trust, and affluence. Subsequently, these brands were consumed as symbols of aspirations, images, and lifestyles.

Manufacturer brands reached consumers through distributors and retailers. For most of the twentieth century, retailers were relatively small, compared with their largest suppliers. This allowed branded manufacturers to ride a wave of quality products, innovation, and mass advertising to establish their power over distribution channels. Manufacturers exploited this power over retailers by becoming branded bulldozers, forcing retailers to accept their products with the associated price and promotion policies.[1] Retailers were usually given the classic "take it or leave it" choice.

Ascendancy of Retailers and Private Labels

Sometime in the 1970s, things began to change, albeit slowly, as retailers started to develop national chains. Some retailers, like Ahold, Carrefour, and Metro, even began to expand internationally, and consolidation of the retail industry from mom-and-pop stores to global players was well under way. Spurred by these pioneers, retailers of consumer packaged goods (CPG), such as Aldi, Auchan, Costco, Lidl, Makro, Tesco, and Wal-Mart, plunged eagerly into global markets over the last two decades of the previous millennium.

Retailers Now Dominate Manufacturers on Size

The bulking up of retailers that started then has changed the balance of power between brand manufacturers and retailers. Twenty-five years ago, the large CPG manufacturers would dwarf their retail customers in size. This is no longer the case. Retailers have now seized the size advantage and the negotiating power that flows from it (see table 1-1).[2]

The shift in the balance of power is not limited to CPG products, since the world's largest retailers also sell significant volumes of non-CPG products. The most striking example is Wal-Mart, whose global sales on non-CPG products are over $150 billion. Non-CPG products also account for a significant amount of sales

TABLE 1-1

Retailers dominate manufacturers on size

	RETAILERS			MANUFACTURERS	
Company	Total sales ($ billion)	Private label %	Private label sales ($ billion)	Sales ($ billion)	Company
1. Wal-Mart	316	40	126	75	1. Nestlé
2. Carrefour	94	25	24	69	2. Altria
3. Metro Group	73	35	26	57	3. P&G
4. Tesco	71	50	36	51	4. Johnson & Johnson
5. Kroger	61	24	15	50	5. Unilever
6. Royal Ahold	56	48	27	33	6. PepsiCo
7. Costco	53	10	5	26	7. Tyson Foods
8. Target	53	32	17	23	8. CocaCola
9. Rewe	51	25	13	20	9. Sara Lee
10. Aldi	43	95	41	18	10. L'Oréal
11. Schwarz Group	43	65	28	18	11. Japan Tobacco
12. ITM (Intermarché)	42	34	14	17	12. Danone

Source: Derived from M+M Planet Retail, 2005; "Fortune Global 500," *Fortune*, July 24, 2006, 113–120; and authors' own calculations and estimates.

of other retail giants, like America's Target ($38 billion) and Costco ($18 billion), Germany's Metro ($32 billion) and Rewe ($10 billion), Japan's Ito-Yokado ($18 billion) and AEON ($20 billion), France's Carrefour ($6 billion), Auchan ($17 billion), and Intermarché ($10 billion), and Britain's Tesco ($11 billion).[3]

Specialty retailers such as Benetton, Best Buy, Fnac, H&M, Home Depot, IKEA, Virgin Superstores, and Zara have also gone global. They have successfully identified global segments in what were fragmented markets, presumably governed by local tastes.

For example, Toys "R" Us caters to the global need of "Moms all want the best for their children: high-quality products and toys that promote learning, spark imagination, and are just plain fun." It has grown into an $11 billion behemoth with approximately sixteen hundred stores in thirty countries.[4] It leverages its worldwide knowledge in areas such as marketing, store operations, and merchandising to give its subsidiaries around the world a clear competitive advantage.

Private Labels Are Growing Faster Than Manufacturer Brands

Private labels have been around for a long time. A&P in the U.S. with its Eight O'Clock Breakfast Coffee and Marks & Spencer in the U.K. with its St. Michael brand have been purveying their own brands for more than a century. Yet, despite some significant exceptions, private labels were seen as poor cousins to the manufacturer brands, with a small share of the overall market that was considered unlikely to become significant. Manufacturers of branded products therefore have been taken aback by the unexpected and continued increase in private label share since the 1970s. A striking example is Germany, Europe's largest economy and the third-largest economy in the world. Private label share increased over the last three decades from 12 percent to a whopping 34 percent!

Retailer private labels, often also referred to as own labels, store brands, or distributor-owned brands, have also grown strongly in other markets. In the U.S., for example, private labels have outperformed manufacturer brands in all but one of the last ten years. They now account for 20 percent of U.S. sales in supermarkets and mass merchandisers as well as a healthy share of sales in department stores, category killers, specialty stores, and convenience stores.[5]

If one examines more closely the share of private labels at the twelve largest retailers in the world, shown in table 1-1, the future looks bleak for manufacturer brands. With the exception of Costco, private labels at these retailers account for more than the overall 20 percent share that private labels generate in the U.S. Increasing consolidation in the retail industry implies that these global retailers are growing faster than the overall market.

But even more, almost every retailer, large or small, wishes to increase the share of its private labels. For example, Coles, the Australian supermarket chain, has declared its intention to increase private label share of its turnover from 13 percent to 30 percent in the near future.[6] In addition, new retail concepts, like the hard discount format of Aldi and Lidl, have emerged, focusing predominantly on private labels and eschewing manufacturer brands. In the U.S., two fast-emerging retailers, Whole Foods and Trader Joe's, also concentrate on private labels. Doug Rauch, president of Trader Joe's, which carries 80 percent private labels, was quoted as saying that it started creating its own products so "we could put our destiny in our own hands."[7]

Not surprisingly, private labels are growing rapidly in the first decade of the twenty-first century. Table 1-2 shows that overall private label *share* as a percentage of the total consumer packaged goods industry is anticipated to grow by more than 50 percent, from 14 percent to 22 percent. The already-developed private label markets of Australasia (greater than 50 percent growth), North America (35 percent plus), and western Europe (increase of 50 percent) will continue to show strong growth as retailers consolidate their gains. And this growth in private label share in these markets is often at the expense of manufacturer brands. For example, for the U.S. in 2005, private label sales of vinegar were up 2 percent to lead the category, while Heinz was second with sales down almost 10 percent.

The less-developed private label markets in table 1-2, Japan and the emerging economies, are anticipated to grow even faster in terms of private label share, albeit from a low baseline. Consumer attitudes toward private labels are already remarkably positive in these regions.[8] Since emerging countries are experiencing higher economic growth, it implies that overall growth in private label sales may be in the double digits. Moreover, this trend is not likely

TABLE 1-2

Consumer packaged goods private label share

	PRIVATE LABEL SHARE (% OF SALES)	
	2000	**Expected 2010**
Worldwide	**14**	**22**
Western Europe	20	30
Central and Eastern Europe	1	7
North America	20	27
Latin America	3	9
Australasia	15	22
Japan	2	10
China	0.1	3
South Africa	6	14

Source: Adapted from M+M Planet Retail, 2004, http://www.planetretail.net/.

to stop in 2010. In the subsequent decade, as global retailers aggressively expand internationally, emerging economies will become the key battlegrounds between private labels and manufacturer brands.

Private Labels Are Ubiquitous

The three best-selling private label categories in food and nonfood may still be predictable—milk, eggs, and bread in food; food storage and trash bags, cups and plates, and toilet tissue in nonfood. However, today's large and sophisticated retailers are able to develop credible private label offerings for categories where traditionally customers were more wary of straying from their favorite manufacturer brand names. Nowadays, store brands are present in over 95 percent of consumer packaged goods categories.[9] Among the fastest-growing categories for private label sales are lipstick, facial moisturizers, and baby food.[10] Even a wholesale club store like Costco, which generally focuses on bulk products, is developing a line of private label cosmetics.

The preceding discussion may mislead the reader into believing that the private label phenomenon is restricted to CPG products and grocery retailers. This is simply not true. Best-in-class retailers and distributors such as Best Buy, Boots, Decathlon, Federated, Gap, IKEA, Home Depot, Lowe's, Office Depot, Staples, Target, Toys "R" Us, Victoria's Secret, and Zara carry a large percentage of, or in some cases exclusively, private labels. The number and types of retailers and distributors that fall under the private label spell continue to increase. Consider three diverse examples.

Apparel is one of the largest sectors for private labels. Private label or store brands now account for 45 percent of total U.S. apparel unit sales, up from 39 percent just two years ago and 35 percent five years ago. In categories like women's skirts and children's clothing, the share of private labels is more than 65 percent.[11] This is partially driven by the resounding success of several private-label-only retail formats such as Gap, H&M, The Limited, and Zara. In response to the value provided by such specialty retailers, upscale department stores like Bloomingdale's and Macy's are also increasing their percentage of sales from store brand merchandise.

Books might seem an unlikely category for private labels. Yet, Barnes & Noble plans to generate 10 to 12 percent of its total sales from private label by 2008. Barnes & Noble began publishing out-of-print books before moving to richly illustrated coffee-table books on gardening, cooking, and lifestyle. In 2002, it dropped the popular CliffsNotes study guide series published by John Wiley and replaced it with its own SparkNotes series, priced at a dollar less. In 2003, the Barnes & Noble Classics series, featuring titles like *Huckleberry Finn* and *Moby Dick*, was expanded into a variety of hardcover and paperback formats in direct competition to Random House's Modern Library and Pearson's Penguin Classics lines.[12]

Financial services may seem very far from the retail world, but private labels abound in the industry. For example, the private label credit card market is overcrowded, with General Electric, Wells Fargo, Citibank, and Bank One among the players that allow retailers to offer store-branded credit cards while managing the entire operation for them. Financial supermarkets like Fidelity and Charles Schwab carry third-party managed funds while simultaneously selling their own funds to investors.

As a result of the success in private labels around the world and in various industries, global private label sales now approach *one trillion dollars*, and counting.

The Transformation of Private Labels

Traditionally, the image that private labels evoked was of white packages with the words *toilet paper*, *beans*, or *laundry detergent* embossed in plain black typeface on them, found somewhere at the bottom of store shelves. Such private labels were "a cheap and nasty substitute for the real thing."[13] But times are changing.

Private Labels Compete on Quality

While low-quality private label products still exist, there is no denying that private labels have made great strides in quality. *Consumer Reports* magazine ranked Winn-Dixie's chocolate ice cream ahead of Breyers, Wal-Mart's Sam's Choice better than Tide detergent, and Kroger's potato chips tastier than Ruffles and Pringles. At the 2005 annual Christmas wine Oscars in the U.K., Tesco Premier Cru, at less than £15 a bottle, was named the best nonvintage champagne. It beat in blind taste tests famous names such as Tattinger and Lanson that can cost twice the price.

A recent German study compared technical characteristics and quality across fifty consumer product categories.[14] In more than half of these categories, the hard discounter private labels (e.g., Aldi, Lidl) rivaled or exceeded the quality of manufacturer brands. Albert Heijn's Excellent, Safeway's Select, Wal-Mart's Sam's Choice, and Vons's Royal Request are some store brands dedicated to high-quality products by retailers. And the risk for consumers to try these private labels keeps decreasing since retailers like Kroger scream, "Try it, like it or get the national brand free!"

Not content with their success, retailers keep raising their quality aspirations. In 2003, Terry Lundgren, chief executive of Federated, which owns the Bloomingdale's and Macy's department stores, observed, "We can sell the highest-end, highest-quality and the most-expensive product carried in the store under a private label." Thus, Hotel Collection by Charter Club, a Macy's own label, sells $1,350 duvets and $275 pillowcases.[15] Similarly, Gap has introduced the 1969 label, which retails at twice the price of most Gap jeans, while The Limited has launched Seven7 jeans to compete against designer jeans by Calvin Klein, Diesel, and Hugo Boss.[16]

Private Labels Are Brands

Brands give us meaning in our role as consumers. Consumers want brands for the quality assurance and the emotional satisfaction they provide. Any product that is not a brand will inherently have limited market appeal. However, brands do not necessarily have to be *manufacturer* brands. They can also be *store* brands. And this is what has happened over the last decade as retailers became bigger and more sophisticated and their private labels became more ubiquitous and successful—providing the necessary mass for investments in branding activities. Retailers now position their private labels as brands in their own right. Their store brands are increasingly imbued with emotion and imagery rather than only with the functional logic that dominated private labels a generation ago.

In contrast to the traditional generic product, picture Texas grocery chain H-E-B's slender glass bottle of Harvest Moon asparagus spears with an elegant label (a soft crescent moon) that makes the Del Monte canned product sitting next to it look cheap.[17] Or consider Decathlon, a 331-store sports equipment retailer that generates over $3.5 billion in sales.[18] It has increased private label share from 33 percent to over 50 percent in a dozen years.[19] Decathlon has developed seven passion brands. The idea behind these own brands is that they are passionate about sports and capture how their customers feel about sports. Each passion brand is developed with a universe in mind. For example, Tribord is all about the water universe focused on sports such as diving, sailing, and surfing, while Quechua targets the mountain universe with sports such as skiing, hiking, and mountain climbing. These are the store brands with which Decathlon is effectively competing against its branded suppliers, like Nike.

Perhaps the best example is Swedish home furnishings retailer IKEA, which "has become a curator of people's lifestyle, if not their lives." Many of the 1.1 *million* customers who visit an IKEA store on an average day consider a store visit fun rather than a chore. IKEA has become an experiential destination, translating into fierce consumer loyalty: "IKEA makes me free to become what I want to be," notes a Romanian customer. And consider a U.S. customer: "Half my house is from IKEA—and the nearest store is six hours away." Given such loyalty, it is not surprising that IKEA's operating margins of 10 percent are among the best in home furnishings and considerably higher than U.S. competitors Pier 1 (5 percent) and Target (8 percent). However, there is still considerable room for growth. As IKEA's CEO Anders Dahlvig notes, "Awareness of our brand is much bigger than the size of our company."[20]

Initiatives to create store brand value are not limited to Western retailers. A compelling example from emerging markets is South Africa's outdoor-equipment retailer Cape Union Mart, with outlets in South Africa, Botswana, and Namibia. Over 80 percent of total sales are own labels. Cape Union Mart has developed an elaborate line of three private labels, catering to different market segments. K-Way is an aspirational brand used for technical clothing and equipment; Old Khaki is a high-fashion range of clothing but styled along the work-wear concept; Cape Union is the mainstream brand, good quality but not suitable for expeditions.

Cape Union Mart adds significant value to its private labels by providing unique in-store experiences. Equipment can be tested on an indoor climbing wall and in a cave. A 12-meter (40-foot) waterfall runs over rocks and forms the backdrop to the shoe department. The running water is soothing and evokes memories of camping trips, with the sound of raging rivers enhancing the core theme of "escapism"—escape from stress. A compelling feature is the two weather chambers, one for customers to test waterproof garments in wet conditions and the other for extreme cold (with a high wind chill factor of –15°C, or 5°F). As design director Ken Lazarus of Cape Union Mart says, "By providing compelling in-store experiences coupled with well priced private-label premium quality merchandise, Cape Union Mart has been able to achieve a successful retail model over other retailers selling comparable manufacturer brands."[21]

Growing Consumer Acceptance of Private Labels

The transformation in private labels has not gone unnoticed by consumers. The improvement in store brands has made them an acceptable purchase alternative for large groups of consumers. Two out of three consumers *around the world* believe that "supermarket own brands are a good alternative to other brands."[22]

Private Label Purchase as Smart Shopping

In line with these positive perceptions, consumers increasingly are seeking store brands. In 2001, 45 percent of shoppers were more likely to switch to a store brand, up from 31 percent in 1996. Moreover, 70 percent of people responsible for household shopping wish that store brand products were available in as wide a selection as branded products. And 54 percent say that they plan to buy more private label products in the future.[23]

Given these attitudes, it is not unexpected to learn that virtually every household in countries like the U.S., U.K., and Germany purchased private label products in the past year. Some of the changes in customer behavior are quite subtle. For example, in the past, consumers were reluctant to buy private label apparel from supermarkets. In the U.K., in five years, Asda has managed to increase the percentage of its customers who buy clothes from 8 percent to one in three.[24] This has propelled the company into becoming Britain's biggest clothing retailer. Clearly, private labels have come a long way from being the ugly ducklings, as compared with their more glamorous and heavily advertised manufacturer-branded rivals.[25]

In the past, private labels were primarily targeted to the poor. Today, while the poor still buy private labels more often than other consumers, one observes even wealthy consumers purchasing store brands.[26] Increasingly, it is considered "smart" shopping to purchase private label products of (supposedly) comparable quality for a much lower price, rather than being "ripped off" by high-priced manufacturer brands. Germans call this tendency "stinginess is brill" (i.e., stinginess is "brilliant").

Smart shopping is not confined to CPGs. In Germany alone, Aldi sells over $6 billion in consumer durables each year, and it is one of the top sellers of such products as PCs and camping equipment.[27] Germany's electronics retailer Saturn has as its slogan "*Geiz ist Geil*" ("Thrifty is sexy"), and a Google search on this slogan yielded 739,000 hits.[28] Discount electronics retailer Media Market has as its slogan "*Ich bin doch nicht blöd*" ("I'm not stupid"). The *Financial Times* notes that in apparel, "shopping is about 'smart consumerism' now . . . there's even a kind of 'one-downmanship' about finding something that's better value."[29]

This trend of private label purchase as smart shopping can also be observed in apparel, where chains like Target (with its Mizrahi line) and Zara cater to the "cheap chic" phenomenon. Even discount giant Wal-Mart benefits from this trend, although to a lesser extent than Target. Eighteen percent of Wal-Mart shoppers have a household income exceeding $70,000.[30]

As a result, private labels have become widely accepted. Their purchase is now driven by much more than simply a desire to economize on expenditures. Private label buyers are found among all socioeconomic strata and in all product categories. They are seen as thoughtful shoppers, who compare manufacturer brands versus store brands, are not easily influenced by advertising, and take pride in their decision-making ability.[31]

Private Labels Are Not a Recessionary Phenomenon

Although private label shares have increased in all developed economies in the last twenty to thirty years, the growth trajectory has not been linear. On the contrary, it has often been speculated that private label buying is something that occurs in recessions. Harvard professor John Quelch argued, "Private label generally goes up when the economy is suffering and down in stronger economic periods."[32] The *Economist* observed that for a long time, consumers regarded private labels as a "cheap and nasty substitute for the real thing, rolled out by retailers during recessions and discarded once the economy picked up again."[33] The German weekly *Stern* wrote, "The harder the times, the better off Aldi is."[34] Thus, past received wisdom was that private label buying is for recessionary times.

A systematic examination of data from four countries (United States, United Kingdom, Germany, and Belgium) spanning multiple decades indeed reveals that private label share increases during recessions and decreases during periods of economic expansion.[35] However, these changes are asymmetric. Private label share increases faster and more extensively during a recession than it falls in the subsequent expansionary phase. In fact, the net increase in private label share in recessions is not completely compensated for by its net decline in expansionary times. Part of private label growth in a recession is *permanent*, caused by consumer learning. As consumers learn about the improved quality of private labels in recessions, a significant proportion of them remain loyal to private labels, even after the necessity to economize on expenditures is over. The onward march of private labels continues across business cycles.

From Manufacturer Brand Loyalty to Store Loyalty

Growing consumer acceptance of store brands results in decreased loyalty to well-known manufacturer brands. A study of American lifestyles indicated that the percentage of twenty- to twenty-nine-year-old consumers who said they stuck to well-known brands fell from 66 percent in 1975 to 59 percent in 2000.[36] More surprisingly, the percentage for sixty- to sixty-nine-year-olds declined from 86 percent to 59 percent. Another U.S. study encompassing such disparate product areas as groceries, apparel, toys, and consumer electronics found that in the last fifteen years, brand loyalty had declined in ten out of the fifteen product areas included.[37]

This does not, however, mean that loyalty is a thing of the past, as is often alleged. Consumers can be, and are, loyal, but not necessarily to manufacturer brands. Increasingly, consumers are first and foremost loyal to a specific retailer. Retailers like Whole Foods in the United States, De Bijenkorf in the Netherlands, Marks & Spencer in the United Kingdom, Auchan in France, El Corte Inglés in Spain, Delhaize in Belgium, Loblaws in Canada, and Aldi in Germany generate intense levels of loyalty among large groups of shoppers. As a result, most consumers first think of Home Depot, the leading retailer, rather than American Standard or Kohler, the leading brand manufacturers, when they have to replace a faucet in their bathroom. Consumers may not be more promiscuous. They have simply transferred some of their loyalty from manufacturer brands to retailers. And private labels, being a unique feature of the retailer in question, are important in forging loyalty to the store.

Examining brand loyalty versus store loyalty for scores of CPG categories among consumers in four continents, we found that about one-third of the consumers are store loyal, half of the consumers are brand loyal, and the remainder are undecided.[38] However, there is considerable variation across categories. Store loyalty is lower in personal care than in household care and food and beverages. Personal care is typically much higher on imagery, motivating consumers to purchase exactly the brand and item they want.

Manufacturer Brands Under Attack

The preceding developments in private labels and the response by consumers have put tremendous growth and profitability pressure on manufacturer brands. In a recent survey, only 29 percent of

U.S. consumers agreed that manufacturer brands are worth the price premium, while only 16 percent believed that store brands are not as good as manufacturer brands.[39] And any social stigma associated with store brands seems to have vanished, since only 6 percent of consumers in the survey reported that they don't feel comfortable serving store brand items in their home.

The benign environment of consolidated media channels and fragmented distribution channels that propelled the rise of manufacturer brands has transformed into a very different landscape populated by fragmented media and consolidated distribution. It is now harder and more expensive for manufacturers to reach consumers directly through media.

Simultaneously, a handful of retailers in any country are increasingly controlling access to the majority of shoppers. Instead of the old TV networks, it is these retailers today that have become the mass channel for communicating to consumers. When combined with their private label threat to branded manufacturers, retailers have the power to seize a larger share of the system profits.

System Profits Migrate to Retailers

A study by The Boston Consulting Group demonstrated the profit implications of private labels and consolidation of retail in the U.S. grocery industry.[40] Between 1996 and 2003, retailers gained five share points of the combined manufacturer and retailer profit pool and more than 50 percent of the *system profit growth*. During this period, manufacturers' total market capitalization grew only 4 percent, well below the 19 percent growth in the S&P 500. Similarly, in the U.K. food industry, as the private label share has increased from 25 percent to 45 percent between 1982 and 2000, the retailers' share of profits has gone from 18 percent to 38 percent, with the manufacturers correspondingly seeing a decline of 20 percentage points in their share of the industry profit pool.[41]

The future will be even more challenging for manufacturer brands, especially if trends in the U.S. follow those of the more advanced European private label markets. Despite the sophistication of its retailers, and contrary to the belief of many U.S. managers, the U.S. is actually *not* leading in private label. To illustrate this point, figure 1-1 plots the *actual* private label share in a country against its private label share as *predicted* by the country's business environment, for thirty-one countries. A position above the 45-degree slope indicates overperformance, meaning that the actual private label share is *higher* than might be expected accord-

FIGURE 1-1

Country private label success chart

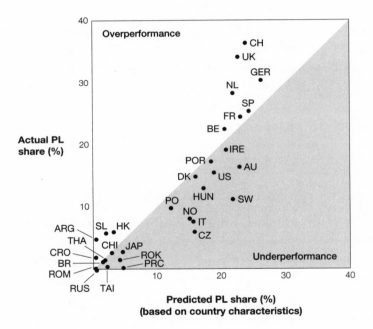

Legend

ARG	Argentina	DK	Denmark	NO	Norway	SW	Sweden
AU	Austria	FR	France	PO	Poland	TAI	Taiwan
BE	Belgium	GER	Germany	POR	Portugal	THA	Thailand
BR	Brazil	HK	Hong Kong	PRC	China	UK	United
CH	Switzerland	HUN	Hungary	ROK	Korea		Kingdom
CHI	Chile	IRE	Ireland	ROM	Romania	US	United
CRO	Croatia	IT	Italy	RUS	Russia		States
CZ	Czech	JAP	Japan	SL	Slovakia		
	Republic	NL	Netherlands	SP	Spain		

Source: AiMark, 2006; http://www.aimark.org/. Reproduced with permission.

ing to the country's characteristics.[42] On the other hand, a position below the 45-degree slope indicates underperformance: actual private label share is *lower* than might be expected based on the country's characteristics.

Figure 1-1 shows that the U.S. is *underperforming* relative to its country characteristics. Why is that the case?[43] One factor is the unusually large size of the U.S., both economically and geographically. This has historically benefited brand manufacturers that could use national advertising to reach huge audiences. The emergence of large nationwide retailers is a relatively recent phenomenon. Even today, many U.S. supermarkets and drugstores are regional players. As a consequence, the retail trade in the U.S. is still much less concentrated than in other developed countries. For example, the combined market share of the top five grocery retailers in the U.S. is less than 30 percent, versus 68 percent in Germany. This has given branded goods manufacturers the upper hand in terms of economies of scale in scale and scope (e.g., advertising).

Moreover, in the U.S., store brands have traditionally received less managerial attention than in Europe. This is due to the strong position of manufacturer brands, low concentration in U.S. retailing, and the less positive image of retailers as employers. In a recent survey among thirty thousand American undergraduates on students' ideal employer, not a single retailer made it into the top fifteen.[44] Compare this with similar surveys in Europe, where year after year, retailers like Carrefour, Marks & Spencer, IKEA, H&M, Zara, Tesco, and Royal Ahold are among the most sought-after employers. Developing strong private label programs requires significant expertise, and retailers are typically not the most preferred employer for the best and brightest in the U.S.

These factors holding back private label success in the U.S. are bound to change through continuing retail consolidation. If the U.S. closes the private label development gap with the U.K. by half, manufacturers will lose tens of billions of dollars in annual sales, and billions of dollars in operating profits will migrate to retailers.

Brand Manufacturers Need to Rethink Strategy

Famous brands, brand icons, industry leaders—nothing is exempt from the pressures from private labels. For example, Mattel's Hot Wheels $0.89 toy cars have seen their sales flag in the U.S. because of increased competition from private labels.[45] In Germany, Tropicana experienced a devastating slide in its volume share from 20 percent in 2000 to 2 percent in 2004 because of cannibalization by private labels.[46]

The rise of private labels and retailer power has forced major brand manufacturers to rethink their strategies. The *New York Times* ran a story in early 2005 titled "What's Behind the Procter Deal? Wal-Mart." The article cited the strong sales and new innovations of store brands at Wal-Mart as a possible factor for the $57 billion acquisition of Gillette by Procter & Gamble.[47] In February 2006, Kraft Foods, Inc., the maker of Oreo cookies and Oscar Mayer lunch meat, announced it was closing twenty plants and laying off as many as eight thousand workers as private labels ate away at its sales.[48]

The manufacturer challenge is exacerbated by the inherent conflict for manufacturers between retailers as customers and retailers as competitors. The areas of conflict are legion. Retailers are inclined to devote the best shelf space to their own brands, while manufacturers obviously disagree. Retailers may feel (often incorrectly, as shown in chapter 6) that they benefit from a large price gap between their own private label and leading manufacturer brands, while manufacturers are wary of such a strategy. Manufacturers desire a high pass-through for their price promotions, while retailers may feel that they gain more by pocketing these promotions rather than passing them on to customers, especially since the profitability of many promotions for retailers is small at best.[49]

Both manufacturers and retailers benefit from product innovations by brand manufacturers, but retailers often want to copy these innovations as soon as possible. This creates an interesting conundrum. Guilbert is the leading distributor of office supplies to business customers in western Europe and is now owned by America's Office Depot. Besides manufacturer brands, it markets the private label Niceday, which includes many office products such as staplers, writing pads, and pens. On the one hand, in 2003, it presented its supplier 3M's Post-it Notes with Guilbert's Product of the Year award in the U.K. On the other hand, one of the most popular Niceday products is a cheaper imitation of Post-it Notes.

Sometimes, the conflict may be less friendly. In the U.K., a major dispute arose between Coca-Cola and J. Sainsbury. Sainsbury's own Classic Cola closely imitated the signs and colors of Classic Coke and captured 17 percent of the British cola market within six months of its introduction. In 2005, Unilever sued Dutch retailer Albert Heijn (a daughter of Royal Ahold) for package imitation of thirteen of its store brand items. Given that Albert Heijn is also Unilever's largest customer in the Netherlands (market share of 25 to 30 percent), such action was not undertaken lightly.

Retailers would like leading manufacturers to engage in private label production, and put pressure on them to share their latest technology, while many manufacturers have vowed never to engage in such practices. For example, in the Netherlands, P&G put the following text on the packaging of its dishwashing liquid Dreft (called Dawn in the U.S. and Fairy in the U.K.): "Dreft does not produce for private labels or imitation products."

Mainstream retailers can react strongly to brand manufacturers supplying to other retailers, most notably hard discounters. Illustrative is the reaction of the vice president of procurement of a large European retailer. During an executive seminar given by one of us on the role of manufacturer brands in the assortment of hard discounters, he stated that if a brand manufacturer would supply the hard discounter, Lidl, he would substantially reduce the amount and quality of the shelf space allocated to the brand in question.

The business press has picked up on the challenges that private labels increasingly place on manufacturer brands. Publications are swamped with headlines such as "Kraft Profit Is Hurt by Private Labels," "Consumers Snub General Mills Price Rise," "Brand Killers: Store Brands Aren't for Losers Anymore," "Retail: Bye-Bye Brands," and "The Big Brands Go Begging" that encapsulate this threat.[50]

The Plan of the Book

Before presenting the plan of the book, we must clarify a definitional issue and a coverage issue for the reader. In this book, we consider a private label to be any brand that is owned by the retailer or the distributor and is sold only in its own outlets. For example, Burberry is not considered a private label even though it has its own retail stores, because the Burberry brand also generates significant sales through department stores. However, brands like Gap, H&M, IKEA, and Zara are store brands because they are sold exclusively in their own outlets. We also use the terms *private labels*, *store brands*, *distributor brands*, *retailer brands*, and *own labels* interchangeably.

In terms of coverage, the underperformance of the U.S., even though that country is the home of some of the world's best retailers, as well as the overperformance of private labels in other countries (figure 1-1) indicates that there is no single "best practices" country. Rather, we can learn about private label success by taking an international view, critically considering successes in different countries. Our focus therefore will be on how best-in-class retailers around the world are enhancing their store brands to make them strong competitors of manufacturer brands. Thus we ask for readers' indulgence in those cases where we use examples with which they may be relatively unfamiliar. To help, we have provided an appendix on the basic facts regarding the retailers referred to in our book.

The book is divided into two parts. The first part examines retailer strategies with respect to private labels, in six chapters. Chapter 2 outlines the role traditional private labels in the form of generics and copycats play in retailers' strategies. Next, we turn to two exciting developments in retailer brands: competing for the quality-conscious consumer with premium store brands (chapter 3) and competing for the rational consumer with value innovator own labels (chapter 4). Chapter 5 explores how retailers are combining various types of private labels to encircle and attack manufacturer brands from all sides with multitiered brand portfolios. Chapter 6 discusses how creating successful private labels involves a lot more than simply offering a lower price. Finally, chapter 7 outlines the role of private labels in maximizing retailer profitability.

In the second part, we examine what manufacturers can do to combat the private label challenge. The manufacturers' dilemma is that they sell to as well as compete with their retailers. This dilemma was best captured by a brand manufacturer in the context of the two largest Australian supermarket chains, Coles and Woolworths: "There's only one thing worse than dealing with Coles and Woolworths, and that's not dealing with Coles and Woolworths."[51] In the U.S., Gap went from being Levi Strauss's largest customer to being its biggest competitor when Gap dropped Levi's to focus on private labels exclusively.

Chapters 8 through 12 focus on how manufacturer brands can survive the onslaught of private labels. Chapter 8 explores the option of "sleeping with the enemy" by supplying private labels to retailers. Alternatively, manufacturers may prefer to focus on their own brands, using several strategies to make the manufacturer brands an attractive alternative to store brands. Chapter 9 examines how to partner effectively with selected retailers and create win-win relationships. Chapter 10 urges brand manufacturers to beat private labels through brilliant innovation. Chapter 11 posits that it is impossible to fight the retailers on all fronts, and instead brand manufacturers must focus their efforts to fight selectively with maximum impact. Chapter 12 discusses how manufacturer brands can create winning value propositions against private labels.

Finally, in our concluding chapter, 13, we draw together the various themes and lessons of the book under the provocative question, Are brands dead? And, we argue, no, brands are not dead. But, as many brand manufacturers are discovering, some of the leading and best-loved consumer brands are now store brands.

Part One

Retailer Strategies Vis-à-Vis Private Labels

TWO FACTS are well known in the developed economies: there are too many brands, and it is an overstored environment. Yet, there always seems to be room for another successful brand or another successful retail chain. Witness the emergence of new iconic brands and successful chains that have either been launched or achieved dominance over the past two decades: Amazon.com, eBay, Nespresso, Old Navy, Red Bull, Starbucks, Tchibo, Trader Joe's, Victoria's Secret, and Zara. What makes a new entrant successful in the face of proliferating brands and stores is the ability to offer something distinctive and desirable with consistent quality. This is the challenge for retailer private labels—with so many brands already out there, what is their unique proposition to customers?

Finding a unique consumer proposition for private labels is exacerbated by the fact that most retailers today manage a multi-brand portfolio of private labels rather than simply having a single store brand, such as Staples or Walgreens. Consider, for example, Wal-Mart, offering a premium Sam's Choice brand and a cheaper Great Value brand of chocolate chip cookie, as well as many other private labels, like Equate OTC (over-the-counter, nonprescription) drugs and Ol' Roy dog food. With multibrand portfolios, retailers have to develop a raison d'être for each of their own brands to exist. For each own label, retailers have to make decisions on the overall strategy, consumer proposition, and objectives for the proposed brand. Once these are articulated, then follow the more tactical decisions on branding, pricing, category coverage, quality, product development, packaging, shelf placement, and advertising or promotion.

Usually, individual retailer store brands have one of four general consumer propositions with which to compete against manufacturer brands and other retailer brands. We refer to them as generics, copycats, premium store brands, and value innovators. Table I-1 outlines the differences between the four types of retail brands on various strategic and tactical dimensions. Of course, within these four types, over time, there are variations and evolution. And between the four types, at the edges, there are overlaps. Yet it is a useful scheme to understand individual brand strategies of retailers. The two traditional retailer strategies vis-à-vis private labels have been generics and copycats. In contrast, premium store brands and value innovator own labels are relatively new approaches by retailers. The separate and joint roles of these four types of private labels in retailers' strategies are discussed in chapters 2 through 5.

At the end of the day, private labels are "merely" tools for retailers to achieve their strategic objectives: market share and, ultimately, profitability. As we argue in chapter 6, building market share for private labels involves a lot more than just price. Chapter 7 highlights the fact that the role of private labels in boosting retailer profitability is actually a lot more complex than the simple stratagem of increasing private label share in one's assortment as much as possible—although this is a strategy followed by many retailers. Using real data and unique insights, we show that overemphasis of private labels may actually decrease retailer profitability.

TABLE I-1

Four types of private labels

	Generic private labels	Copycat brands	Premium store brands	Value innovators
Examples	No-name black-and-white packages marked *soap, shampoo, bread*	• Walgreens shampoo • Osco vitamins • Quill office products	• President's Choice • Body Shop • Tesco Finest	• Aldi • H&M • IKEA
Strategy	Cheapest—undifferentiated	Me-too at a cheaper price	Value added	Best performance-price ratio
Objectives	• Provide customer with a low-price option • Expand customer base	• Increase negotiating power against manufacturer • Increase retailer share of category profits	• Provide added-value products • Differentiate store • Increase category sales • Enhance margins	• Provide the best value • Build customer loyalty to store • Generate word of mouth
Branding	No brand name, or identified as first price label	Umbrella store brand or category-specific own labels	Store brand with subbrand or own label	Meaningless own labels to demonstrate variety
Pricing	Large discount, 20%–50% below brand leader	Moderate discount, 5%–25% below brand leader	Close to or higher than brand leader	Large discount, 20%–50% below brand leader
Category coverage	Basic functional product categories	Originates in large categories with strong brand leader	Image-forming categories, often fresh products	All categories

(continued)

TABLE 1-1 *(continued)*

	Generic private labels	Copycat brands	Premium store brands	Value innovators
Quality to brand leader	Poor quality	Quality close to branded manufacturers	Quality on par or better, advertised as better	Functional quality on par with brand leader but with removal of "non-value-adding" product features and imagery
Product development	None; product put up for contracts to manufacturers with lagging technology	Reverse engineered using manufacturers with similar technology	Considerable effort to develop best products with similar or better technology	Considerable effort and innovation in terms of cost-benefit analysis
Packaging	Cheap and minimal	As close to brand leader as possible	Unique and source of differentiation	Unique but cost-efficient
Shelf placement	Poor; less visible shelves	Adjacent to brand leader	Prominent eye-catching positions	Normal as all over store
Advertising/promotion	None	Frequent price promotions	Featured in advertisements but limited price promotions	Store not own-label advertising, normal promotion schedule
Customer proposition	Sold as cheapest-priced product	Sold as same quality but lower price	Sold as best products on market	Sold as best value—price of generics but objective quality on par with brand leaders

Competing on Price with Traditional Private Labels

Percentage of all private labels that are copycats:
50 percent

Despite all the buzz surrounding new developments in the private label landscape, such as premium store brands, we should not forget that traditional private labels—generics and copycats—are still the dominant types of store brands around the world. And retailers that venture into private labels typically start here. Hence it is appropriate to start this discussion of retail strategies vis-à-vis private labels with these still-ubiquitous types of store brand.

Generic Private Labels

Private labels, especially in the U.S., started as cheap, inferior products. Historically, they did not even carry the name of the store and were therefore called generics. Usually, the package with black letters on a white background simply identified the product, like paper towels or dog food. Most consumers saw them for what they were—undifferentiated, except in their poor quality, but at a very low price. These cheap, shoddy products, however, did offer lower-income and price-sensitive customers a purchase option, and as a result enabled the retailer to expand its customer base. Generics were all about the lowest possible price.

In terms of supply chain, generics did not add a lot of complexity for the retailer. They appeared only in the basic, functional, low-involvement categories like paper goods and everyday canned foods. And within each category, they were usually offered in one size and one variant only, thereby accounting for relatively few additional stock-keeping units (SKUs) for the retailer. Retailers rarely ran price promotions on generics. The retailers generally put these generic products out for bid to manufacturers, either those specializing in private labels or brand manufacturers selling their excess capacity.

The Decline and Revival of Generics

Typically, generics did not account for a large proportion of the retailer's volume, and as a result they were not strategically important to the retailer. Generics suffered from poor shelf placement, usually on floor-level, less visible, retail shelves. Over time, generics have lost shelf space and importance to copycat store brands, premium store brands, and value innovator own labels, as shown in figure 2-1.

There has, however, been a recent resurgence in the generics consumer proposition in Europe, though not as the old "black and white" generics. Many European retailers, with advanced private label programs, are converting what used to be generics into an important element of their multibrand portfolios. To respond to the intense price pressure from hard discounters like Aldi, Lidl, and Netto, mainstream retailers have been forced to develop a dedicated private label that identifies the lowest price at which a product is available in the store. By having such a first-price

FIGURE 2-1

Private label evolution

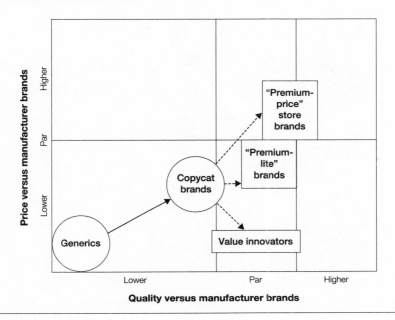

Quality versus manufacturer brands

private label line, traditional retailers such as Albert Heijn, Carrefour, Delhaize, and Sainsbury can demonstrate that they have a basket that is price competitive against the hard discounters.

Three Branding Strategies for Generics

These price-fighter private labels may be a store brand with a subbrand, a stand-alone own brand, or a consortium brand. For example, Tesco and Sainsbury have used *the store brand with subbrand* approach to anticipate and limit the onset of hard discounters in the United Kingdom. Tesco has a Value line, while Sainsbury's Low Price economy range (see figure 2-2) encompasses more than three hundred food and household products.

South Africa's Pick 'n Pay, one of Africa's largest supermarket chains with more than three hundred supermarkets and fourteen hypermarkets in southern Africa, has its No Name line to fight

FIGURE 2-2

Sainsbury cheap white labels

Source: Jan-Willem Grievink, "Retailers and Their Private Label Policy" (presentation given at the 4th AIM Workshop, June 29, 2004). Reproduced with permission.

superefficient Shoprite. To counter quality concerns often associated with generics, there is a money-back guarantee on the packaging of the No Name, stating that if the customer is not satisfied, "we will gladly give you DOUBLE THE MONEY BACK" (capitals in the guarantee). To give further credibility to this guarantee, it is signed by Pick 'n Pay's legendary founder, CEO Raymond Ackerman.

In contrast, in 2003 Carrefour was finally forced to introduce a line of low-priced private label goods under a *stand-alone brand name* "1" after losing significant market share in France to hard discounters. The assortment under "1" now exceeds two thousand products and generates $1.6 billion in annual sales for Carrefour. The brand attempts to be 6 to 7 percent cheaper than the hard discounters and adopts the everyday low prices (EDLP) strategy, but it is doubtful that it generates any significant profits for Carrefour.

To leverage economies in sourcing beyond those that would otherwise be available to a single retailer, Ahold and eight other European retailers have formed an alliance that negotiates very hard with private label manufacturers on hundreds of products, from paper goods to soft drinks, which are then sold under the *consortium brand* Euroshopper.[1]

Such generics or a first-price range of products do help the retailer serve the price-sensitive consumer and limit the onset of price-oriented competitors. However, it is not entirely clear that these generics generate the required profitability to justify their shelf space. Furthermore, they may end up cannibalizing the retailer's own higher-priced and higher-margin private label range. Yet, the hope for retailers is that such a line attracts price-conscious customers, whose shopping basket ultimately ends up with a mix of low-margin generics as well as some higher-margin nongeneric products. Thus, while the first-price range may not be very profitable in its own right, it may still attract profitable shoppers.

Copycat Store Brands

Generics, especially in the U.S., lost their share of the shelf space to retailer private labels that often carry the name of the retailer as a brand, referred to as store brands. These store brands are copycats in the sense that they imitate the leading manufacturer brands in the category. For example, Wal-Mart's Equate brand of dental rinse compares itself on the front of the package to its branded competitor, Plax. Similarly, Target's dental rinse product explicitly references a leading manufacturer brand, Wintergreen Listerine. The drugstore chains CVS and Walgreens also have similar copycat store-branded mouthwashes.

Copycat Brand Strategy

Often, copycat store brands are uncomfortably close in terms of packaging, as the Cif (Unilever) and Nescafé (Nestlé) examples demonstrate in figure 2-3. Placing these look-alike store brands

FIGURE 2-3

Retailer copycat brands

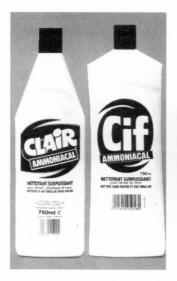

Source: Photos by Jean-Noel Kapferer, 2006. Reproduced with permission.

adjacent to the leading brand encourages both brand comparison and brand confusion on the part of shoppers.

Retailers aggressively promote copycat brands using price promotions and comparative messages. For example, in August 2003, Quill, the direct office products retailer, in an online ad promoted a bundle of fourteen Quill brand products for $29.99 against the comparable manufacturer brand items for $141. No wonder Quill private labels now account for one-third of its business.[2]

To ensure quality, retailers analyze the contents of a leading manufacturer brand and then re-create the product step by step, a process called reverse engineering. In this sense, they are free riding on the manufacturer's innovation, research, product development, and image-building efforts for its brand. Since there are few research and development or sales and marketing expenses for the retailer, and the products are aggressively outsourced for low-cost manufacturing, the price on such copycat store-branded products is considerably lower than the referent manufacturer brand while still delivering high margins to the retailer, at least in percentage terms. For example, Reckitt Benckiser's Vanish is priced in the Netherlands at $11.50 per kilogram, compared with $6.34 per kilogram for the Kruidvat store-branded copycat.

Copycats Drive Profits from Manufacturers to Retailers

Copycat store brands by retailers do not face the risks associated with new product introduction, because they only introduce such copycat brands once the manufacturer's new product has become a hit. For example, only recently have retailers begun launching store-branded flavored waters. In categories where new products are the lifeblood of the industry, this can be a considerable advantage since new products usually have a high miss-to-hit ratio. By adopting only the hits, copycat retailers do not have to absorb the costs of the misses.

It is therefore not surprising that the toy industry in the U.S. is in trouble. Successful toys are few and far between. When such hits do come along, they are rapidly duplicated by lower-cost manufacturers located in China for Wal-Mart and other retailers.[3] The promise of such copycat private labels is that they are about the same quality as the branded leader but at a much lower price.

By introducing such copycat private labels in large categories with a strong brand leader, the retailer effectively creates some competition for the brand leader. This increases the retailer's negotiating power with the brand leader as well as the other manufacturer brands in the category. As a result, the retailer generates larger category profits, both from the higher margins on its own private label and from the higher margins induced from manufacturers under the threat of favoring the store brand. Copycat brands are all about driving revenues and profits from manufacturer brands to retailers. We now describe two retailers—Walgreens and Zara—from different continents and operating in different categories, that successfully employ a copycat strategy.

Walgreens Copycat Brands

With $677 in sales per square foot and an average of 3.6 million daily customer visits, Walgreens is the largest drugstore retailer in the U.S. Walgreens pioneered the notion of making the drugstore a convenience destination rather than just a pharmacy stop. Of its nearly 5,000 stores, about 1,200 are open twenty-four hours a day, and with satellite links between the stores, prescriptions can be filled twenty-four hours a day. Drive-through pharmacies are a feature at around four out of five stores.[4]

At Walgreens, prescription drugs made up approximately 63 percent of the $42 billion in sales in 2005, while general merchandise was responsible for 25 percent and nonprescription drugs accounted for 12 percent. Private labels are important in the pharmaceutical industry, making up almost half of the sales of vitamins, a third of mineral supplements, and a quarter of multivitamins. In addition to vitamins, private labels also make up a significant proportion of analgesics and oral care sales. Walgreens is the private label leader among drugstores, obtaining 12 percent of its dollar sales from private labels, compared with 7 to 8 percent at CVS, Rite-Aid, and Brooks.

Aggressive Price Comparisons

Central to Walgreens's private label strategy is price. Through side-by-side shelf displays, it aggressively encourages customers to make favorable price comparisons between manufacturer brands and its own equivalent products. Electronic displays communicate the deals of the week to shoppers. Its private label goods are heavily promoted via circulars, in-store displays, and shelf talkers, as well as a weekly thirty-minute television program on health issues, named "Walgreens Health Corner."

Its brochures educate customers on diabetes care and compare its private label glucose monitors to the national brand. For example, Becton Dickinson's Logic Blood Glucose Monitor costs $74.99, compared with $17.99 for Walgreens's brand. In oral care, Walgreens's Fresh Breath Supreme Toothbrush is sold for just $1.99, compared with Oral-B's Indicator Toothbrush, priced at $2.99. The Walgreens private label line is meant to signify value for money. Its "Compare and Save" offers contrast Walgreens's products with manufacturer brands—for example, its whitening toothpaste ($1.99) versus P&G's Crest whitening toothpaste—with a "You Save $1.00" sign on the shelf to reinforce the message.

In addition to price-oriented store brands, Walgreens does have a few other brands in different categories. In 2003, it introduced a $9.99 digital camera under the name Studio 35, and for an additional $9.99, shoppers can have one-hour processing of their prints. It sells gourmet Belgian-style chocolates under the Truffelinos name. Walgreens is also the exclusive U.S. distributor of the upscale Swedish brand of beauty products IsaDora. Despite these exceptions, the thrust of Walgreens's private label program is focused on copycat store brands.

Zara—The Copycat Fashion Brand

Zara, the enormously successful Spanish apparel chain, is a copycat brand making high fashion universally accessible.[5] In 2006, Zara's 885 stores had a selling area of more than 9 million square feet in 62 countries. With sales of $5.3 billion in fiscal year 2005, Zara had become Spain's best-known fashion brand and the flagship brand of the $8.1 billion holding group Inditex. Zara earns a net margin (before interest and taxes) of 16 percent, and annual sales growth approaches 20 percent. Inditex's stock market listing in 2001 had turned Amancio Ortega, its founder, into the world's twenty-third-richest person, with a personal fortune that *Forbes* magazine estimated at $12.6 billion.

Fast Fashion

Zara strives to deliver fashion apparel, usually knock-offs of famous designers, at reasonable costs to young, fashion-conscious city dwellers. They use a team of two hundred young, talented, yet unknown designers. These designers, who are usually recent graduates of top design schools, create designs based on the latest fashions from the catwalk and other fashion hot spots, which are easily translatable to the mass market.

Zara is a master of picking up-to-the-minute trends and churning them out to stores around the world in a matter of weeks. After Madonna's first concert in Spain during a recent tour, her outfit was quickly copied by Zara. By the time she performed her last concert in Spain, some members of the audience were wearing the same outfit. In 2003, when the crown prince of Spain announced his engagement to Letizia Ortiz Rocasolano, she wore a white pantsuit for the occasion. In just a few weeks, the same white pantsuit was hanging from Zara's clothes racks all over Europe, where it was snatched up by the ranks of the fashion conscious.

The in-house designers present new items of clothing to customers twice a week, in response to sales and fashion trends. Thus the merchandise of any particular store is fresh and limited. To produce at such short notice requires that Zara maintain a vertically integrated supply chain that distributes the clothes through a single state-of-the-art distribution center. Unlike its competitors that outsource most of their production to low-cost countries like China, more than 50 percent of Zara's garments are manufactured in Europe. The speed at which it can copy successful items means that Zara sometimes has the copycat designs in its stores even before the famous designers can have their clothes on the racks of the traditional retailers.

Zara Brand Management

Zara is an exclusively private label store format. It even tends to deemphasize the Zara brand on its clothes because that gives more flexibility to the consumer. The consumer can either talk about the clothing as a smart buy or instead choose to quietly mix it with other designer clothes and project the image of having spent a lot of money. The success of Zara has led the fashion shows of Milan and Paris to change their rules and restrict attendance in order to deny Zara personnel the opportunity to see and copy the original designs.

Zara spends only 0.3 percent of sales on advertising, usually to emphasize the attractiveness of its copycat strategy. In contrast, its competitors, like H&M, spend 3 to 5 percent of sales on advertising. The savings that result are plowed by Zara into showcasing the merchandise at the best and most privileged locations of major cities, like Regent Street in London, Rue Rivoli in Paris, Fifth Avenue in New York, or Avenidas das Americas in Rio de Janeiro. For Zara, the store window display is the major vehicle for advertising to the consumer. The windows, refreshed every two weeks, are large and dramatic, and feature the merchandise as the star.

Chapter Takeaways

Successful Generics

- Account for a small percentage of a retailer's total sales because they suffer from poor margins.

- Provide a purchase option for extremely price-sensitive but quality-insensitive shoppers.

- Attract profitable customers, despite inadequate profitability at the product level, through cross-selling of higher-margin products.

- Help combat the threat of price-driven and private label–focused hard discounters like Aldi.

Successful Copycat Private Labels

- Free ride on the brand manufacturer's investments in research, product development, and advertising in order to offer a comparable product at a cheaper price.

- Aggressively promote against the manufacturer brands with price comparisons on the shelf and in their advertising.

- Increase the negotiating power versus brand manufacturers, especially in categories with dominant manufacturer brand players.

- Operate in categories that depend on a constant stream of new products where the copycat retailer does not need to absorb the cost of failures.

THREE

Competing on Quality with Premium Store Brands

Price premium for Tesco Finest chocolate over Cadbury:
65 percent

RATHER THAN RESTRICTING themselves to the traditional generics and me-too copycat store brands described in the previous chapter, retailers are now becoming savvier. They are beginning to recognize that while the classic copycat branding strategy does help as a tool against manufacturer brands, it does not help differentiate the store against other retailers. It does not provide a reason for the consumer to buy at this retailer in favor of another retailer, since every major retailer has an equivalent private label (as the mouthwash example in the previous chapter demonstrated). And often the only thing separating one retailer store brand from the other is the name on the label.[1] To escape this commoditization, retailers are investing in premium store brands.

The emergence of the "premium" private label is one of the hottest trends in retailing. While this premium private label phenomenon has attracted considerable attention in both the popular and the academic press, it has rarely been tightly defined in terms of premium on *what* and compared with *what*. Is it premium quality or premium price or both? And is it premium as compared with the leading manufacturer brands or the traditional copycat retailer brands?

Two Types of Premium Store Brands

Historically, the "premium" in premium private labels seems to have referred mainly to the contrast with the copycat retailer brands rather than with leading manufacturer brands. The premium store brands are superior in price and quality to the traditional copycat store brands. However, compared with leading manufacturer brands, they were priced lower but advertised as being of superior quality.

In terms of objective quality, the aspiration is to be of better quality than manufacturer brands. But even objective quality is relatively subjective in many categories. For example, is a unique feature or better packaging considered higher quality? For the most part, one can conclude that these premium store brands are, on average, at par with manufacturer brands with respect to quality, and sometimes even better. For example, thirteen of Kroger's Private Selection products, its premium private label, have earned the Good Housekeeping Seal of Approval, while Albertsons, one of Kroger's biggest rivals, has won industry awards for its store brand cognac, called Origine.[2]

The important distinction between premium store brands and traditional copycat brands is the clear vision of the retailer to differentiate on quality vis-à-vis the manufacturer brands combined with the absence of any attempt to copy the packaging of the leading manufacturer brands. Retailers wish to differentiate their premium private labels explicitly from other manufacturer and retailer brands.

Within premium store brands, we distinguish between two types:

- "Premium-lite" store brands, shown in figure 2-1, are those that espouse the proposition "better and cheaper." The aspired-to consumer proposition is to be equal to or better in quality than leading manufacturer brands while selling at a discount.

- "Premium-price" store brands, on the other hand, are those retailer brands that are both higher in price and superior in quality, compared with leading manufacturer brands. The aspired-to consumer proposition here is to be the best that money can buy.

As the following discussion demonstrates, premium-price store brands are still few and far between, while premium-lite brands are becoming very popular.

Premium-Lite Store Brands— Better and Cheaper

The premium-lite store brand starts with leading manufacturer brands as the standard and then attempts to make a superior product at a lower price. If retailers can pull this off from a product development perspective and convince customers of the performance from a marketing perspective, then life can become unbearable for manufacturer brands. It is the holy grail of retailer private label strategy. This is the ambition of retailers around the world, regardless of retail type or size, as the following examples demonstrate.

Consider Staples, the office products and supplies retailer in the U.S., with more than a thousand products sold under the Staples brand, like yellow self-stick notes, stainless steel shears, and ink cartridges for laser printers. The executive vice president of supply chain management observed, "Our strategy is to develop the Staples brand, not just offer consumers private-label items. We are putting the Staples logo and brand on products, infusing better quality than national brands, and offering the product at a discounted price."[3] As a result, Staples is investing in product development. In 2004, Staples filed for more than twenty-five patents and hired Michael Kent, formerly a product and package-design guru at BIC.

At Ukrop's Super Markets, a Richmond, Virginia–based chain in the U.S., the vice president of category management observed that Ukrop's "wants to offer a product that is equal to or higher in quality to the leading national brand at a lower price."[4] Similarly, Costco contends that it will not develop a Kirkland Signature product, which is its own label, unless it can make it better and cheaper than the leading manufacturer brand.[5]

In Europe, where this premium-lite store brand trend originated, Ahold, the owner of Albert Heijn supermarkets, claims that it does not want to position its private label as a discount label, but rather on a balance between price, quality, and uniqueness. Albert Heijn still wants its private labels to be cheaper than manufacturer brands, but beyond that, it would also like to position the store brands on the unique recipe of the product and its quality.[6]

Similarly, Australia's Woolworths sells a premium-lite private label called Select that aspires to provide the best quality in the range for the category while still providing a significant price advantage to customers, relative to comparable quality manufacturer brands.[7] (Note that Woolworths is present in various countries, such as the United States, United Kingdom, South Africa, and Australia, but they are separate companies, having very different assortments and positioning.)

Loblaws's President's Choice—Premium-Lite Strategy

Canadian retailer Loblaws has over 1,050 stores and 500 associated stores, where it offers 5,000 private label products. Private labels make up 30 percent of total sales. Its premium President's Choice brand includes grocery products, financial services, and even mobile phone services. The President's Choice brand has generated impressive customer loyalty.

President's Choice aims to compete directly against the major manufacturer brands. In its marketing, rather than focus on price,

President's Choice emphasizes the quality of the ingredients and the care with which the products are prepared.[8] It claims, for example, that President's Choice olive oil has been "harvested from trees planted more than 80 years ago and produced from the first cold pressing of sun-ripened olives." Similarly, since Kellogg had two scoops of raisins in its cereal, President's Choice cereal had to have twice the number of raisins while still being cheaper.[9]

To develop products that can compete with manufacturer brands on quality and unique features, Loblaws invests in market research and close relationships with private label suppliers. For example, Loblaws's market research indicated that customers wanted a richer cookie than that provided by the market leader, Nabisco's Chips Ahoy! The Decadent chocolate chip cookie under the President's Choice label was therefore 39 percent chocolate chips, compared with 19 percent chocolate chips by weight in Chips Ahoy! In addition, real butter replaced hydrogenated coconut oil, and quality chocolate substituted for artificial chips.[10] The resulting Decadent product became Canada's market leader in chocolate chip cookies despite being sold only in the 20 percent of the market held by Loblaws.[11]

Loblaws initially introduced the President's Choice line as a way to differentiate itself from rival grocers. But as the line became very popular, the chain began licensing it to retailers across the U.S., where Loblaws had no stores of its own.[12] The success of President's Choice inspired Wal-Mart to launch its own premium-lite private label, called Sam's Choice.

Premium-Price Store Brands— The Best You Can Buy

While most premium store brands are still somewhat cheaper than leading manufacturer brands, there are indeed some premium private labels now that are more expensive than manufacturers' brands. Rather than perceiving them as a poor cousin to manufacturer brands, many consumers, particularly in Europe, will pay more for better-quality private labels than manufacturer brands.[13]

Premium-price store brands were pioneered in Europe, especially in the United Kingdom by retailers like Marks & Spencer, Sainsbury, and Tesco. Sainsbury has a premium private label range called Taste the Difference that competes head-on with manufacturer brands and other retailers on quality, not price. The challenge is built into the brand name! It runs across eight hundred products and accounted for sales of more than $800 million in 2005.

Britain's Marks & Spencer (M&S) is a clothing, food, and household goods retailer with an exclusive private label focus. Customers perceive Marks & Spencer's food as gourmet, restaurant-quality food, and therefore Marks & Spencer is able to attract a price premium. Its Per Una Due underwear and St. Michael clothing brands are also highly sought out. Marks & Spencer store brands are perceived as premium quality, with 70 percent of U.K. shoppers believing they offer better quality than other department and supermarket chains.[14]

South Africa's Woolworths follows the same premium-price store brand strategy. It has a strong private label focus, selling nearly all its foods and general merchandise products at premium prices under the Woolworths name. With this strategy, Woolworths caters to the high-income segment in South Africa.

In the United States, Victoria's Secret in lingerie has been able to develop several premium-price private label brands. These brands are premium priced compared with the mainstream brands, though cheaper than the top-end designer brands, where the sky can be the limit. Owned by The Limited, Victoria's Secret Collections in intimate apparel, beauty products, sleepwear, hosiery, and fashion encompass many private labels, including Body by Victoria for seamless shaping using microfiber or cotton, Very Sexy for provocative lingerie, and Signature Cotton for everyday cotton comfort. In intimate apparel, Victoria's Secret is the number-five brand in the U.S., with 9 percent of respondents saying it is the label they prefer.[15] This has helped it generate sales of $3 billion from one thousand stores.

Tesco Finest: Premium-Price Private Label

To understand premium-price store brands, we examined Tesco's pricing strategy in a few categories as it related to the Tesco Finest line. (See figure 3-1.) For example, in orange juice, both Minute Maid and Tropicana were priced below the Tesco's premium store brand, Tesco Finest! There was no manufacturer brand priced above Tesco Finest.

In the wholemeal (whole wheat) breads category, Tesco Finest sold at 82P (pence), compared with the manufacturer brand Kingsmill at 78P. However, this was less than the premium Kingsmill Gold bread, which retailed at 98P. Kingsmill has successfully managed to stretch its brand up and differentiate a Gold line from a standard line.

In milk chocolate bars, Tesco Finest at 89P for 100 grams was priced above the category leader Cadbury, priced at 54P, but significantly below specialty brands such as Lindt at £1.29. Similarly, among cheddar cheese, Tesco Finest at £9.29 per kilogram is able to extract a price premium over Colliers and Pilgrims Choice but not over Cracker Barrel, which retails at £9.90 per kilogram.

One usually observes premium-price store brands in fresh foods and prepared foods. In these categories, retailer brands are able to extract a premium over manufacturer brands because they can promise real additional value. For example, in orange juice, Tesco promises freshly squeezed, which cannot be easily replicated by the manufacturer brands, because the latter have a longer logistics cycle.

To be a premium-price store brand, the private label must be able to price above some of the leading manufacturer brands in the category. However, there will be niche and specialty brands that are priced higher than the premium-price retailer brands because most retailers have a mass-market strategy. The point is that a premium-price store brand will sometimes be the highest-priced product in the category, but more often there will be some manufacturer brands that will sell at an even higher premium.

Tesco has used the strength of its premium Finest label to extend it into nonfood categories such as bath and body products,

FIGURE 3-1

Tesco brand portfolio price positioning

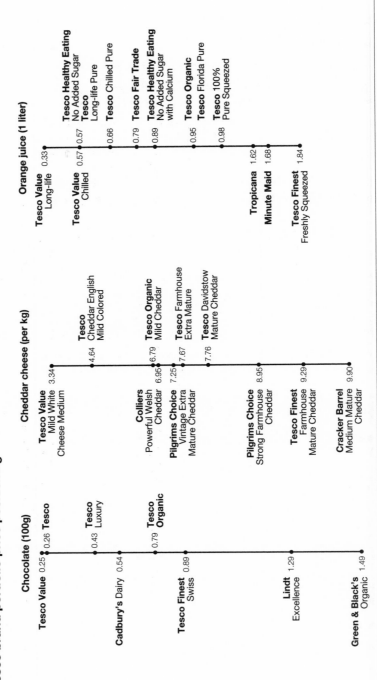

Chocolate (100g)

Tesco Value 0.25 ● Tesco 0.26

Tesco 0.43 Luxury

Cadbury's Dairy 0.54 ●

Tesco 0.79 Organic

Tesco Finest 0.89 Swiss

Lindt 1.29 Excellence

Green & Black's 1.49 Organic

Cheddar cheese (per kg)

Tesco Value 3.34 Mild White Cheese Medium

Tesco 4.64 Cheddar English Mild Colored

Colliers 6.95 Powerful Welsh Cheddar

Tesco Organic 6.79 Mild Cheddar

Pilgrims Choice 7.25 Vintage Extra Mature Cheddar

Tesco Farmhouse 7.67 Extra Mature

Tesco Davidstow 7.76 Mature Cheddar

Pilgrims Choice 8.95 Strong Farmhouse Cheddar

Tesco Finest 9.29 Farmhouse Mature Cheddar

Cracker Barrel 9.90 Medium Mature Cheddar

Orange juice (1 liter)

Tesco Value 0.33 Long-life

Tesco Healthy Eating 0.57 No Added Sugar

Tesco 0.57 Long-life Pure

Tesco Value 0.57 Chilled

Tesco Chilled Pure 0.66

Tesco Fair Trade 0.79

Tesco Healthy Eating 0.89 No Added Sugar with Calcium

Tesco Organic 0.95

Tesco Florida Pure 0.95

Tesco 100% 0.98 Pure Squeezed

Tropicana 1.62

Minute Maid 1.68

Tesco Finest 1.84 Freshly Squeezed

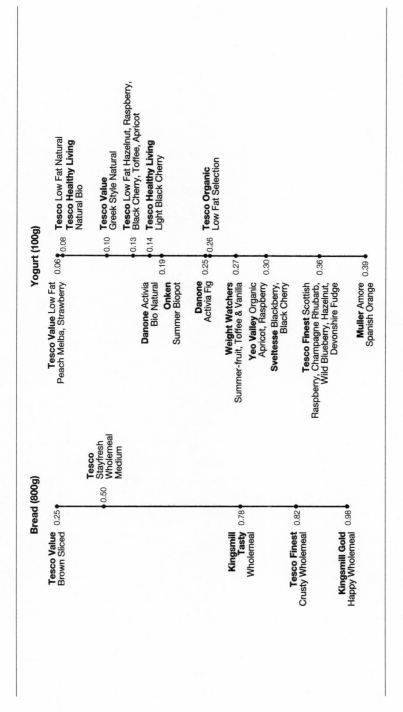

Bread (800g)

Tesco Value Brown Sliced — 0.25

Tesco Stayfresh Wholemeal Medium — 0.50

Kingsmill Tasty Wholemeal — 0.78

Tesco Finest Crusty Wholemeal — 0.82

Kingsmill Gold Happy Wholemeal — 0.98

Yogurt (100g)

Tesco Value Low Fat Peach Melba, Strawberry — 0.06

Tesco Low Fat Natural
Tesco Healthy Living Natural Bio — 0.08

Tesco Value Greek Style Natural — 0.10

Tesco Low Fat Hazelnut, Raspberry, Black Cherry, Toffee, Apricot — 0.13

Tesco Healthy Living Light Black Cherry — 0.14

Danone Activia Bio Natural — 0.19

Onken Summer Biopot — 0.25

Danone Activia Fig — 0.26

Tesco Organic Low Fat Selection

Weight Watchers Summer-fruit, Toffee & Vanilla — 0.27

Yeo Valley Organic Apricot, Raspberry — 0.30

Sveltesse Blackberry, Black Cherry — 0.36

Tesco Finest Scottish Raspberry, Champagne Rhubarb, Wild Blueberry, Hazelnut, Devonshire Fudge

Muller Amore Spanish Orange — 0.39

and towels. A striking illustration is the Tesco Finest Platinum credit card.

Managing a Premium Store Brand

Many retailers are now offering a top-end range of private labels, which are of equal or higher quality than the leading brand. Irrespective of whether these premium store brands are premium priced compared with manufacturer brands, to support these premium store brands, retailers will need to focus on product enhancements and invest in marketing competence.

Product Enhancement

In principle, a premium private label must offer high quality and represent unique products. Often, the premium store brand carries specialty private label products that contain unique ingredients that cannot be found elsewhere. For example, Trader Joe's chocolate sandwich cookies, a competitor to Oreos, are made with higher-quality ingredients. The Traders Joe's cookie does not contain trans fat, which results from adding hydrogen to vegetable oil in order to increase the shelf life and flavor stability of foods, but which increases the risk of coronary heart disease.

Similarly, premium private labels may offer unique flavors. In yogurts (see figure 3-1), Tesco Finest sells at 36P per 100 grams, with flavors such as Scottish Raspberry, Devonshire Fudge, Wild Blueberry, and Champagne Rhubarb. In contrast, Danone Activia Bio Natural is priced at 19P, while Danone Activia Fig is 25P. In other manufacturer brands, Weight Watchers is priced at 27P, while Yeo Valley and Sveltesse are priced at 30P. Only one brand at Tesco, Muller Amore Spanish Orange at 39P, was priced above Tesco Finest.

These premium store brands have distinctive packaging, a far cry from the bland generics or copycat packaging of the past. There is no attempt to confuse customers and make them think that these are manufacturer brands, as is the case with copycat store brands. The strategy is to develop a unique positioning for the retailer.

Developing unique products, flavors, and packaging requires retailers to partner with the best manufacturers available, and private label manufacturers to invest codevelopment time and effort in developing dedicated and unique products for retailers. Private label manufacturers will be motivated to do so only if their relationship with retailers is either based on trust and commitment or protected by contractual guarantees. Therefore, retailers following a premium store brand strategy have to mature beyond simply outsourcing private label production based on the lowest price.

Invest in Marketing Competence

How have retailers managed to build better products? Most importantly, there has been a great change in attitude among retailers and how they view their private labels. Most leading private label retailers now take an active role in the positioning and manufacturing specifications of the product. It is no longer about just slapping their logo on whatever comes off the assembly line.[16] They carefully invest in product development, market research, advertising and promotion, packaging design, and so on. In order to do so, leading private label retailers have had to upgrade their marketing competence. For example, Tesco has recruited lots of marketers from consumer goods companies like Unilever.

Consider the U.S. department store JCPenney as an example of retailer investments in private labels. At 40 percent of sales, it has the highest level of private label penetration when compared with its competitors. JCPenney's flagship private label brand, Arizona, was ailing. The company hired Jeff Bergus, who had previously held design posts for Geoffrey Beene and Izod, to turn it around. He did some research and found that the average Arizona customer was actually forty-five years old, not seventeen to twenty-four years old as JCPenney had envisioned.

Transforming the Arizona label required sending designers to Avril Lavigne concerts to scan the audience for inspiration. The new TV ad campaign launched for Arizona featured young models wearing strategically placed denim and barely buttoned blouses. This approach does not seem that different from best practice for manufacturer brands, often considered leading edge with respect to marketing. Arizona is now a billion-dollar brand for JCPenney and a major contributor to its turnaround.

Premium Store Branding Strategies

Retailers follow different premium branding approaches in order to make it easy for consumers to identify these products as the retailer's best quality. A number of retailers adopt a *subbrand* with clear store identification for their premium range, like AH (for Dutch retail chain Albert Heijn) Select or Safeway Select (with the tagline "take a vacation from ordinary items"), to communicate that it is the top-end of their private label range. Similarly, Saks Fifth Avenue has the Platinum line, rumored as being produced in the same Italian factory as Armani clothing.[17]

Other retailers develop a *separate premium brand*. This strategy is prevalent at Wal-Mart with Sam's Choice, at A&P with Master Choice, at Loblaws with President's Choice, and at Kroger with Private Selection (with the tagline "go ahead and spoil yourself"). It helps distinguish the premium line from the standard line. For example, Shaw's Signature brand, launched in 2001, includes three hundred items in grocery, dairy, bakery, and meats. Despite using premium ingredients, the Signature brand represents at least a 5 percent savings from manufacturer brands. In contrast, Shaw's standard private label products offer a 10 to 20 percent savings.[18]

Since the store may have limitations with respect to its ability to achieve a premium positioning with consumers, some retailers adopt a *cobranded* strategy with a prominent brand manufacturer. For example, several of Costco's Kirkland Signature range products are cobranded with famous names, such as Starbucks on the Kirkland Signature blend house coffee, Hershey and Nestlé on candy, Quaker on cereal, and Whirlpool on major appliances.[19] Similarly, U.S. supermarket retailer Publix premier ice cream has a tie-in with Butterfinger. This allows the store's premium brand to achieve a higher-level positioning in the category than would be otherwise possible. The downside is that margins have to be shared with the co–brand owner.

An alternative approach is to *delink* the premium line with the store. The retailer brands its premium products under labels with no mention of the store brand. This strategy allows the premium brand greater positioning and pricing flexibility since it does not have to reconcile its offer with the overall store image. For example, for its premium health and beauty care line, Duane Reade has Apt. 5, Fred Meyer has Curfew Colors, Albertsons has Identity, while CVS has Essence of Beauty. Giant Eagle has launched a premium private label brand of pasta and related products called Laurenti to capitalize on the customer demand for high-quality products. The line contains thirty products and is around 33 percent more expensive than the retailer's midtier label but cheaper than competing manufacturer brands.

The disadvantage of the stand-alone premium brand strategy is that it does not raise the image of the retailer's store as much as the closely linked premium brand approach does. Shoppers perceive these to be stand-alone premium own labels as brands in their own right and may often be unaware that these private labels originate from the retailer. This is the case with Macy's Style&co. clothing line, which is sold alongside other fashion labels. Consider the experience of a shopper, Barbara Harkleroad, recounted in the *Miami Herald*.[20] It is reported that she used to buy designer brands like Liz Claiborne and Jones New York until she discovered Style&co. For a significant savings, she found she could get a comparable T-shirt or Polo shirt. But when questioned, she had no idea that Style&co. was a Macy's own label.

Exclusive Line as a Premium Store Brand

Sometimes the unique brand may be an exclusive to the retailer by a designer, such as Martha Stewart housewares at Kmart or Cheryl Tiegs clothes at Sears. Kohl's often signs one-year exclusive deals or licensing agreements, such as exclusive rights with

Quicksilver sportswear for the Tony Hawk brand or with Polo Ralph Lauren for Chaps for men. Strictly speaking, these cannot be considered to be retailer private labels, since the brands are owned by the designers rather than by the retailers. However, in terms of retailer strategy, their role is similar to that of premium private labels.

America's Target has used the exclusive designer label strategy very successfully to compete against and differentiate itself from Wal-Mart. Target's Mossimo was formerly a department store apparel brand for men and women; it is now sold exclusively at Target stores and is very popular with consumers, as is Target's Michael Graves housewares line. Target's other brands include a makeup line by Sonia Kashuk, casual clothing line Cherokee (which it is exclusively licensed to sell in the U.S.), juniors' clothing line Xhilaration, Kitchen Essentials by Calphalon, Waverly home accessories, and a bedding collection by Woolrich. It has an exclusive deal with Hilary Duff (an American actress and singer) to carry the brand's lifestyle products. Its upscale designer offerings include dedicated Target lines by Isaac Mizrahi and Liz Lange.

Target is now the second-largest mass retailer in the U.S., after Wal-Mart. It differentiates itself from its main competitor by offering higher-end, trendier merchandise while keeping its prices low. It encourages customers to "Expect more. Pay less." It aims to maintain consistent pricing of its merchandise, and a lot of effort is put into displays and arrangements in-store. The result of these premium private labels is the ability of Target to attract a younger, more upscale, fashion-aware, and urban clientele than Wal-Mart, thereby moving beyond simply competing on price, where Wal-Mart will win every time.

Pros and Cons of Premium Private Labels

Retailer private labels have come a long way. Banish the old image of cheap, low-quality toilet paper or canned beans packaged in black and white. Today, most retailer brands compete on value for money, having upgraded quality, image, and price. Sometimes, as the Tesco Finest range exemplifies, they can be more expensive than famous manufacturer brands with long histories such as Cadbury, Danone, and Tropicana.

The Benefits of Premium Store Brands

If product development and launch costs are kept under control and the retailer is able to convince the customer on superior quality, premium store brands are highly profitable for retailers. As figure 3-1 demonstrated, the high prices at which these products sell, compared with manufacturer brands, means that, theoretically, margins on these products for retailers should be very large. Relative to manufacturer brands, the retailer does not have to spend similar amounts on advertising the premium store brands, running retailer promotions, or maintaining a sales force.

Premium labels like Tesco Finest, AH Excellent, Arizona, and President's Choice engender store loyalty from customers, who will specifically go to a retailer to purchase an item. Wal-Mart's ReliOn brand of diabetes medication is another store brand that attracts high consumer loyalty and makes Wal-Mart a destination store for ReliOn brand loyal consumers.

The premium store brands also help raise the image of the entire private label offering of a retailer. Investments in premium private label quality have paid off for retailers because the independent and reputable *Consumer Reports* magazine has ranked many of the premium private label products of Wal-Mart, Safeway, Winn-Dixie Stores, Albertsons, and The Kroger Company among the top ten brands in many categories, including crunchy peanut butter, tuna, raisin bran cereal, ice cream, and strawberry yogurt.[21]

A McKinsey study revealed that developing a strong brand in the retail industry results in real financial benefits.[22] It examined the brand strength (index of quality, distinctiveness, and consistency) of four types of retailers in the U.S.: superstores (Kmart, Target, Wal-Mart), department stores (Bloomingdale's, Saks, Neiman Marcus), general merchandisers (JCPenney, Sears), and big-box retailers (Circuit City, Best Buy). Within each type of retailer, a higher brand strength of a retailer resulted in greater sales per square foot for the retailer.

The Costs of Premium Store Brands

As retailers upgrade their private labels to become more like brands, they start facing some of the same cost structures and risks that manufacturer brands do. For example, Saks Fifth Avenue launched three new private label brands in 2004, but none did as well as expected. The poor job that Saks did of forecasting sales forced higher markdowns and lower margins.

In 2005, merchandising experts, purchasers, designers, and packing experts at America's Staples collaborated to introduce six hundred to seven hundred new packaging designs.[23] And Super-valu introduced Carlita in its attempt to create a brand that will appeal to Hispanic Americans. Supervalu spent over a year conducting market research, hired brand consultants, and even had its top executives take Spanish lessons.[24] The costs of launching such a premium brand for a retailer, as brand manufacturers are already aware, can be rather high. And unlike brand manufacturers, retailers have a more limited ability to recoup these new-product investments because store brands sell only in the particular retailer's stores. Even the most global of retailers tend to be present in only thirty countries. In contrast, large-manufacturer brands sell at all retailers and all over the world.

In many product categories, a premium position is difficult to achieve without imbuing the brand with some intangible imagery. Packaging and in-store communication such as displays have been used successfully by retailers of premium store brands. However, mass-media advertising is still an important, if not indispensable, tool to create brand imagery. It is also very expensive, and the sales base may not be large enough to amortize such investments.

As retailers get into the business of developing new products and new brands, they must not forget that brand manufacturers have had years of practice in designing, developing, marketing, and selling new products and brands. Yet, most new products and brands fail. To summarize, as retailer brands ape manufacturer brands in product development and marketing, they begin losing their original advantage of lower costs.

Choosing Selectively to Compete with Premium Store Brands

Despite all the claims by retailers that they are developing more than copycat retail brands, the truth still remains that most of this is ambition rather than reality. It is true that retailers today are frequently developing packaging that helps position the store instead of just trying to mimic the manufacturer brands. There are also instances where the retailer brand has unique features or higher quality than manufacturers' brands. But this is more the exception than the rule. The retailer's private label proposition continues for the most part to be close to the quality of manufacturer brands, and therefore of acceptable quality, while being cheaper.

Retailers need to be selective in picking their battles with manufacturer brands for premium private labels. Retailers who succeed in building strong store brands attack categories that allow opportunities for own-label differentiation. The private label product fulfills a need based on a want, where products were missing within a category such as ethnic foods, diet foods, and fair-trade foods.[25]

Premium price private labels are feasible in value-added meal solutions as consumers are increasingly looking for, and willing to pay for, convenience. In 1996, basic ingredients like lettuce and tomatoes accounted for 65 percent of the retailer's fresh food sales, and by 2006 this percentage has declined to 37 percent. Instead, ready-to-cook components like freshly cut pineapple, ready-to-heat meals like prepared pasta, and ready-to-eat meals have increased from 35 percent to 63 percent, averaging a growth in excess of 15 percent a year.[26]

Chapter Takeaways

Successful Premium Store Brands

- Differentiate the retailer from other retailers and thereby generate store loyalty.

- Beat the manufacturer brands on objective quality.

- Offer unique products, ingredients, and flavors.

- Come in distinctive packaging that emphasizes the differences with manufacturer brands rather than mimicking them through the copycat strategy.

- Aspire to price at par with the mainstream manufacturer brands and command a premium price to some of them.

- Build the explicit quality challenge in their selling proposition.

- Contain some brand imagery.

Retailers with Successful Premium Store Brands

- Invest in market research to find consumer needs that are unfulfilled by manufacturer brands.

- Seek out manufacturers with distinctive capabilities rather than simply subcontracting to the lowest-cost manufacturer.

- Brand the premium line by:

  - Using a store brand with a subbrand (e.g., Tesco Finest) to build an image consistent with a premium positioning, or

  - Delinking the store with the stand-alone premium-positioned brand (e.g., The Limited Seven7 jeans), or

  - Seeking a higher-status partner (e.g., Cheryl Tiegs at Sears) to cobrand the premium line.

- Imbue the premium line with brand imagery, using in-store communication and mass-media advertising.

- Conduct a rigorous investment analysis, taking into account that the retailer not only obtains higher margins but also bears the product development and marketing costs and risks of failure and markdowns.

- Pursue opportunities to sell the store brand (e.g., President's Choice) at noncompeting retailers to attain a sufficient return on investment.

Competing for the Rational Consumer with Value Innovator Own Labels

Private labels as a percentage of Aldi's $43 billion in sales:
95 percent

As RETAILERS began to analyze the contents of the leading brands and according to their findings recreated them to produce copycat and premium store brands, they discovered that there were opportunities beyond simply copying the branded product. In fact, by brutally confronting each element of cost in the product against the objective value added to the consumer, they could create a good, perhaps even better, quality product at remarkably low prices. This included stripping away most, if not all, of the elements of imagery, like expensive packaging and "superfluous" features.

The champions at this type of value innovator retailer brands have been the hard discount chains like Aldi, Lidl, and Netto in Europe. Outside the consumer packaged goods industry, the Swedish apparel chain H&M and the Swedish furniture and home furnishings chain IKEA have pursued this strategy with great success. In the U.S., Wal-Mart and Costco have also successfully adopted this approach in a few product categories. However, the pioneer at this strategy and the biggest story in European retailing in the past two decades has been Aldi.

Aldi—The German Hard Discount Phenomenon

The hard discount store pioneered by Aldi is a small outlet of about 15,000 square feet (1,000 to 1,500 square meters). It carries only 700 lines of stock, compared with, say, 100,000 items in a large Wal-Mart Supercenter or 25,000 at a typical supermarket. Aldi has a private label focus and carries between 90 and 95 percent of its own label products. The more than 7,400 stores worldwide generated $43 billion in sales. Aldi has a market share of almost 20 percent in Germany. Even in the U.S., Aldi has 740 stores, besides owning the Trader Joe's chain.

Limited Assortment Is Key

The limited assortment of 700 SKUs is key to Aldi's strategy. Aldi argues that focusing on the items that are most frequently used and offering these as Aldi brands makes shopping at Aldi both simple and a great value. Customers are not confused by row after row of products differentiated by brand name only. Although Aldi sells prepackaged meats and baked goods, its stores don't have fresh meats, fish, or bakeries, and have only a limited assortment of produce. As a result, customers usually have to supplement their purchases by shopping in a traditional supermarket.

The private label policy is to use different brands (in fact, merely made-up labels) in different categories so that despite the overwhelming focus on private labels, it appears that the customer has choice. Instead of Coke, it has Bueler Cola, and rather than Kleenex tissues, Royal Avenue. Millville breakfast cereals,

Casa Mamita refrigerated tortillas and salsa, Snack Rite crackers, Havana Lane chocolate ice cream, D-san laundry soaker, Goliath plastic wrap, Beaumont coffee, Oxi-fix stain remover, Alio dish detergents, Kirkwood chicken—the list goes on. It is a house-of-brands strategy rather than the branded house strategy followed by most retailers, such as Whole Foods, Safeway, and Tesco.

To make the shopping experience interesting despite a limited selection, Aldi offers an exciting selection of nongrocery items known as "Surprise Buys." These items, which change every Thursday, are available only while stocks last. Examples were the Medion personal computer, an Aldi own label, for less than £500 in the U.K. or a notebook computer at less than €1,000 in Germany. Extensively advertised and promoted in-store, the Surprise Buys help drive store traffic since they are often sold out within a couple of days, and in extreme cases, a couple of hours.

Top Quality at Low Prices

Aldi's aspiration is to offer top-quality products at incredibly low prices. The company achieves this by focusing strictly on the essentials and never stops looking for ways to cut prices further. All the products are developed in conjunction with leading suppliers to the highest quality standards. The only exception is coffee, which is processed in Aldi-owned plants. Often, the suppliers are leading packaged goods companies selling excess capacity. There is continual in-house quality testing along with independent laboratory analysis. The commitment to quality is reinforced by the fact that every product in the store is guaranteed.

Most comparisons of prices across retail stores have designated Aldi as the winner. In Australia, the Aldi Goliath plastic wrap retails at A$1.29 (Australian dollars) for a 60-meter roll, compared with A$3.71 for Glad. In the U.S., Costco sells two six-packs of bagels for $3.45, while Aldi has single pack of six bagels for 99¢. Similarly, Costco has big shrink-wrapped packs of 8-ounce yogurts for about 50¢ each, while Aldi's are 29¢ each and can be purchased individually. In Germany, P&G's Ariel laundry detergent sells for €4.65 for 30 tablets at the Edeka supermarket chain, and Henkel's Persil is €5.79 for 30 tablets at Metro, both comparing unfavorably to Aldi's Tandil brand, which retails at €2.99 for 36 tablets.[1] A basket of Aldi products is an incredible 50 percent cheaper than the same basket filled with branded goods.

Of course, the preceding price comparisons do not provide information on quality differences. But this is where Aldi has been especially successful. It aggressively promotes the independent quality assessments made of its products. Its U.K. Web site, for example, has a special page devoted to what English publications say about Aldi-branded products (a selection of which appears in table 4-1).[2] In Germany, their products have managed to win several independent quality and taste tests. As a result, Aldi is Germany's third-most-respected corporate brand, just behind Siemens and BMW and, amazingly, ahead of DaimlerChrysler.[3] An astonishing 89 percent of German households shopped at least once at Aldi last year. No wonder, Klaus Jacobs, who owned Jacobs Coffee (now part of Kraft), was quoted in a German business magazine as saying, "Our number one competitor is clearly Aldi."[4]

Lower System Costs

Since Aldi concentrates on seven hundred SKUs, its turnover per SKU is much higher than any other retailer's, giving it greater negotiating power against its suppliers. This focus allows the company to work with suppliers to get the price-quality ratio right. But Aldi's price advantage is based less on the lower price paid to its suppliers and more on the difference in processing costs between it and other retailers. In other words, Aldi is simply more efficient at getting the products from the supplier to the consumer.

At Aldi the total costs added to its procurement price from suppliers is about 13 to 14 percent (2 percent each for logistics, rental, overhead, and marketing, plus about 5 percent for staff). In contrast, traditional supermarkets, including the mighty Wal-Mart, are twice as costly on each of the cost components and

TABLE 4-1

Kudos for Aldi-branded products

Medion Titanium MD8385 Base Station £499.99 each	*Buy It* guide, *Computer Active* "Another undeniably good offer from the Aldi/Medion stable and well recommended if you're in the market for a new or second PC." Overall ★★★★★
Soupreme Tomato Soup 27p, 400g	*Take a Break* "Has a smashing tangy flavour and a nice smooth texture. I love it. More please!"
Temptations Puff Pastry Twists 79p, 150g	*Woman's Own* "Deliciously crisp and golden pastry twists with a rich flavour of Gruyere cheese." Cheese Straws Taste Test Winner
Premium Gravad Salmon £1.99, 200g	*Family Circle* "It's good quality Scottish smoked salmon . . . tastes delicious, and at a great price."
Ameristar Premium Lemonade 39p, 2 litre	*Chat* "You can smell the lemon before you start to drink. And when you do, it's delicious." —WINNER
Centanni Olive Oil £1.85, 750ml	*House Beautiful* "Enjoy good quality olive oil at an affordable price."
Bramwells Flame Roasted Tomato and Red Pepper Chutney 69p, 200g	*Good Food* "Very colourful and tomatoey with an excellent taste."
Fletcher's Cream Sherry £3.29, 75cl	**Malcolm Gluck, Superplonk column,** *The Guardian* "Remarkable undertone of toffee and crême brûlée."
Chateau Selection Claret £2.99, 75cl	**International Wine Challenge 2003 & Robert Joseph's** *Good Wine Guide 2004* "Supple and ripe with user-friendly tannins."
Worldwide Spicy Tomato Salsa 69p, 300g	*Best* Best Test Winner
Ransome's Vale Shiraz Petit Verdot £3.99, 75cl	**Oz Clarke © Brides/The Condé Nast Publications Ltd.** "Two of the world's beefiest grape varieties create this big, spicy, blueberry-flavoured party pleaser."

Source: "What the Papers Say" page from Aldi's U.K. Web site (http://uk.aldi.com).

therefore need to add double that amount (28 to 30 percent) to their procurement prices.

To obtain its deep discount positioning, Aldi buys inexpensive locations mostly on city outskirts or less popular streets, builds cheap warehouses, employs minimal staff, and displays products on pallets rather than shelves. Unlike the local pricing employed by most retailers, every store in the country has exactly the same prices. Aldi touts this as its belief that consumers should pay the same amount for their groceries regardless of where they live. It helps reinforce Aldi's consumer champion image.

Checkouts are spacious and scanning is lightning-fast so that even the biggest shopping list can be taken care of with speed and without frustration. Shoppers have to bring their own shopping bags to the store or buy one for a small price. They must pay a refundable deposit for the grocery cart; this eliminates the need to have clerks round up carts all over the parking lot.

Aldi alone accounts for half of the total German private label sales. When the CEO of one of the largest CPG companies visited his company's European headquarters, the president for Europe wanted to show his boss the competitor he was most concerned about. He took his boss to an Aldi store!

Aldi Imitators

The success of Aldi has led to its being often imitated. Its most successful imitator has been Lidl & Schwarz of Germany, with 5,000 no-frills discount stores throughout Europe that tend to carry about 800 different items. Lidl has somewhat less of a private label focus than Aldi, being about 65 percent private label, compared with Aldi's 95 percent. However, its overall sales are in the same ballpark. By emulating Aldi's low-cost operating methods, Lidl is challenging and even outpacing its rival in some markets, notably in France and Britain and lately even in Germany.[5] The large numbers of Mercedeses and BMWs parked in Aldi and Lidl parking lots reinforce the old adage that poor people need low prices, while rich people love low prices.

In the U.S., the hard discounters are sometimes referred to as "dollar stores" and have been growing at 14 to 17 percent a year. It is anticipated that this sector will be the fastest-growing concept in Canada and the United States. The leading North American players in this sector are Dollar General with 7,320 stores, Family Dollar with 5,466 stores, Dollar Tree with 2,735 stores, Supervalu with 1,287 stores, and Aldi with 780 stores. While the core market for dollar stores in the U.S. is families with an annual income of less than $30,000, a quarter of Americans with incomes over $100,000 shopped at them at least once in the last six months.[6]

Save-A-Lot is one of the fastest-growing retailers in the U.S., now with sales exceeding $4 billion from 1,200-plus stores. It targets the poor, often located in inner cities and usually ignored by the large supermarkets and mass merchandisers. The company has extremely low prices. A study in the Memphis area found that Save-A-Lot's prices were 11 percent lower than Wal-Mart's for similar store-branded products.[7] For example, a pound of bananas cost 29¢ at Save-A-Lot, compared with 48¢ at a nearby Wal-Mart Supercenter. The competition led Lee Scott, Wal-Mart's CEO, to observe to investors, "You certainly aren't going to underestimate the hard discounter."[8]

Like all the dollar stores in the U.S., Save-A-Lot tends to have a lot more manufacturer brands, compared with its European counterparts. But it carries only 1,250 items and mixes store brands with only the best-selling manufacturer brands in each category. By combining its own distribution centers with best sellers, it has extremely low stock and high inventory turns. Margins and operating costs are kept low by cutting frills—products are displayed in cardboard boxes, and customers have to pay a dime for bags. The high stock turns allow acceptable return on assets despite relatively low margins.

In the U.S., the Albrecht brothers (who own Aldi) acquired Trader Joe's in 1979 and have since then made it very successful, using a twist to the Aldi formula. The stores offer gourmet-style food and wines at bargain prices. It is now a chain of more than 250 stores, with sales growing at an average of 23 percent since 1990. It is adding about fifteen to twenty stores a year and eschews most promotion activities. It is 80 percent private label format with an opportunistic assortment strategy. Trader Joe's purchase managers are looking for bargains all over the world, and only if a great deal on a product is available will they acquire it. Thus the products change all the time, and customers learn to browse the store. However, like Aldi, it relies on tightfisted cost control, low-rent real estate, and bargain prices.

H&M—The Value Innovator Fashion Brand

Swedish clothing chain H&M was founded in 1947.[9] By 2006, it had close to 50,000 employees and around 1,200 stores in twenty-two countries. Its 2005 sales were $7.5 billion, which yielded a profit of $1.7 billion. H&M's business concept is to offer fashion at the best price. In order to offer the latest fashion, H&M has its own buying and design department. And in order to offer the cheapest price, it sources 60 percent of its clothes from Asia and the rest from other low-cost producing areas. It achieves the best price by:

- Having few middlemen

- Buying in large volumes

- Having a broad, in-depth knowledge of design, fashion, and textiles

- Buying the right products from the right market

- Being cost conscious at every stage

- Having efficient distribution

H&M Branding

H&M's clothing lines in menswear, women's wear, and children's wear, as well as its cosmetics range, target cost-conscious shoppers. Despite being totally private label, H&M employs a mix of own labels and subbrands to create some feeling of brand choice. For example, within H&M women's wear are different subbrands like Hennes (women age twenty-five to thirty-five), L.O.G.G. (casual sportswear), Impuls (young women's trends), BiB (plus-size line), Woman (classic), Clothes (current trends), MAMA (maternity), and Rocky (youth fashion). Similarly, there are also different subbrands within the men's and children's lines.

Unlike Aldi, which focuses on utilitarian products and targets large families, H&M is a different type of value innovator private label. Because H&M is in the apparel industry and targets youth, it cannot divorce itself from imagery and emotion in its branding. Therefore, H&M devotes 5 percent of its revenues to advertising. Its high-profile ad campaigns featured celebrities, such as Pamela Anderson, Claudia Schiffer, Johnny Depp, Naomi Campbell, Jerry Hall, and Madonna wearing its low-cost clothes. Initially, its advertising campaign was a shock to the industry because it used celebrities previously seen wearing only haute couture but suddenly appearing in H&M ads. These celebrity ads always carried the low H&M price of the clothes, such as the famous Naomi Campbell billboard ad in which she is wearing a $10 H&M swimsuit! When teenagers started stealing H&M billboard ads, the company started offering them for free. More recently, dedicated collections by star designers Karl Lagerfeld and Stella McCartney have continued to create buzz among its customers.

Managing a Value Innovator Own Label IKEA-Style

IKEA, the furniture and home furnishings retailer, operates in thirty-three countries and generates a turnover in excess of $18 billion. The combination of low production and low process costs allows IKEA to offer stylish furniture at incredible low prices. Like Aldi and H&M, IKEA reinforces the two lessons for successful value innovator private labels.

Continuous Search for Lower Cost

Not only do the value innovator retail brands like IKEA, Aldi, and H&M start at low prices, they strive to continuously push the cost envelope. The process of driving down production costs starts from the moment a new item is conceived and is pursued relentlessly throughout the product life cycle. In the case of new products, the price cuts can be substantial over time as the companies learn how to lower costs through more efficient production methods and replacing expensive materials with cheaper ones. For example, at IKEA, the price of a basic Pöang chair fell from $149 in 2000 to $99 in 2001 to $79 in 2002.[10]

At IKEA, prices are continually being reduced instead of being raised. Although IKEA's prices are typically 30 to 50 percent below competitors' prices, the 2005 catalog had an average price cut of 2 percent, compared with the previous year's prices.

Process-Related Savings Are Key

In exchange for the low prices, IKEA demands that customers engage in self-service, self-assembly, and self-transportation of purchases. This helps the company achieve lower costs throughout the system, compared with the traditional furniture retailer.[11]

The traditional furniture stores are beleaguered by expensive independent designers, high work-in-progress inventory, labor-intensive handicraft manufacturing, transportation and inventory of finished goods, fragmented marketing, costly retail locations, elaborate displays, and expensive delivery to the consumer. As figure 4-1 reveals, IKEA instead uses cost-conscious in-house design, interchangeable parts, high-volume component manufacturing, parts inventory (rather than more expensive finished product inventory), extensive computerization of logistics, its natural Scandinavian image, relatively inexpensive peripheral locations, and simple display facilities, leaving final transportation and assembly to the consumer.

FIGURE 4-1

IKEA's unique value network

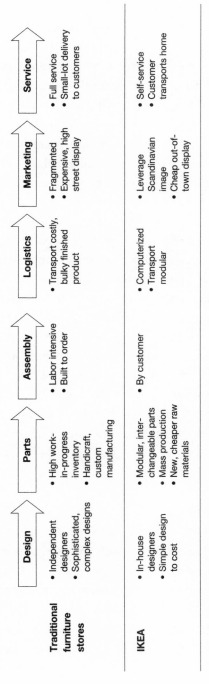

	Design	Parts	Assembly	Logistics	Marketing	Service
Traditional furniture stores	• Independent designers • Sophisticated, complex designs	• High work-in-progress inventory • Handicraft, custom manufacturing	• Labor intensive • Built to order	• Transport costly, bulky finished product	• Fragmented • Expensive, high street display	• Full service • Small-lot delivery to customers
IKEA	• In-house designers • Simple design to cost	• Modular, inter-changeable parts • Mass production • New, cheaper raw materials	• By customer	• Computerized • Transport modular	• Leverage Scandinavian image • Cheap out-of-town display	• Self-service • Customer transports home

Source: Nirmalya Kumar, *Marketing as Strategy* (Boston: Harvard Business School Press, 2004), 183.

Evaluation of the Value Innovator Model

The core strength of the value innovator model is delivering good-quality products at unbeatable prices. The significantly lower prices, compared with those of the competition, are not only a result of product-related savings. Beyond product savings, these value innovator retailers generate significant process-related savings, compared with the traditional retailer selling mostly manufacturer brands. Thus, the quality of the product need not be compromised.

The lower product and process costs allow value innovators to provide the best value for money while not hurting their profitability. In contrast, it is doubtful whether traditional retailers have adequate profitability on their range of first-price private labels (see generics in chapter 2). However, value innovator retailers are among the most profitable in the world. For example, Aldi's EBITDA (earnings before interest, taxes, depreciation, and amortization) of over 6 percent of sales is higher than the EBITDA earned by retailers like Carrefour and Ahold. The personal fortunes of value innovator founders such as IKEA's Ingvar Kamprad ($23 billion), Aldi's Karl and Theo Albrecht ($18.5 billion and $15.5 billion, respectively), and H&M's Stefan Persson ($11 billion) attest to the profitability of this retail model.

Targeted Positioning

Nevertheless, the key success factors underlying the value innovator model also are its main challenges. One key success factor is its precisely targeted positioning, which enables great efficiencies in logistics and other stages in the value-adding chain. Rather than being everything to everybody, these retailers focus on a fairly precisely defined consumer segment. However, the more successful the value innovator retailer becomes, the less room there is to grow since most people in the target segment have already become customers. There is a limited segment—albeit as Aldi proves, a rather large one in Germany for packaged goods—that can be served effectively.

To maintain growth, the value innovator has to either (1) target new segments or (2) expand internationally, rolling out its concept globally. If it chooses the former option, it risks losing its targeted positioning. Anyone not belonging to H&M's target segment may be turned off by its blasting, in-your-face music and cluttered stores, as one of the authors whose daughter drags him into the local H&M can attest.

International expansion is a second option. As IKEA has convincingly demonstrated, a similar target segment did exist in other markets outside its Swedish home market, even in an industry as "local" as furniture and home furnishings. However, international expansion is fraught with risks and may add overhead, logistics, and other costs to the system. The very fact that it took IKEA decades to become profitable in the U.S. is a sober reminder that even the world's most sophisticated value innovators can stumble badly.

Cost of Shopping

The costs of shopping—as distinct from the costs of buying—are higher for customers of value innovator retailers. Because value innovators need to reduce process costs, they pass on many functions to the consumer and also ask them for certain sacrifices. For example, given Aldi's limited assortment, its customers have to visit other stores as well to buy manufacturer brands they value—I may be willing to purchase Aldi dry pasta but not its cola—and products not carried by Aldi (e.g., fresh fish). Visiting multiple stores is costly, both in time and effort; thus it increases the costs of shopping.

Or consider IKEA. Once customers have gone through the endless checkout lines, they have to transport the furniture home. And then it takes a lot of time and frustration to figure out the incomprehensible assembly instructions, let alone to put the pieces of furniture together.

Value innovators may be inclined to reduce the costs of shopping—for example, by expanding their assortment, both in breadth (more categories) and in depth (more SKUs, including manufacturer brands). As a result of Lidl's greater success in some markets, Aldi has started negotiations with leading brand manufacturers to add their brands to its assortment. However, this threatens to undermine the very basis of its success.

Chapter Takeaways

Successful Value Innovator Own Labels

- Aim for objective product quality on a par with manufacturer brands at unbeatable prices, with a constant search to lower the prices continually.

- Achieve lower prices through rigorous system processing cost savings (e.g., low overheads, limited assortment, minimal displays, low staff intensity, efficient logistics) rather than by compromising on product quality.

- Eschew image factors such as expensive packaging.

- Encourage independent quality assessments.

- Create fancy labels to give the feeling of choice in a predominantly private label environment.

- Compensate for their lower dollar margins with higher asset turnover and growth potential that helps create significant wealth for their owners.

- Pass on many shopping functions to the consumer.

- Focus on an underserved target segment.

- Do not stray too far from this target segment to avoid the risk of losing the competitive cost advantage.

FIVE

Encircling Manufacturer Brands with Retailer Brand Portfolios

Wal-Mart's annual private label portfolio sales:
$115 billion

WHILE THE INDIVIDUAL private label follows one of the four propositions of generic, copycat, premium, and value innovator, most retailers manage a brand portfolio, which incorporates multiple types of store brands. By having a portfolio of own labels, a retailer can penetrate several different segments simultaneously. Traditionally, savvy segmentation of the total market has been a domain where branded goods manufacturers excelled. Nowadays, though, retailers implement a sophisticated mix of segmentation strategies to construct their own-brand portfolios.

Portfolio Segmentation Strategies

We broadly distinguish three portfolio segmentation strategies, based on price, category, or benefit.

Price-Based Segmentation

A price-based segmentation approach to a brand portfolio requires having at least two, and often three, store brands that help appeal to different price segments. European retailers, especially supermarkets, now implement a three-tiered private label strategy, with a low-end offering, a medium or standard range, and a premium store brand. For example, Sainsbury, in the U.K., has a low-priced line called Basics, the standard Sainsbury line, and the premium Taste the Difference product range. The three-tier price segmentation allows mainline supermarkets to fight their two perceived enemies: hard discounters and manufacturer brands. Carrefour in Spain communicates that in a particularly powerful way. At the front of each store, three baskets of products with accompanying cash register receipt and total are displayed, one filled with manufacturer brands (total price of the basket: €72.67), one with its own "Carrefour" copycat brand (€45.47), and one with its value brand "1" (€29.06). The display screams to shoppers, We can compete with Aldi if you are price sensitive, and with manufacturer brands if you are quality sensitive.

Category-Based Segmentation

Category-based private labels span a number of different products but within a specific merchandise category. This is often, though not always, a house-of-store-brands strategy—that is, where independent brands, which are not affiliated with one another or with the retailer, are sold next to one another. Since they are in separate categories, they are not competing with one another. The brand spanning a category can help communicate the unique brand associations and benefits that are important to the category in question. This can also be advantageous when there is no obvious connection between the retailer and the category or there are conflicting associations between categories (e.g., all-purpose cleaners are sold on functional performance but beauty products on image).

For example, Intersport, the largest sports equipment retailer in the world, with 4,700 stores in twenty-five countries, does not really have any identity except positioning itself on choice.[1] It therefore develops category brands, such as Etirel for clothes, Techno Pro for tennis, Nakamura for bicycles, and McKinley for winter sports, to communicate the necessary brand image for each category.

An additional benefit of the category approach to private labels accrues to retailers that rely largely on private labels, like Aldi, IKEA, and Gap. They can use a house-of-store-brands approach to create the feeling of choice for the consumer despite not carrying any brands. Historically, this was French retailer Intermarché's approach, with 240 private labels including Paturages in dairy, Paquito in nonalcoholic beverages, as well as May and Apta in health and beauty. Consumers often perceive these as secondary national brands selected by Intermarché for their quality and more affordable price.[2]

Whole Foods, in the U.S., has a range of private labels. Its 365 Organic Everyday Value brand targets price-sensitive customers, while its Authentic Food Artisans label is aimed at the more high-end food connoisseur. But its other brands are category based, including Whole Kitchen (frozen), Whole Treat (desserts), Whole Catch (fish), Whole Ranch (meat), Whole Kids Organic (children's food), and Allegro (coffee).

Benefit-Based Segmentation

A benefit-based segmentation strategy builds the individual store brands around the specific needs of a customer, as distinct from the customer's price sensitivity or category type. Retailers are aware of the changes in consumer lifestyles and needs. For example, the increase in the public's awareness of food safety and health means that organic ranges and foods purported to be healthy are increasing in popularity. In response, Kroger recently launched Naturally Preferred, its own brand of high-quality natural and organic products.

Additional trends, such as the popularity of low-carbohydrate diets, the rise of food allergies, and the increasing popularity of vegetarianism, have led to changing consumption patterns among consumers. Longer working hours and the increase in the proportion of working women have contributed to increasing demand for convenience foods, ranging in levels of preparation from pre-washed salads to ready meals. Building private label ranges around customer needs, such as organic, healthy living, free-from, fair-trade, and low-fat, allows a retailer to address differing consumer lifestyles.

Sainsbury, for example, has two benefit-based store brands: Be Good to Yourself and Blue Parrot Café. Launched in 1999, the Be Good to Yourself line contains over two hundred products that were "specially developed to help you towards a healthier lifestyle, offering lower fat and lower calorie foods that are bursting with flavour." The brand's promise is to be low-fat and salt-reduced, to contain equal or lower sugar levels than standard products and only colors permitted by the Hyperactive Children's Support Group, and to have restricted additives. Product packaging has clear labels to allow easy identification of nutritional content, including fat content.

The Be Good to Yourself brand was developed to make it easy for customers to shop for low-fat products, and in recognition of the fact that these customers are very valuable to Sainsbury, as revealed by customer loyalty cards. Consistent packaging across product categories and in-store promotions helped increase visibility of the range. Additionally, the brand aims to assure customers who perceive low-fat products as compromising taste. It is targeted at female consumers, especially mothers, who are aware of the benefits of a low-fat diet but are not prepared to compromise on food enjoyment or convenience. The brand has been highly successful and was identified as one of the top twenty-five U.K. brands in 1999.[3]

Sainsbury's Blue Parrot Café includes 250 products. Started in 2000, this brand is addressed at parents concerned about the nutritional quality of the food consumed by their children. The line was also developed in recognition of the fact that children influence the buying decisions of around half of households ("pester power"). The products promise to deliver great taste with improved nutritional quality and are aimed at attracting children age five to eleven. The Blue Parrot's "Beady Eye Promise" is to provide food with restricted colors and preservatives, only natural flavorings, controlled fat and salt levels, no flavor enhancers, and a choice of products sweetened with sugar or with artificial sweeteners. A traffic light system on the packaging indicates the product's nutritional profile and ingredient quality.

France's Carrefour presents another illustration of benefit-based segmentation. Its value line ("1") and the standard Carrefour store brand are complemented by several sophisticated own labels that cater to specific benefit segments: Reflets de France for the need for local authenticity; Carrefour Bio for environmentally conscious consumers; Escapades Gourmandes for the desire to escape to specialty gourmet foods; J'aime for products synonymous with health and fitness needs; and Destination Saveurs for international products that fulfill the need for novel, unexpected, and foreign experiences.

Complex Store Brand Portfolios

The leading private label retailers, especially mass merchandisers and supermarkets, are combining the three types of store brands—generic, copycat, and premium—with the three types of segmentation—price-based, category-based, and benefit-based— to create complex private label *portfolios* (see table 5-1). Wal-Mart and Tesco are two excellent examples of best practice in managing multibrand portfolios.

Wal-Mart

With $316 billion in sales and $11 billion in net income in 2005, Wal-Mart is the world's second-largest corporation. It prides itself on finding the best value for its customers, as expressed by its motto "Always Low Prices. Always." It draws 100 million

TABLE 5-1

Retailer brand portfolios

Retailer	Examples of some private labels carried by the retailer
Macy's (department)	I·N·C (youth fashion clothing), Charter Club (women's clothing), Tasso Elba (men's clothing), Style 2 (men's clothing), Club Room (men's clothing), American Bag (men's clothing), Hotel Collection (bedding), Alfani (suits), Tools of the Trade (cookware), The Cellar (dinnerware), Greendog (children's clothing), First Impressions (baby clothing)
Kohl's (department)	Sonoma (bath, bed, dining, home decor, kitchen, clothing), Croft & Barrow (women's clothing), apt. 9 (fashion clothing)
Walgreens (drugstore)	Deerfield Farms (cereal, dried fruits, candy, snacks), Secrets of Paradise (bath line), Land Before Time (children's vitamins, diapers), Walgreens (pharmacy, personal)
Home Depot (DIY)	Hampton Bay (ceiling fans, lighting, outdoor living), Behr (paint), Mills Pride (cabinets), Glacier Bay (kitchen and bath), Ryobi (power tools), Ridgid (Power tools), Toro (outdoor)
7-Eleven (convenience)	Big Eats (deli and baked goods), Slurpee (beverage), Big Gulp (beverage), Quality Classic Selection Spring Water, Santiago Cerveza de Oro (beer), Big Brew (coffee), Big Bite (hot dog), 7-Eleven Speak Out Wireless Services (mobile phone)
Office Depot (office supplies)	Office Depot (office supplies, printer and fax supplies, office furniture protection plans, credit cards), Viking (office products), Nice Day
Toys "R" Us (toys)	Animal Alley (plush), Fast Lane (toy cars and trucks), Fun Years (musical toys), Especially for Baby (baby furniture and accessories), Dream Dazzlers (dress-up sets)
Rite-Aid (drugstore)	Pure Spring (bath and body), Soaked in Tickles (children's line), Salon Plus and Style Masters (beauty care), Umberto Giannini (hair care line)
Limited Brands (apparel, beauty and personal care)	The Limited (apparel), Express (apparel), Victoria's Secret (lingerie), Bath & Body Works (personal care), Henri Bendel (lingerie), PINK (lingerie), C.O. Bigelow (personal care)
Decathlon (sports)	Decathlon Cycle (bicycles), Domyos (fitness equipment and clothing), Inesis (racket sports and golf), Tribord (water sports), Quechua (mountain sports), Kipsta (team sports)

customers per week to its 5,000 stores in ten countries. Wal-Mart had made its founder, Sam Walton, the richest American at the time of his death in 1992. In 2005, five of the fifteen richest people in the world were his surviving wife and four children!

Sam Walton opened the first Wal-Mart Discount City store in 1962. The store's original format was the discount store with no perishables, which nowadays tend to be around 100,000 square feet. In 1998, Wal-Mart started opening Supercenters, modeled after Carrefour of France, which are over double the size and a hybrid between a supermarket and a discount store. Supercenters include specialty stores and aim to be a one-stop shop for families doing their shopping. Many of the original discount stores have been converted to Supercenters. More recently, neighborhood markets that are smaller and located in urban centers have been tested. Finally, Sam's Club is a warehouse club, focusing on a limited number of large SKUs but delivering them at an extremely low cost.

Wal-Mart's original focus was very much on manufacturer brands, but now it is estimated to sell almost 40 percent private labels. In 1992, the Great Value line of private label grocery products was launched with 350 items. While it started out as a "me-too" value equivalent, the line soon became known as innovative, with many first-to-market items, such as lactose-free powdered milk, low-sugar orange juice (for low-carb dieters), and micro-wavable turkey gravy. It has introduced products aimed at specific customer segments, such as fruit nectars for the Hispanic community, and regional items, such as jambalaya mix or red beans and rice mix in the South.[4] With over $5 billion in sales and 1,300 products in 2005, Great Value was the top-selling brand in the U.S. grocery market. To penetrate the quality-conscious segment, in the late 1990s, Sam's Choice was launched as the premium line of grocery items.

Besides the price-based segmentation approach, Wal-Mart has also successfully implemented a portfolio of category-specific store brands. One of its most successful categories is Ol' Roy dog food. Named after Sam Walton's favorite hunting dog, the Ol' Roy range has five dry formulations, for different stages in a dog's life, as well as wet food and specialty products, such as Moist & Meaty, dog biscuits, and jerky treats. In 2004, it was the number-one-selling dog food in the U.S. Nutritionally the same as national brands, Ol' Roy costs significantly less.

Among Wal-Mart's clothing lines are trendy George and classic Faded Glory. George was developed by Wal-Mart's Asda stores in the U.K. and was internationally acclaimed as having the best price-quality ratio in men's clothing. Faded Glory is a $3 billion brand and was named the best-fitting jeans on the market by *Consumer Reports*. Levi Strauss—which had refused to allow Wal-Mart to carry its brand—reported a drop in its sales of jeans from $7 billion to $4 billion.[5] Equate health care products include shaving cream, soap and hair care products, over-the-counter medications, and pregnancy tests. Wal-Mart also has the home electronics brand Durabrand, which includes televisions, CD players, surround sound systems, and related products.

Wal-Mart's private label share is best in class in sixteen categories—more than any other retailer in the United States.[6] But it has penetrated certain categories more successfully than others. In categories such as breakfast meats, trash bags, frozen seafood, and ice cream, Wal-Mart has managed to acquire only an average or below-average private label share.

Tesco

Tesco was founded in London in 1924 by Jack Cohen, who espoused the "pile it high, sell it cheap" approach. It became Britain's leading supermarket in the mid-1990s, and its turnover in 2005 was $71 billion, with pretax profits exceeding $3 billion. While its food business dominates sales, its nonfood business (including clothing, home entertainment, stationery, news and magazines, as well as health and beauty) amounts to $11 billion. It has also launched a retailing services business, which includes online shopping, personal finance, and telecoms.

Present in thirteen countries, Tesco has 2,365 stores and 350,000 employees. In the U.K., it operates four different store formats: Tesco Express, which are neighborhood convenience stores; Tesco Metro in city centers for workplace shopping; Tesco Superstore for weekly shopping; and Tesco Extra stores, which are out-of-town hypermarkets that also stock nonfood items.

Central to Tesco's success are its twelve thousand private label product lines, which accounted for over half of the company's revenues, compared with 27 percent ten years ago! Tesco uses all three forms of segmentation—price, category, and benefits—to create its brand portfolio and deepen its penetration of the U.K. market. The Tesco brand architecture appears in figure 5-1.

Tesco has a brilliant price-segmented offering that caters to those on a budget and to those for whom price does not matter, but they are all looking for value.[7] Tesco has three price ranges of private labels: Tesco Value (low price), Tesco (medium or standard quality), and Tesco Finest (premium). As figure 3-1 demonstrated, the three price lines put a pincerlike grip on the manufacturer brands, often beating them both at the bottom end and at the top end.

FIGURE 5-1

Tesco brand architecture

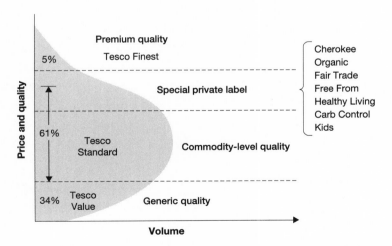

Source: Adapted from Jan-Willem Grievink, "Retailers and Their Private Label Policy" (presentation given at the 4th AIM Workshop, June 29, 2004).

Tesco Value. Tesco's Value range, launched in 1993 in response to Aldi's entry into the U.K., was made up of forty-one commodities or food staples for the average family. It has since grown to over two thousand products. The Value line was ideally placed to take advantage of the downward pressure on prices in the U.K. in recent years. Retailers were battling among themselves to outdo one another on price cuts. Between April 2004 and 2005, Tesco had invested over $500 million in price cuts, and it planned to invest a further $120 million. The cost of the original forty-one products in the Value range has fallen by about a third. In the words of Tesco's marketing director, Tim Mason, "The media has been talking about 'bargain Britain' in recent weeks. I believe Tesco Value [range] has been a driving force in bringing prices down for shoppers. That is why today we sell a Value iron for under a fiver, a pair of jeans for £3 and a kilo of potatoes for 40p."[8]

Tesco Standard and Finest. Its standard Tesco brand aims to provide good-quality products at a lower price than the manufacturer-branded equivalent. On the top end, Tesco's Finest range provides ready meals and chilled foods, and focuses on delivering superior quality for the high-end consumer, delivered in premium packaging. It is not considered cheap to arrive as a guest with a Tesco box of Finest Belgian chocolates. What is remarkable about the Tesco Finest line is that it is a premium-price store brand. The Value and Finest ranges are both extremely popular—and interestingly are not mutually exclusive when it comes to attracting customers, since 77 percent of customers buy from both ranges. Tesco has also managed to maintain clear distinctions between its various private label offerings.

Benefit-Based Tesco Subbrands. In the important food and prepared meals category, Tesco has created the following benefits extensions of the standard Tesco line:

1. *Tesco Carb Control.* A line of bakery products and ready and frozen meals naturally low in carbohydrates or low-carbohydrate versions of the standard product. This is

targeted at dieters who are trying to restrict their carbo-
hydrate consumption.

2. *Tesco Free From.* A range of 125 products for people
   with food allergies or intolerances. All products are
   gluten and wheat free, and many are also free from milk,
   soy, egg, maize (corn), yeast, or artificial additives.

3. *Tesco Healthy Eating.* Half the fat and a lower calorie
   intake than corresponding products, for those aiming to
   control the fat and calorie content of their diet.

4. *Tesco Organic.* A line of organic products for consumers
   concerned with pesticide residues in food or the environ-
   mental impact of agriculture and the environment.

5. *Tesco Serves One.* Single-serving prepared food, targeted
   at the single-member household.

6. *Tesco Simple Solutions.* Prepared convenience food that
   is preseasoned and requires minimal preparation by the
   consumer.

7. *Tesco Fair Trade.* A range of products whose producers
   are from developing countries and receive above-
   market prices for items, targeted at ethically conscious
   consumers.

Category Store Brands. In the clothing category, the category brands are further subsegmented by benefits as follows:

1. Cherokee, for low-cost, high-quality fashionable casual
   wear for young men and women

2. Back to School, for durable and good value school uni-
   forms for children and teenagers

3. Florence & Fred, for low-cost fashionable work wear
   and evening wear for women

4. F&F, for low-cost fashionable work wear and casual
   wear for men

In addition, there is Tesco Kids, a range of products, including ready meals, toiletries, and other items, aimed to be both attractive and beneficial to children and their parents.

Tesco has been an amazing story over the past two decades, turning from an industry follower with a cheap image into the dominant industry leader. The private label portfolio has been critical in its march to the leadership position. The various private label brands have given Tesco the ability to serve almost all segments effectively within a single store and become the U.K.'s supermarket. In its advertising, it communicates this rather effectively. Over time, it has managed to upgrade its image to a level where the Tesco Finest range in certain categories can command a premium price against the manufacturer brands.

Managing Store Brand Portfolios

As retailers move from a single store brand to actively managing multibrand private label portfolios, they can face additional challenges. The three types of store brands combined with three types of segmentation can ultimately lead to very complex portfolios. If the retailers' own brands are not smartly differentiated, they may just end up stealing each other's sales, just as Old Navy initially siphoned off Gap sales by offering similar merchandise at cheaper prices.[9]

Store Brand Proliferation

Enamored by complex private label portfolios, some retailers have gone too far with store brand proliferation. This has led to brand rationalization programs. For example, Winn-Dixie replaced sixty private labels with its store brand. Carrefour also found that its three-basket display described earlier led some consumers to compare the "1" value line with the standard Carrefour line instead of comparing it against hard discounters like Aldi. As a result, some consumers started observing that the Carrefour standard line is overpriced compared with the "1" line.

Cannibalization

Overlapping store brands can lead to cannibalization. To avoid cannibalization, America's Target has given considerable thought to positioning its two private labels in grocery. Archer Farms is premium quality. All Archer Farms products are created with the very best ingredients so consumers "can expect the greatest flavor in each and every bite," while Market Pantry positions itself on price. On shelves, Target positions Archer Farms products next to premium brands, while Market Pantry–branded items sit next to lower-priced brands. Shelf location is important, because Target consciously seeks to prevent the consumer from making direct price comparisons between its two private label brands.

Failure Risks

In pushing their private labels, retailers must beware of the significant negative consequences of poorly managed private labels.[10] A single product failure in the private label range can have a backlash on the retailer's overall image. The customer may start believing that if the retailer's doughnuts are not good, perhaps its bread will be the same. Does the customer spend enough effort in processing the differences between the value line and the premium line to keep the failure in the value line apart from the quality in the premium line?

Variety Reduction

A proliferating store brand portfolio requires all the brands to find adequate shelf space. The temptation for the retailer can be to assign the scarce shelf space to its brands at the expense of manufacturer brands. Some manufacturer brands may even have to be dropped to make space for the new private labels. For example, the orange juice category at Tesco, shown in figure 3-1, has several Tesco brands. As a result, it has become hard for some shoppers to find the manufacturer-branded orange juice products at Tesco stores. This may turn off a large segment of the customers who feel that their choice is being constrained by the retailer. Even the Swiss retailer Migros, which has been historically anti–manufacturer brands, is now adding branded products from Nestlé, Ferrero, and L'Oréal to give consumers choice.

The new reality of private labels has necessitated the overturning of many prevailing industry assumptions regarding their quality and price. In addition, traditionally it was believed that focused retailers like Aldi, Victoria's Secret, Whole Foods, and Zara are more easily able to create brands customers are passionate about. In contrast, large multicategory retailers struggle because they are trying to be all things to all people. However, as Target and Tesco demonstrate, a big box does not have to be just a box; it can be an intense brand that consumers fall in love with.

The challenge to retailers as they build their private label brands is to somehow develop a relationship with their customers, above and beyond simply price considerations. Essentially, the question is, If the price were the same, would any customers purchase the store brand in preference to the manufacturer brand? To date, very few retailers can answer yes to this question, and even there, only in a limited number of categories.

Chapter Takeaways

Successful Retailer Brand Portfolios

- Adopt a sophisticated mix of price-based segmentation, category-based segmentation, and benefit-based segmentation strategies to deepen the retailer's penetration into all consumer segments.

- Use price-based segmentation to create at least two private labels ("value" and "standard"), but increasingly a third price tier ("premium") to attack the mainstream retailer's twin enemies of value innovators and manufacturer brands.

- Employ category-based segmentation to give shoppers a sense of choice and make it easier to imbue the category-specific private labels with unique and relevant brand associations.

- Exploit benefit-based segmentation to give the retailer the flexibility to cater to changes in consumer lifestyles and needs by building individual store brands around specific needs.

- Limit store brand proliferation, cannibalization, spillover effects of product failures, and perceived variety reduction for consumers in order to avoid the shortcomings of complex store brand portfolios.

- Manage the costs of a complex retailer brand portfolio that may mitigate the ultimate advantage on which much of the appeal of store brands is based—better value for money in each price tier.

SIX

Creating Successful Private Labels Is About More Than Just Price

Manufacturer brands' price premium
if quality is at par with private labels:
37 percent

A S THE PREVIOUS CHAPTERS DEMONSTRATE, there is considerable variety in private labels. However, except for a few "premium priced" private labels mostly in the food category, private labels overwhelmingly still sell at a discount to major manufacturer brands. Thus, industry wisdom holds that private labels sell on price.

It is undeniably true that buying private labels helps consumers save money. A telling illustration is that an Internet search on "Buying private labels saves money" yielded 13.9 million hits![1] This has led managers in both retail and manufacturer organizations to believe that the larger the price gap is between private labels and manufacturer brands, the more successful private labels are. Yet it is far from obvious that successful private labels are all about lower prices compared with manufacturer brands.

FIGURE 6-1

Global private label share and price gap

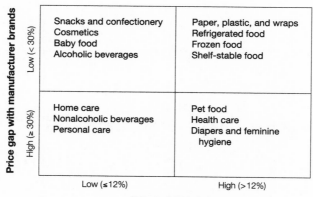

Source: Derived from ACNielsen, *The Power of Private Label 2005* (ACNielsen Global Services, 2005).

Figure 6-1 provides the global private label share and the price gap between private labels and manufacturer brands for fourteen CPG categories.[2] We see that in some categories where the price gap is *large*—home care, nonalcoholic beverages, and personal care—private label share is *low*. On the other hand, private labels command a *high* market share while the price differential is *small* for refrigerated, frozen, and shelf-stable food, as well as for plastic, paper, and wraps. Clearly, reality is more complex and subtle than simply recommending that retailers lower their private label prices to drive private label share.

Perceived Quality Versus Price as Driver of Private Label Success

How can private labels apparently be successful without having to rely on the price weapon? Economic theory holds that the price consumers are willing to pay for a product depends on the utility they derive from consuming the product. A major source of utility is the *perceived quality* of the product. Perceived quality is defined as the degree of perceived performance excellence of the product.[3] How well does the brand perform its functions in the eyes of the consumer?

Consider how one U.S. consumer thinks about Crest toothpaste: "I knew from experience that Crest was most effective for, you know, the enzymes in my mouth. I mean, being the tooth freak I am, I know everybody's saliva is different and the way it combines with toothpaste to combat cavities is different, and Crest is just right for me and the type of saliva I have."[4]

Perceived Quality, Not Price, Drives Private Label Success

A good illustration of the importance of quality is the performance of the private label of the leading Dutch retail chain Albert Heijn, a subsidiary of Royal Ahold. We studied the performance of AH, Albert Heijn's copycat store brand, across nineteen CPG categories.[5] In four categories (e.g., evaporated milk, coffee), it is very successful, commanding, on average, a national market share of 15 percent, while the price gap with the leading manufacturer brands is only 12 percent. This is all the more impressive if one realizes that AH is sold only in Albert Heijn, which commands a market share of 25 percent. On the other hand, in the other fifteen categories (e.g., margarine, beer, cornflakes, pantiliners), AH is considerably less successful. It commands a much lower market share (on average, 7 percent) while being 21 percent cheaper than the leading manufacturer brands!

At first sight, the results seem an anomaly. A small price gap with leading manufacturer brands is associated with a large market share for AH, and a large price gap with a small market share. How is that possible? That is because in categories in which AH is successful, consumers believe that it is of considerably higher quality. In fact, the average perceived quality rating (on a 7-point scale) for the four top categories is 5.3 versus 4.6 in the other categories.

But how does that drive the market success of AH? To understand this, let us consider the price sensitivity of consumers and the perceived quality difference between leading manufacturer brands and AH. When we combine these two dimensions, this results in a two-by-two matrix (see figure 6-2) with four cells: random buyers, brand buyers, private label buyers, and toss-ups.

- *Random buyers* are not particularly price sensitive and see little difference in quality.

- *Brand buyers* are consumers who are low on price sensitivity and perceive a large quality difference between leading manufacturer brands and the store brand. They will buy a manufacturer brand.

- *Private label buyers* are price-sensitive consumers who perceive a small quality gap between leading manufacturer brands and the store brand. They will purchase the store brand.

- *Toss-ups* are consumers who are high on price sensitivity and perceive large quality differences between leading manufacturer brands and the store brand.

The key battleground is among toss-ups and random buyers. However, the strategy to induce them to buy private labels is very different. Random buyers can be attracted to the private label by using in-store stimuli that guide the shopper to the private label, such as favorable shelf facings, shelf tag-ons, and end-of-the-aisle displays. Toss-ups will usually purchase a manufacturer brand since for most consumers quality is more important than price.[6] This is especially true if the manufacturer brand regularly runs price promotions, which will appeal to the toss-ups' high price sensitivity.

Private labels can convert toss-ups into private label buyers only if they convince consumers that the quality of the private labels is comparable to, if not better than, the quality of the manufacturer brands. And this is exactly what Albert Heijn has been

FIGURE 6-2

Four types of buyers

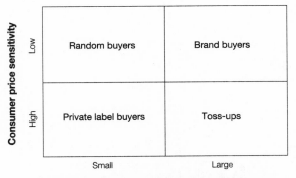

Perceived quality gap with manufacturer brands

able to achieve in its four successful categories (e.g., evaporated milk, coffee). In these categories, Albert Heijn has closed the perceived quality gap with leading manufacturer brands. Consequently, many toss-up consumers have become buyers of AH. This, together with the segment of private label buyers and a hefty share of the random buyers (by giving AH favorable shelf facings), leads to the high market share observed in these categories. In the other categories, AH has been less successful in closing the perceived quality gap. Hence, it can only attract customers that are high on price sensitivity (i.e., private label buyers) by charging a much lower price than manufacturer brands.

Perceived Quality Gap Varies Across Categories

The Albert Heijn case illustrates that the perceived quality of the AH copycat brand varies across categories. However, it concerns one specific store brand. Table 6-1 takes us one step further by looking at the perceived quality gap between manufacturer and store brands in *general*. The findings are based on sixty-six CPG categories as perceived by U.S. consumers.[7]

TABLE 6-1

Perceived quality gap between manufacturer and store brands

Store brand better (2%)	Quality equivalent (9%)	Small quality gap (44%)	Large quality gap (40%)	Very large quality gap (5%)
Electric light bulbs	Bleach	Baby food	Antismoking products	Beer
	Frozen fish	Bean and ground coffee	Batteries	Candy bars
	Frozen vegetables	Breakfast cereals	Canned soup	Diapers
	Frozen meat	Butter	Carbonated soft drinks	
	Soft cheese	Canned fruit	Cookies	
	Vitamins, minerals, and supplements	Cat food	Deodorants	
		Crackers	Dog food	
		Dentifrice/toothpaste	Facial tissues	
		Dish detergent	Hair-coloring products	
		Fabric softener liquid	Hand creams	
		Floor cleaners	Heavy-duty detergent	
		Frozen pizza	Household cleaners	
		Frozen dinners/entrees	Ice cream	
		Frozen poultry	Mayonnaise	
		Hair-conditioning products	Mustard and ketchup	
		Hairsprays	Paper towels	
		Hard cheese	Peanut butter	
		Jam	Razor blades	
		Margarine and spreads	Salty snacks	
		Mineral water	Sanitary napkins/tampons	
		Oral care (mouthwashes and floss)	Shampoo	
		Pasta	Spaghetti sauce	
		Processed cheese	Spirits	
		Pure fruit juice	Table wine	
		Shaving foams and soaps	Toilet tissues	
		Shower and bath additives	Toothbrush/dental accessories	
		Tea		
		Toilet soap		
		Yogurt		

Source: AiMark, 2006; http://www.aimark.org/. Reproduced with permission.

Table 6-1 shows that:

1. At the category level, perceived quality can still vary significantly between manufacturer and store brands.

2. In 89 percent of the categories, manufacturer brands are perceived to be of better quality than store brands.

3. In 45 percent of the categories, the perceived quality gap is managerially significant (i.e., large or very large quality gap).

This last result indicates that there is still the opportunity for the best manufacturer brands to differentiate themselves by being "simply better."[8] However, the fact that in more than 50 percent of the categories the quality gap is small implies that the writing is on the wall for CPG companies—improve quality or suffer the consequences.

Manufacturer Brands' Irrational Price Premium

Are consumers willing to pay more for better quality? After all, it is nice that they value quality, but better-quality products often cost more to produce, which translates into higher prices. Thus, the question is whether products of higher perceived quality also command a higher price in the marketplace.

The news is encouraging for manufacturers. Consumers are often willing to pay a disproportionate price premium for better quality, because quality typically weighs more heavily than price in purchase decisions.[9] We examined the relationship between the perceived quality gap and the price premium commanded by manufacturer brands over private labels for CPGs in France, one of the world's most important and competitive private label markets. The analysis was based on seventy-five CPG categories.[10] Here's what we found:

- In categories where the perceived quality of manufacturer brands exceeds the quality of store brands, the average price premium for manufacturer brands is 56 percent.

- In quality-equivalent categories (i.e., categories where consumers do not perceive a quality difference between manufacturer and store brands), the price premium commanded by manufacturer brands is 37 percent.

- Finally, in categories where the perceived quality of store brands exceeds the quality of manufacturer brands, the price premium for manufacturer brands is 21 percent.

The French findings are consistent with evidence from the United States:[11]

- A recent study (using "objective" quality as reported by *Consumer Reports*) finds that a 1 percent quality gap between manufacturer and store brands is associated with a 5 percent price gap.

- The price premium that manufacturer brands command in quality-equivalent markets is the same as in France, or 37 percent.

- In 33 percent of the cases, consumers perceive manufacturer and store brands as quality equivalent; however, they are willing to pay the same price for the store brand as for the manufacturer brand in only 5 percent of the cases.

What does this all mean?

1. The perceived quality gap between manufacturer and store brands is an important factor driving the price gap in the marketplace.

2. Quality is not the entire story. There is a "residual" price gap that cannot be explained by quality perceptions. Recall that we found that in categories where consumers *do*

not perceive a quality difference between manufacturer and store brands, the price premium commanded by manufacturer brands still is a substantial 37 percent. Consumers are unwilling to pay equivalent prices for store brands even if they perceive them as quality equivalent.

This last result is rather depressing for retailers. Why are consumers willing to pay a price premium for manufacturer brands, even when they do not perceive a quality difference between manufacturer and store brands? The reason is that manufacturer brands have a clear advantage on brand imagery.

Brand Imagery and the Price Gap

Manufacturer brands offer something intangible that most private labels do not (yet) offer. They allow consumers to identify with the values imbued in the brand, and help consumers express who they are and how these brands fit into their lifestyle and self-concept. *Brand imagery* refers to the personalized social-emotional bond the consumer has with a brand. What does the brand stand for, and does that appeal to me? Consumers show no difficulty in assigning personality characteristics to brands, in thinking about brands as if they are animated, humanized, and personalized.[12] For example, brands like Marlboro, Harley-Davidson, Jack Daniels, and Levi's glamorize American ideals of the West, strength, and masculinity, while sophisticated brands like Gucci, Chivas Regal, Revlon, and Mercedes are associated with aspirational imagery such as the upper class, glamour, and sexiness.[13]

These image components, regardless of the functional qualities of the product, can be extremely important to people. Two brands may be quality equivalent, but if one brand is stronger on image, it will generate higher utility in the target segment. Consumers are willing to pay a price premium for image utility.

Using the French CPG data mentioned earlier, we found:

- The average price premium commanded by manufacturer brands in categories that are *low* on imagery (e.g., floor cleaners, kitchen paper, canned green beans) is 38 percent.

- The average price premium commanded by manufacturer brands in categories that are *high* on imagery (e.g., deodorants, hair-coloring products, whiskey) is 61 percent.[14]

Thus, the price premium associated with brand imagery is, on average, 23 percent. Brand imagery contributes significantly to the price gap, even in such "mundane" categories as CPGs.

Importance of Brand Imagery Varies Across Consumers

The weight placed on brand imagery in any given category differs among consumers. For some consumers, the brand of coffee, fountain pen, suit, or even car tire is an important aspect of their self-concept, while others could not care less. In an interesting study, Professor Susan Fournier explores the emotional ties three U.S. females have with certain brands.[15]

Jean (married, fifty-nine years old) has powerful emotional brand attachments in food categories connected to her core identity as an Italian-American wife and mother. She has strong emotional ties with tomatoes (Pastene), olive oil (Bertolli), tomato paste (Contadina), bread crumbs (Progresso), and even the pan in which she cooks her spaghetti sauce (Revere Ware).

Kay (recently divorced, thirty-nine years old) shows few emotional bonds with brands, but personal care brands are emotionally charged. More specifically, Mary Kay and Dove are central to her feelings of the need to retain a youthful appearance, and offer a unique opportunity to exert a sense of independence since these brands were rejected by others in her household. She also embraces Gatorade, Coca-Cola Classic, and Reebok running shoes. Because of her personal history, Reebok has become a symbol of her vitality, independence, and overall self-sufficiency.

Vicky (unmarried, twenty-three years old) is the most involved with brands in general and the most emotionally loyal to specific brands in particular, ranging from perfumes (Opium as nighttime seductive, Intimate Musk as everyday friend), makeup, and lingerie to ice cream and baked beans. By being faithful to her brands, her core self-image remains intact. It really bothers her that in the area she moved to, they don't sell B&M Baked Beans.

This study reveals that imagery is not inherent to specific categories but rather can be created in any category with astute marketing. If somebody can miss baked beans, one can miss anything. Working with one of the world's largest CPG companies, we learned that ourselves. We wondered how there could possibly be any image utility associated with paper towels. In response, the president of the global paper unit of that company pointed out that it had been able to achieve just that in the United States, while admitting that it had not really tried to do that in Europe. As a result, the company has a much higher price premium and market share in the United States than in Europe. Whether a manufacturer brand or a store brand possesses image utility depends not only on the individual consumer but also on the marketing strategy of the company.

Some Generalizations Across Consumers

Although the importance of brand imagery varies across consumers, some generalizations still emerge:[16]

- Younger consumers attach more importance to brand imagery because of their greater desire for social acceptability, besides being more image conscious in general (this is consistent with Vicky's being most involved with brands).

- Singles and couples attach more importance to image utility than larger families.

- Poorer consumers give more weight to brand imagery. This seems paradoxical since they stand to gain most from purchasing lower-priced store brands. However, it allows them to show the world that they are also "sophisticated" consumers. Thus, the fact that the poor buy private labels more often than the rich is because they have to, not because they want to.

Implications for Retailers

We have learned that there is a lot more to private label success than price. We can formalize these ideas by drawing on economic theory. Consumers will purchase a private label if the price premium for the manufacturer brand *exceeds* the utility the consumer derives from the surplus in perceived quality and imagery (if any) generated by manufacturer brands. If the price premium is *less* than the gap in quality and image utility, the consumer will choose the manufacturer brand.

Thus, private labels do not have to compete on price alone. Beyond managing the price gap, they can also compete on two nonprice strategies. We will discuss them first before turning to managing the price gap.

Decreasing the Perceived Quality Gap

One way to decrease the perceived quality gap with manufacturer brands is to increase the *objective (actual) quality* of the private label by using better materials, procurement from top-notch suppliers, and so on. Objective quality, in turn, is positively correlated with perceived quality, although the correlation is far from perfect.

A second path to decreasing the quality gap is to adopt a *copycat* strategy, whereby the retailer introduces a private label as a me-too product that is very similar to a (leading) manufacturer brand (see also chapter 2). The copycat strategy accounts for more than 50 percent of the store brand introductions in the CPG industry.[17] Illustrative is the strategy of the U.S. grocery chain Dominick's in the ready-to-eat cereal market. Its store brand imitates manufacturer brands that are sales leaders in their respective segments and are among the largest brands in the overall cereal market: Cheerios, Frosted Flakes, Rice Krispies, Corn Flakes, Raisin Bran, and Froot Loops.[18]

Copycat is an effective retailer strategy to decrease the price premium commanded by manufacturer brands. In France, the price gap between manufacturer brands and private labels in categories where private labels have successfully implemented a copycat strategy is, on average, 30 percent, while the price gap is 69 percent in categories where the degree of (package) similarity between manufacturer and store brands is low.[19]

Decreasing the Image Gap

Another way to avoid the price game is to imbue one's store brand with imagery. Traditionally, compared with manufacturer brands, private labels have fared much worse on brand imagery than on perceived quality (let alone objective quality). But as we discussed in chapter 3, there are more and more examples where private labels are narrowing the image gap too. Think about Pick 'n Pay's (South Africa) line of Foodhall, Loblaws's (Canada) President's Choice, and Macy's (U.S.) The Cellar (dinnerware).

Retailers are also starting to advertise their store brand in the media. As noted by Brian Sharoff, president of the Private Label Manufacturers Association: "Ten years ago, retailers focused on the top national brands in television advertising. Today, Kroger, A&P and Safeway are all doing terrific advertising that lets shoppers know. 'This is the only place you can get our brand.'"[20] Britain's Tesco and the Netherlands' Albert Heijn are among the biggest advertisers in their countries.

By decreasing the perceived quality and/or brand imagery gap with manufacturer brands, the retailer increases the attractiveness of its private label. This allows the retailer to increase the price of its private label and hence to move the game from price to non-price competition.

Increasing the Price Gap Between Manufacturer and Store Brands

The retailer might also play the classic price game. In this case, it attempts to increase the price gap between its store brand and the manufacturer brand to ensure that the price premium commanded by the manufacturer brand exceeds the gap in perceived quality and image utility with the store brand.

One way to increase the attractiveness of its private label is to increase the price of the manufacturer brands. In general, that is a risky strategy because the prices of manufacturer brands are readily comparable across retail chains. Consumers use prices for manufacturer brands charged by different retailers to form an impression of a retailer's overall price image. However, sometimes retailers disfavor manufacturer brands that they imitate by charging higher prices, while lowering the price of manufacturer brands that they do not imitate.[21]

The obvious alternative is to offer the private label at a low price so that the price gap between the manufacturer brand and the retailer's own private label becomes sufficiently large—at least for a sizable market segment—to compensate for the lower perceived quality and/or image utility of the store brands. This raises the question, What is the optimal price gap between private label and manufacturer brands for the retailer to maximize its category sales?

The Optimal Price Gap for the Retailer

The optimal price gap depends on the price sensitivity of the manufacturer brands, the price sensitivity of the store brand, and the effect of manufacturer and store brand prices on each other.[22] Too big a price gap reduces the sales the retailer derives from manufacturer brands. However, and counterintuitively, it may also reduce private label revenues. Why is that the case? As we will show later, this is because the retailer "is leaving money on the table."

Wharton professors Stephen Hoch and Leonard Lodish conducted a rigorous field experiment on the optimal price gap for analgesics involving all eighty-four stores of a U.S. grocery retailer.[23] Three price gaps (15 percent, 33 percent, and 50 percent) were created by holding constant the prices of all manufacturer brands' SKUs and by raising or lowering the price of the comparable store brand SKUs. The pretest price gap was about 33 percent. The experiment ran for six months, and results were compared with those of the previous six months. We focus on the two new price gaps (15 percent and 50 percent). The results are summarized in table 6-2.[24]

The results present a consistent picture. As one would expect, unit sales for manufacturer brands *decrease* with larger price gaps (15 percent versus 50 percent), albeit with a modest −3.5 percent. There is a more substantial *increase* of 23 percent in private label

TABLE 6-2

Price gap analysis for analgesics in U.S. grocery chain

	PERCENT CHANGE IN UNIT SALES		
Price gap	**Manufacturer brands**	**Private label**	**Total category**
15%	0	0	0
50%	−3.5%	23.0%	4.2%

	PERCENT CHANGE IN $ SALES REVENUE		
Price gap	**Manufacturer brands**	**Private label**	**Total category**
15%	0	0	0
50%	−3.4%	−9.2%	−3.5%

Source: Adapted from Stephen J. Hoch and Leonard M. Lodish, "Store Brands and Category Management" (working paper, Wharton School, Philadelphia, PA, 1998).

demand when the price gap widens from 15 percent to 50 percent. Total category *unit* sales are 4.2 percent higher, with a large price gap. However, this comes at the expense of a considerably lower average price, as the price of the private label decreases 41 percent (from 85 percent to 50 percent of the price of the brands). This suggests a rather low price sensitivity of the private label. A 23 percent increase in unit sales for a 41 percent decline in prices indicates a price elasticity of –0.56. This means that a 1 percent decrease in the price of the private label leads to a 0.56 percent increase in unit sales.

When price elasticities are between 0 and –1, volume moves less strongly than price—that is, lowering prices destroys value. And that is what is evident in sales revenue figures (table 6-2). The retailer's category sales *revenues* are 3.5 percent *higher* in the 15 percent price gap condition!

The key takeaway of this important study is that the demand for private labels may be not particularly sensitive to (1) the absolute level of the price of the store brand and (2) the price gap with the manufacturer brand. Retailer category revenues may be higher if the retailer charges higher prices for its private label.

Bringing It All Together

We are not arguing that competition on price is not a viable strategy. Price gap management is a vital component of any private label strategy, as shown in this chapter. However, focusing disproportionately on price means that often the retailer leaves money on the table. Investing money in improving objective and perceived quality (e.g., through brand imitation) and creating imagery for the store brand are often more effective. Moreover, it directs mainstream retailers away from head-to-head competition with hard discounters, battles they increasingly find hard to win, given radically different business models (see chapter 4).

Chapter Takeaways

Successful Retailer Private Label Strategies

- Manage the price gap with manufacturer brands by varying the prices of the private labels rather than by increasing the prices of manufacturer brands, since the latter has a detrimental effect on the retailer's overall price positioning.

- Understand that there is a large variation across categories with respect to perceived quality of store brands vis-à-vis manufacturer brands.

- Recognize that more consumers are quality sensitive rather than price sensitive, and therefore a small quality gap may matter more than a large price gap.

- Concede that even in quality-equivalent markets, manufacturer brands command a price premium of 37 percent, and this price premium is due to the superior brand imagery of manufacturer brands.

- Compete on both price and nonprice aspects. But given the importance of non-price aspects (quality and brand imagery), it is especially attractive for store brands to compete by improving quality, reducing quality gaps through copycats, and creating brand imagery.

- Maintain a small price gap between manufacturer brands and the store brand, since contrary to what one may expect, retailer revenues are higher with smaller price gaps.

SEVEN

Maximizing Retailer Profitability Using Private Labels

Retailer gross margins on private labels versus manufacturer brands:
25–30 percent higher

THERE IS A WIDESPREAD BELIEF among retailers and brand manufacturers that retailers make greater profits when they sell private labels instead of manufacturer brands. While working with one of the world's largest consumer packaged goods companies, we heard its top managers wondering why retailers were selling their brands at all, given that the store brands were so much more profitable for the retailer! But is selling private labels truly more profitable for retailers? Is this always true? Or are there certain conditions under which this may not be true?

Retailers believe that the higher profits they generate selling private labels flow from four sources:

- *Better profit margins* because the retailer earns a higher margin and unit dollar profit on its own private label products

- *Greater leverage* because the presence of private labels in a category allows the retailer to negotiate a better margin on manufacturer brands

- *Building store loyalty* because private labels help differentiate the retailer, and consumers who purchase these store brands can only do so at the retailer in question, thereby making consumers more loyal to the store

- *Higher customer profitability* because the shopper who favors private labels is considered to be more profitable for the retailer (higher margins on private labels and greater store loyalty) than a shopper who largely purchases manufacturer brands from the retailer

We discuss each of these in turn and demonstrate that the story is a lot more nuanced than it appears at first sight. At the outset, we note that this discussion pertains to mainstream retailers that carry both manufacturer and store brands. The business model for value innovators such as Aldi and Lidl, but also H&M and IKEA, is completely different. They sell low-priced private labels, yielding unbeatable value to consumers and huge profits to the value innovator because of superior and innovative organization of the value chain (see chapter 4).

Better Profit Margins on Private Labels

In a *Discount Merchandiser* survey, retailers rated "better profit margins" as the most important reason for carrying store brands.[1] Private labels generate higher margins because store brand suppliers have virtually no market power. The private label supplier market has all the characteristics of what economists describe as "perfect competition."

There are many private label manufacturers. For example, 1,638 companies participated in a recent private label trade show in Amsterdam. Or think of the thousands of Chinese shoe manufacturers. The market share of any individual private label supplier is usually low. Product differentiation by definition is virtually absent, and they sell to professional retail buyers who are well informed about product quality and availability.[2] Retailers often set the technical specifications and ask private label manufacturers to bid on contracts.

In such perfectly competitive markets, standard economic theory dictates that the retailer will be able to drive the acquisition price of its private label down to the point where marginal costs of production equal average costs. Therefore, the retailer will capture most of the total system profits, resulting in high retailer gross margins on private labels.

Gross Margins Are Higher

The data clearly supports economic theory. On average, the retailer's gross margin on private labels is 25 to 30 percent higher than its gross margin from manufacturer brands. To illustrate, if the gross margin on manufacturer brands is 20 percent, the average gross margin on the store brand is 25 to 26 percent. However, there is considerable variation between categories.

In the health, beauty, and cosmetics category, private labels tend to have much higher gross margins than manufacturer brands. The category is characterized by strong manufacturer brand names, heavy brand advertising, and high personal relevance to consumers. Thus, manufacturers need to offer retailers smaller gross margins than they do in other categories. The result is that gross margins for retailers on store brands in health, beauty, and cosmetics become relatively more attractive than on manufacturer brands.

Dollar Profit per Square Foot Is the Appropriate Measure

So far so good, but gross margins are only part of the story with respect to retailer profitability. Profit optimization requires that profitability be calculated in monetary (dollar) terms with respect to the critical resource of a company. For brick-and-mortar retailers, shelf space is the critical resource. Hence, simply concentrating on private label gross margins is misleading. Dollar profit per square foot is the measure of profitability that retailers should focus on. Four factors intervene between gross margin and dollar profit per square foot of shelf space.

First, retailers typically extract from brand manufacturers many additional discounts and off-invoice allowances, such as slotting allowances, listing fees, promotion deals, advertising and merchandising allowances, and credit for return of unsold merchandise. These are absent in the case of private labels.

Second, brand manufacturers provide various "free" services, like transportation, warehouse and store labor, and merchandising help for retailers. For private labels, the retailer usually must bear all the costs of these services. Taking these two factors into account implies that the difference between private labels and manufacturer brands on *net* margins is less than on *gross* margins.

Third, manufacturer brands usually retail at a considerably higher price than private labels. Thus, even when the net margin as a percentage on manufacturer brands is lower, the absolute dollar profit per unit sold may still be higher than for store brands (e.g., 20 percent of $2.00 is higher than 25 percent of $1.50).

Fourth, shelf space turnover, referred to as *velocity*, is often much higher for manufacturer brands. European data indicates that, on average, the velocity of (leading) manufacturer brands is at least 10 percent higher. If anything, our work with companies indicates that this is a conservative estimate.

Industry wisdom believes that higher private label shares translate into higher dollar profits. For example, according to Christian Haub, CEO of the A&P supermarket chain, "Private label for us is clearly a huge opportunity . . . We know that every percentage-point improvement is associated with significant increases in profit-dollars."[3] But is this really true once the preceding four factors are taken into account?

Profitability Analysis Studies

A study commissioned by PepsiCo in the Canadian market showed "the national brand to be more profitable than private labels once all factors, including deal allowances, warehousing, transportation, and in-store labor were taken into account."[4] A similar study in the U.K., commissioned by Coca-Cola, reveals similar differences in the profitability of store brands versus Coca-Cola. A study of saltine crackers finds that the percentage margin is higher for the store brand, but—because of the lower selling price—dollar profits are actually lower.[5] A McKinsey study covering sixty food categories claimed "almost half of the private label products produced less profit per cubic meter than brand leader counterparts."[6]

The Boston Consulting Group studied the economics of fifty SKUs at two major U.S. retailers and found "on average, that branded and private label were near parity on penny profits but differed widely by category and item." For example, although private label and branded cereals yield the same gross dollar profit, 31¢ per item sold, the private label cereals are less profitable because of low velocity. On the other hand, the dollar profit on private label diapers ($1.49) is so much higher than the dollar profit on the leading manufacturer brand (43¢) that the 50 percent higher velocity of the branded diapers could not compensate for this difference.[7]

Table 7-1 summarizes the key findings of what is probably the most extensive profitability analysis to date. It provides results— aggregated across more than two hundred product categories— for private label versus manufacturer brands for a major U.S. supermarket chain.[8] For illustrative purposes, we assume an average retail price for the private label of $1. Based on proprietary European data, we further assume that shelf turnover of national brands is, on average, 10 percent higher than shelf turnover of private labels. As mentioned earlier, this is probably a conservative assumption.[9]

TABLE 7-1

Profitability analysis of private labels versus manufacturer brands (U.S. grocery retail chain)

	Private labels	Manufacturer brands
Gross margin	30.1%	21.7%
Net margin	23.2%	15.9%
Price*	$1.00	$1.45
Dollar contribution	$0.23	$0.23
Velocity per square foot (index)	90	100
Direct product profitability	21	23

*Assumed price of private labels is $1.00.

Source: Adapted from Kusum L. Ailawadi and Bari A. Harlam, "An Empirical Analysis of the Determinants of Retail Margins: The Role of Store Brand Share," Journal of Marketing (January 2004): 159.

Table 7-1 demonstrates that, in general, one cannot assume that retailers have higher profitability on private labels. The higher gross margin on private labels compensates for the lower private label prices, and, therefore, the penny profits are the same on both private labels and manufacturer brands. In fact, at many retailers, such as Kroger, the policy is to earn identical penny profits on private labels and manufacturer brands. Yet, as table 7-1 indicates, velocity, or shelf space turnover, is of crucial importance. Because of high brand awareness and advertising support, leading manufacturer brands can enjoy significantly higher velocity.

Greater Leverage over Brands

Apart from higher margins on private labels, retailers listed "bargaining tools with branded manufacturers" as one of the prime benefits of introducing a private label in the category.[10] The presence of own labels helps the retailer negotiate better terms with branded manufacturers.[11] Even the most valuable brands in the world are not immune to this pressure. A former high-level marketing executive of Coca-Cola conceded that Coca-Cola significantly lowered the wholesale price of its products in response to the introduction and aggressive shelf placement of a premium store brand by a large supermarket chain.[12]

Private Labels' Impact on Manufacturer Brand Margins

Retailer margins on manufacturer brands vary widely across categories. Under what conditions is a retailer able to extract higher margins from brand manufacturers? According to industrial economics theory, the margin secured by a party is directly related to its *market power*. The greater the power of its store brand in a category, the more margin the retailer should be able to extract from manufacturer brands. Empirical research reveals that this theory is remarkably accurate.

In one study, it was found that the retail margin for Quaker Oats increased after the introduction of a store brand, indicating that the retailer gained power.[13] In another important, large-scale U.S. study, Dartmouth College professor Kusum Ailawadi and CVS vice president for market intelligence, Bari Harlam, demonstrated that a retailer's margin on *manufacturer brands* is higher for categories where the retailer's private label commands a larger share.[14] The supermarket chain in the study commanded, on average, four percentage points higher gross margin on manufacturer brands in those categories where its private label had a large market share than in categories where its private label had a small market share.

Despite the overall tendency, the relationship between store brand share and retailer gross margin on manufacturer brands is not a linear one—greater store brand share does not necessarily lead to higher margins on manufacturer brands. As figure 7-1 shows, at very low and very high levels of store brand share in a category, important deviations from linearity may occur—even a reversal of the effect!

FIGURE 7-1

Private label share and retailer bargaining power

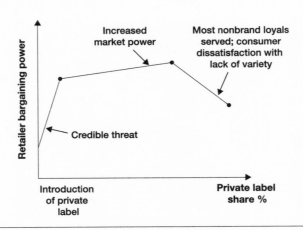

Presence of Private Labels Constitutes a Credible Threat

The mere introduction of a private label in a category can significantly affect the supply terms negotiated between the retailer and branded goods manufacturers, even when the store brand market share is very small.[15] The store brand constitutes a "credible threat" to the manufacturer brands because the retailer could promote its own brand through activities such as flyers, displays, and greater shelf space at the expense of manufacturer brands. However, the threat of private labels is credible only if a store brand is actually introduced, since this entails significant up-front fixed costs for the retailer. In other words, a retailer threat to introduce a private label in a category is not credible; only an actual introduction is beneficial for negotiating better supply terms with branded goods manufacturers.

The credible threat phenomenon explains the presence of store brands in categories where they are unsuccessful. For example, consider the cooking margarine category in the Netherlands.[16] The market is dominated by two powerful Unilever brands, Croma and Becel. The store brands of two leading supermarket chains, Albert Heijn and C1000, have few loyal purchasers, a low ability to attract random buyers in the marketplace, and consequently a very low market share. In this category, inventory costs are very high since the SKUs have to be stored in cooled shelves, called chillers. Chillers are a scarce resource in supermarkets, with high opportunity costs. There is only one reason why the Dutch retailers allocate expensive chiller space to their own unsuccessful private labels—they constitute a credible threat to Unilever and keep the latter "honest."

Overemphasis on Private Labels

Retailers that carry both private labels and manufacturer brands in a category may end up overemphasizing their own labels. To explore this, recall that consumers in a particular category can be divided into four groups: brand buyers, private label buyers, random buyers, and toss-ups (see figure 6-2).

Brand buyers will never purchase private labels—unless the price difference between brands and private labels becomes outrageous. For simplicity, we will assume that brand manufacturers manage this price gap since, at the end of the day, the number of "Marlboro Fridays" is very low. Random buyers and toss-ups are not loyal to any product alternative, but will purchase the private label if the price gap between the manufacturer brand and the private label exceeds some threshold. Of course, this threshold differs between individuals.

If the store brand is very successful, it has captured not only private label buyers but also a significant number of the random buyers and toss-ups. In this situation, the brand manufacturer has little incentive to reduce the wholesale price of its brand any further because brand buyers would purchase anyway. Consequently, the retail margin on the manufacturer brand will be lower than when the brand manufacturer would still be competing for a significant part of the segment of random buyers and toss-ups.[17]

Overemphasis of private labels can also strengthen the negotiating position of the branded goods manufacturer through another dynamic. If the retailer places too much attention on its store brands—for example, by giving them overwhelming shelf space—it may cause dissatisfaction among the retailer's customers. Suddenly, shoppers cannot find their favorite brands anymore and start feeling that their choice is being restricted. This is essentially what happened to British retailer J. Sainsbury. It had to deemphasize its private labels because consumers resented the lack of variety and started to patronize rival chains.

Private Labels Build Store Loyalty

Private labels were often introduced as "best-value" products, but increasingly, as mentioned in chapter 3, retail chains have improved their quality in order to raise the image of the chain. Through this strategy, retailers hope to encourage consumer loyalty to the retailer rather than to manufacturer brands. This constitutes the third reason why retailers believe that selling private labels generates more profits than manufacturer brands.

Store Brands Help Retailer Differentiation

From a retailer's perspective, manufacturer brands are commodities, available at many competing retail chains. By introducing store brands, the retailer differentiates itself from other chains. This increases the psychological costs for its customers to switch retailers since they will not be able to purchase their favorite store brands at competing retailers, and therefore have to go through cognitively demanding evaluative processes involving other brands, including the store brands of other retailers.

Store brand differentiation in turn leads to greater customer loyalty toward the retailer. As one British retailer put it, "Customers' loyalty is a fundamental reason for having own labels. If you have a nucleus of products which customers see as having a quality image, there is an inevitable dynamic created." This is a view echoed by a French retailer: "Private label is what consumers want; it makes them loyal to the chain." But are private label shoppers more loyal to the retailer?

Private Labels and Store Loyalty

Empirical evidence indeed supports the strong relationship between purchasing of private labels and store loyalty. One study of U.S. households found that a 1 percentage point increase in store brand purchasing is associated with a 0.3 percentage point increase in store loyalty. For example, if a particular household increases the share of purchases allocated to the retailer's store brand by 10 percentage points, the "market share" of the retailer for that household increases by 3 percentage points.[18]

Another U.S. study examined the relationship between store loyalty and private label buying, while controlling for more than ten psychographic correlates of store loyalty (e.g., price consciousness, quality consciousness, shopping enjoyment, and variety seeking).[19] The positive relation between private label buying and store loyalty remained, even after controlling for a host of other variables.

Results from international studies are similar. Figure 7-2 examines the relationship between store loyalty (share of the shopper's weekly food expenditure spent at Carrefour) and private label share across some of the different countries in which the French retail giant Carrefour operates. It shows a strong correlation ($r = 0.73$) between the share of Carrefour's private label in total sales and loyalty to the store. Finally, a global study involving consumers from more than twenty countries found that, on average, heavy private label buyers were considerably more store loyal than other customers.[20]

FIGURE 7-2

Private labels build store loyalty at Carrefour

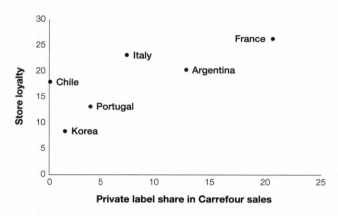

Source: AiMark, 2006; http://www.aimark.org/. Reproduced with permission.

Private Label Shoppers Are More Profitable

While private labels build store loyalty, are private label shoppers also more profitable? Received wisdom holds that loyal customers are more profitable.[21] But does this hold true for private labels, which are lower priced and attract more price-sensitive shoppers?

Higher Gross Margin Percentage

Table 7-2 presents a profitability analysis for a large U.S. drugstore chain, based on purchase records of 41,335 customers, who made a total of 347,214 shopping trips over a six-month period.[22] Customers were divided into four groups, according to their private label buying intensity: light (0–10 percent), medium (10–20 percent), heavy (20–35 percent), and very heavy (greater than 35 percent).

Clearly, the gross margin as a percentage of sales is higher for heavy private label buyers. This is consistent with the evidence

TABLE 7-2

Are private label buyers more profitable?

	MEAN VALUE OVER SIX-MONTH PERIOD FOR CONSUMERS WHOSE PRIVATE LABEL SHARE IS:			
	0–10% Light	10%–20% Medium	20%–35% Heavy	> 35% Very heavy
Total sales	$251	$263	$216	$129
Gross margin	30.3%	32.1%	34.7%	36.8%
Total gross margin dollars	$77	$85	$70	$48

Source: Adapted from Kusum L. Ailawadi and Bari A. Harlam, "An Empirical Analysis of the Determinants of Retail Margins: The Role of Store Brand Share," *Journal of Marketing* (January 2004): 161.

earlier in the chapter that private labels command higher gross margins. However, because of the substantially lower price points for private labels, compared with manufacturer brands, the dollar sales for heavy and very heavy private label buyers are actually lower than those for light private label buyers.

The decline in sales dollars is especially dramatic for very heavy private label buyers (greater than 35 percent). For this segment of the market, the fall in dollar volume is driven by more than simply lower private label prices. These consumers typically operate under financial constraints and cherry-pick at multiple stores. Therefore, they buy less from any single retailer. They also tend to purchase store brands wherever they shop because they consider them good value. Thus, they are loyal to the value proposition offered by store brands in general, rather than being loyal to any particular store brand and retailer.

Lower Gross Margin Dollars

If we combine information on gross margins with information on dollar sales, we obtain dollar gross margins by segment. As table 7-2 shows, consumers who engage in medium private label buying (10–20 percent) are the most profitable. Heavy and very heavy private label buyers are actually less profitable than light private label buyers. These findings would be even stronger if net margins and velocity were considered.

Conclusion: Are Private Labels More Profitable for Retailers?

So, are private labels more profitable than manufacturer brands for retailers, or not? Is it indeed true that "every percentage-point improvement in private label share is associated with significant increases in profit-dollars" for the retailer? Our discussion shows that such a sweeping statement may not always be true and that the actual situation is quite complex. On the affirmative side, there is strong evidence that for retailers:

- The introduction of a private label in a category leads to higher retail margins on manufacturer brands.

- Private label is a powerful instrument to make consumers loyal to the retailer.

However, on the negative side, there is compelling evidence that for retailers:

- When compared with manufacturer brands, private labels often do not generate higher dollar profitability per square foot of shelf space.

- Heavy private label buyers may not be more profitable; shoppers purchasing some private labels are more profitable than those buying no private labels, but too much emphasis on private labels may be counterproductive.

The negative evidence is puzzling. If private labels are not more profitable to retailers, why is the private label share of many of the world's leading retailers so high and increasing (see table 1-1)? Table 7-2 indicates that when private label share exceeds 20 percent, retailer profits may actually decline. However, the private label share for most leading retailers is considerably above 20 percent. How can we reconcile these conflicting findings? Are all these retailers wrong? We believe a more nuanced conclusion is warranted.

Higher dollar profitability per square foot for manufacturer brands, as table 7-1 reveals, is driven by their higher prices and more rapid shelf space turnover. The *higher price* argument applies when one compares manufacturer brands with generics and copycat store brands, but not when one compares against premium store brands, which usually retail at the price discount of 10 percent or less, and sometimes may even be higher in price than manufacturer brands. Thus, for premium store brands, the profitability picture is dramatically different. The dollar contribution of the manufacturer brands would be, in our estimate, 25 percent lower than the dollar contribution of premium store brands.

More rapid shelf space turnover of manufacturer brands may also be a thing of the past. This is especially true when one considers that most private labels replace secondary manufacturer brands (those that are not number one or two in the category), which are usually not supported by massive advertising. In addition, retailers have begun to advertise their store brands more aggressively and are becoming increasingly sophisticated in using in-store communication to impact consumer choices at the point of purchase. All of these changes should favorably increase the velocity of private labels vis-à-vis manufacturer brands.

The historically lower customer profitability of the heavy private label buyers is also impacted by the changing character of store brands. The drugstore chain on which the profitability analysis is based (see table 7-2), although huge, follows a relatively unsophisticated copycat strategy. On the other hand, as we have seen in chapter 5, retailers like Tesco, Carrefour, and Wal-Mart follow a sophisticated private label strategy, including the introduction of premium private labels. Since premium private labels compete much less on price but rather on superior quality, heavy purchasing of private labels should not lead to lower profitability.

In conclusion, we still believe that mainstream retailers can give too much emphasis to private labels, leading to dissatisfied consumers and reduced profitability—Britain's J. Sainsbury can attest to this. However, for sophisticated retailers following a multi-tier strategy, we also believe that the optimal private label share is considerably higher than 20 percent—perhaps 40 to 50 percent.

Chapter Takeaways

To Maximize Retailer Profitability Using Private Labels

- Do not focus on gross margins of store brands versus manufacturer brands.

- Conduct a comprehensive profitability analysis incorporating gross margin, dollar profit, and velocity for store brands versus manufacturer brands.

- Use the presence of private labels in a category to negotiate higher gross margins from manufacturer brands.

- Avoid overemphasis of private labels in a category because it can enhance manufacturer brands' bargaining power as customers seek variety.

- Consider the trade-off between loyalty and profitability. While shoppers who purchase a higher proportion of private labels from a retailer tend to be more loyal to the store, heavy buyers of value or copycat private labels are less profitable for the retailer because that reduces the dollar value of the shopping basket.

- Recognize that the negative conclusions about private label profitability vis-à-vis manufacturer brands are less likely if the retailer carries an extensive premium private label range.

Manufacturer Strategies Vis-à-Vis Private Labels

I N THIS PART, we turn to the question that keeps brand manufacturers awake at night: How should they combat the large retailers and this new reality of private labels? Is there anything manufacturer brands can do to stop the onslaught of store brands?

Some companies, as they observe the continued growth of private label share, wonder whether their future lies in producing private labels in order to profitably employ their capacity. Rather than trying to beat private labels, perhaps it is better to join the party. Chapter 8 examines the viability of brand manufacturers' becoming producers of private labels by exploring two options: (1) the "dual strategy" model, where the manufacturer produces both its own brands and private labels for retailers, and (2) the "dedicated private label manufacturer" strategy, where the manufacturer concentrates exclusively on producing private labels for retailers.

For most brand manufacturers, producing private labels is at best a peripheral activity. One may argue that it only tightens the noose. Their central mission is to sell their brands profitably and grow their market share. They want to beat private labels with their brands and want to know how to do it.

Let us share the bad news first. Our years of working with leading brand manufacturers around the world have taught us that there is no silver bullet. There is no single answer that will solve the brand manufacturers' problem vis-à-vis private labels. Whatever marketing consultants or gurus may claim, no such magic potion exists. But through hard work and consistent effort, brand manufacturers can address the private label threat head-on by pursuing four strategic thrusts: partner effectively, innovate brilliantly, fight selectively, and create winning value propositions. We will discuss these four actions in chapters 9 through 12.

They are not to be pursued in isolation but rather as a combined, concerted, and frontal attack—only then is there a chance for victory. And the secret lies in their execution rather than in the grand plans. But beware—there are no guarantees; one must accept that retailers also have several aces up their sleeves. As Edwin Artzt, the former Procter & Gamble CEO, famously said: "We're not banking on things getting better. We're banking on us getting better."

One note of caution is to be noted up front. We find that before brand manufacturers can beat private labels, they must first achieve a significant change in their mind-set. When discussing private labels with brand manufacturers, our biggest frustration is usually the inability of many executives, especially those from the U.S., to accept the new reality of private labels. Many of these executives dismiss private labels as inferior and instead focus exclusively on the competing manufacturer brands. Working with a leading U.S. company, we were impressed by the amount of benchmarking it did on objective quality, market share, consumer attitudes, and so on. However, we were dismayed to find out that it had benchmarked only against other manufacturer brands, not against private labels. It never occurred to the company that it was competing with private labels too!

But underestimation of private labels is not the prerogative of U.S. executives only. One of us recently participated in a brand strategy session with the CEO and the top management team of one of the largest and most widely admired European CPG companies. The CEO contemptuously dismissed private labels with the argument that they were of inferior quality. He reminded everyone that they had five hundred scientists working on product development, while the retailer had only one. It never occurred to the CEO that perhaps they had far too many researchers involved.

Or that the retailer could purchase high-quality products from brand competitors or from dedicated private label suppliers. Retailers do not necessarily need a five-hundred-person product development department to produce quality private labels.

Most high-powered executives started their careers when retailers were relatively unsophisticated, peddling unbranded generics, and being local rather than global in scope. As a result, those running the large manufacturer brands, with MBAs from prestigious business schools—which to exacerbate things, give hardly any attention to private labels either—had an arrogant attitude toward retailers. Most of them did not consider retailers, or the executives who populated them, as their intellectual or social equals. And certainly, manufacturers did not see private labels as worthy competitors to their cherished brands. However, as retailer brands have transformed, there is a need to change the brand manufacturer mind-set.

Today, we should not think of the retail challengers as private labels. Rather, they are more appropriately referred to as retailer brands or store brands, and retailers behave accordingly by communicating this to their customers. For example, Carrefour uses shelf tags stating: "Carrefour, c'est aussi une *marque*" (Carrefour is also a *brand*; emphasis in the original). Even a low-price, mass-market player like Wal-Mart recognizes the need for brand building. In September 2005, Wal-Mart had an eight-page insert in *Vogue* and hosted its first runway show during New York Fashion Week. Wal-Mart also acquired its own brand of blue jeans, called Faded Glory, paying extra to retain the original design team. Faded Glory is today a $3 billion brand, and independent tests by *Consumer Reports* named it the best-fitting jeans on the market, beating Wrangler and Liz Claiborne. Levi Strauss, which had refused to allow Wal-Mart to carry its brand, saw its sales of jeans drop from $7 billion to $4 billion.[1] To combat this, Levi Strauss had to celebrate its 150th anniversary by developing and launching a fashionable, but less expensive, "Levi Strauss Signature" brand exclusively for Wal-Mart.

If brand manufacturers are going to be successful in fighting private labels, it is imperative that they recognize that retailer brands:

- Have become a permanent feature of the competitive landscape
- Are of good quality
- Are brands in their own right

Unless brand manufacturer strategies are based on a completely honest understanding of the reality now on them and the reality that is about to hit them, they will fail. As it is, they have a real fight on their hands vis-à-vis private labels.

EIGHT

Mfctr. PL

Produce Private Labels for Greater Profits

Buyers and sellers at Private Label Manufacturers
Association trade show: 10,000

IN THE FACE of increasing private label share in the market-place and idle capacity in their production facilities, brand manufacturers are tempted to become private label producers. There are two alternative strategies for manufacturers to pursue with respect to private label production: first, a *dual* strategy, where the firm manufactures both its own manufacturer brands and private labels for retailers. Alternatively, the manufacturer can become a *dedicated* private label producer.

2 options
a) Dual
b) only PL

Dual Strategy

Private label production by brand manufacturers is a ubiquitous phenomenon. In the U.S. alone, it has been estimated that over half of the brand manufacturers also engage in private label production. These manufacturers are typically secretive about it, lest it reduce the equity of their own brands. Nevertheless, by visiting industry trade shows and checking displays and program guides, one can get an idea of the companies involved in private label production. For example:

- Alcoa (which owns Reynolds Wrap aluminum foil) also produces private label foil, wrap, plastic bags, and disposable storage containers.

- Bausch & Lomb provides private label eye care products and nonprescription nasal remedies.

- Birds Eye supplies retailer brands with frozen vegetables and canned soup.

- Del Monte manufactures private label canned soup, broth, and gravy.

- McCormick offers spices, seasonings, salad dressings, and party dips as private labels.

- H. J. Heinz sells excess capacity to retailers for canned soup and baby food.

In contrast, other brand leaders vow that they will not engage in private label production. Examples of companies that have said so at various times include Coca-Cola, Heineken, Kellogg, Procter & Gamble, Gillette, and Nestlé (in coffee).[1]

The decision of whether or not a brand manufacturer should engage in private label production is not an easy one, since several considerations come into play. It is not a simple black-or-white decision but requires a careful trade-off of the pros and cons. The arguments for producing private labels by brand manufacturers fall into two categories: generate additional profits and have a greater influence over the category.

Profitability

Supplying private labels often starts on an opportunistic basis. The brand manufacturer has some spare capacity because of a temporary imbalance between supply and demand. A private label order can be used to fill the spare capacity. In that case, any contribution over and above the variable costs of production is incremental profit. In the short run, this makes good business sense.

However, the long run is nothing but the accumulation of many successive short runs, and when seen from this perspective, the enhanced profitability is often illusionary. Only when the company fills capacity on a purely *ad hoc*, strictly *occasional* and *temporary* basis, is it sound business practice to consider any income above variable costs as a contribution to profits. However, what starts as an ad hoc opportunity often leads to repeat business. Consequently, full costs should be computed, but then the profitability picture can change dramatically.

Private label production consumes capital and valuable management time. While it is easy money because the manufacturer does not have to fight for shelf space, it weakens the necessary focus on the manufacturer's own brands. It is like a narcotic: the short-run contribution to the sales and profits effect is exhilarating, with the long-run effect being that you cannot live without it, even when it torments you. We have noticed all too often that companies overlook the obvious alternative: bring production capacity in line with the sales potential of one's own brands, either by closing factories or by spinning off private label activities. This avoids the firm's being trapped in private label production to keep the machines running, and frees capital and management time that can instead be devoted to the firm's own brands.

Ralston Purina and Dean Foods are two U.S. companies that have reduced production capacity by spinning off private label production. In 1994, Ralcorp Holdings was carved out of Ralston Purina and is now a leading producer of private label foods in the U.S., with sales of $1.7 billion. In 2005, Treehouse Foods was spun off from Dean Foods; it sells private label pickles and nondairy powdered creamers, among other things, with sales of about $700 million.

Two Examples

Illustrative of the problems associated with the profitability argument is our experience in working with a beverage company. The vice president of marketing of this company claimed that private label production was profitable. However, the controller argued that that was only true if all fixed costs (e.g., depreciation, maintenance, some labor expenses) were allocated to the company's own brands. Since the company had been engaged in private label production for a number of years, this did not make sense from an accounting (or any reasonable business) perspective. If costs were properly allocated, private label production incurred losses rather than profits, and the company was subsidizing private label through its own brands! This is a situation we have encountered in other companies as well. And this does not even take into account the cannibalization of own brand sales.

Figure 8-1 provides an example for a U.S. food company that manufactures both its own brand and a private label.[2] Its own brand sells for $1.59 per pound, versus $1.29 per pound for the private label product. From an ad hoc, short-run perspective, private label production made sense, since the private label's *contribution* of $0.23 was equal to the *profit* earned on the company's own brand. But that business model is only sustainable—even in the short run—if the company sells enough of its own brand to cover the fixed costs.

It gets worse when seen from the long-run perspective as fixed costs would then have to be incorporated in determining private label profitability. As a result, the company would have to sell four units of the private label product to generate the same profit as on one unit of its own brand. Is that likely? We believe that is often not the case, and if private label sales cannibalize the manufacturer's own brand, the profitability picture only becomes poorer.

We worked with one food company whose cost structure resembles that in figure 8-1. The company's flagship brand has a market share of 50 percent. If the company incurred "fair share" cannibalization, it would lose one unit of its own brand for every two units sold of the private label, resulting in a sharp reduction in net profits: per million units of private label sold, it would lose $110,000. The company would only remain profit neutral if it lost just half of its fair share—that is, per four units of private

FIGURE 8-1

The real costs of private label production: Example of a U.S. food company

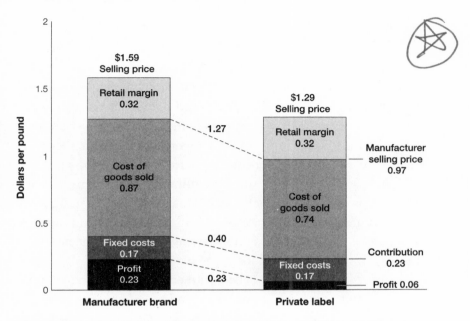

Source: John A. Quelch and David Harding, "Brands Versus Private Labels: Fighting to Win," *Harvard Business Review*, January–February 1996, 104.

label product sold, it lost only one unit of its own brand. Even the vice president of marketing had to admit that was unlikely.

In considering cannibalization of one's own brands, the focal manufacturer must also consider competitive dynamics. If by not engaging in private label production, it would still lead to a private label presence because a competitor would then produce it for the retailer, then the focal firm should ignore the negative effects of cannibalization of private label production.

Manage the Category

A brand manufacturer can also engage in private label production to manage the category. It allows the firm to strengthen its relationship with the retailer—after all, the manufacturer demonstrates its cooperative behavior by supplying private label products. As Paul Luchsinger, CEO of Ontario Foods, observes, "One reason manufacturers choose to do this is to cultivate better relations with retailers."[3]

The hope is that because the brand manufacturer is also a private label supplier to the retailer, the retailer will reward it with more favorable shelf allocation for the manufacturer's own brands, joint promotions, and so on. The brand manufacturer also learns more about the needs and behaviors of private label buyers, which, after all, constitute an important segment in many markets. Proponents of private label production also argue that engaging in this activity increases the brand manufacturer's control over the retailer. It is in a better position to manage the price gap between its own brand and the private label, and it can manage the quality of the store brand. There is no denying that these are powerful arguments. But are they valid?

Much of the strength of the arguments resides in the assumption that the retailer will respond in kind to cooperative behavior by the brand manufacturer. Unfortunately, there is not much compelling evidence to support this assumption. Working with various European and U.S. companies, we never were able to uncover hard evidence that making private label products enhances the relationship with the retailer and leads to preferential merchandising support for the brand manufacturer's own brands. In fact, private label contracts can increase a brand manufacturer's dependence on a few large retailers, forcing the manufacturer to disclose strategic information on its cost structure and share its latest product technology. This can result in bare-knuckle margin pressure every time a private label contract is up for renewal.[4] And common business sense dictates that this is to be expected. In most markets, brand power equals market power, and with respect to private labels, the retailer has the brand power. It can play off one private label supplier against another and appropriate most, if not all, of the channel profits. To do otherwise would imply that the retailer is not maximizing shareholder value.

But what about the frequently heard argument: "If I don't do it, my competitor will do it." This is probably true, but it underestimates the adverse organizational and marketing dynamics associated with private label production. Account managers will have more difficulty justifying a trade price premium for the manufacturer brand, especially when it has neither superior performance nor sales volume. Moreover, private label production can lead to "organizational schizophrenia."[5] The manufacturer brand mentality of long-term investment and (image-based) differentiation is inconsistent with the private label production mentality of short-term flexibility and lowest costs. Organizational schizophrenia can be alleviated to some extent by placing manufacturer brand and store brand production in separate units, with different account managers. However, there is still potential for between-unit competition for the same retail accounts and shelf space, and reduced production efficiencies.

Sobering Lessons from Dual Strategy Experiences

Since the dual strategy of adding private label production is so seductive for brand manufacturers and so frequently employed in practice, we explore three examples of companies from diverse industries. Each of these companies employed the dual strategy but faced significant challenges in making it work. We believe their experiences will be illuminating for those brand manufacturers who are tempted by the dual strategy.

Campina—Refocusing on Brands

The European dairy cooperative Campina (2005 sales over $4 billion) appears to have recognized the downside of private label manufacturing before it was too late. In March 2005, it announced that profits were dragged down by private label production: "Basic dairy is produced under private labels at the lowest possible cost. However, the return on these products continues to give cause for concern."[6]

Fortunately, in recent years, it has ramped up brand-building efforts through innovation and marketing. While private label sales flagged, Campina's key consumer product brands, including Campina, Landliebe, and Mona, bolstered their share of Campina's total revenues from 21 percent in 2001 to 44 percent in 2005. Ria Feldman, spokesperson for Campina, explains: "Branding is helping Campina to develop value-added products that are harder, or even impossible, for supermarkets to copy and sell as private label."[7] Campina's experience underlines a willingness to move away from margin-squeezing private label production into the more lucrative area of branded, added-value products—an approach that has produced considerable success for a handful of international dairy firms, like New Zealand's Fonterra.

United Biscuits—Resizing Capacity

In the late 1980s, United Biscuits (UB) was the brand leader in the U.K. sweet biscuit (cookie) market.[8] It decided to go heavily into private label production as a way to fill production capacity and to maintain short-term profits. Its focus on private labels came at the expense of its own brands. It underinvested in marketing and innovation, and consequently its brand equity eroded. Consumers increasingly came to view store brands as offering comparable quality and better value. Not surprisingly, private label share continued to grow in the sweet biscuits category, also at the expense of UB's own brand. The long-run effects of this short-term strategy took some time to emerge but became increasingly evident. In the period 1988–1994, operating margins halved, and in 1995, the company racked up considerable losses.

In 2000, UB was acquired by three private equity groups and Kraft Foods. Since its acquisition, UB has successfully turned around its biscuit business. Rather than filling up spare capacity with private label production, it has moved to reduce its production capacity as part of its ongoing program of restructuring. At the same time, the flagship McVities brand and UB's other U.K. brands have posted growth of 7 percent annually, helped by a substantial increase in marketing investment in both new and existing brands. Branded sales now constitute nearly 90 percent of the total sales of over $2 billion. Nowadays, UB is "focused on maximizing the value of the group through profitable branded growth."

Apli Paper—Facing a Dilemma

Apli is a family-owned Spanish company with a turnover of $72 million and sales in over one hundred countries. The company is one of the ten leading producers of self-adhesive labels in Europe and the absolute leader in Spain. Its main brand is Apli, which it sells through distributors.

Some years ago, the company started manufacturing private labels for distributors for four reasons. First, it wanted to utilize its spare capacity. Second, it was believed that this would help strengthen relationships with key distributors. Third, it was argued, "If we don't do it, our competitor will." Fourth, the additional volume would give the firm greater purchasing power vis-à-vis its suppliers.

Both the branded product and the private label are produced at the same factory for efficiency. The quality between them differs, but not significantly. Instead, the firm attempts to differentiate the branded product through packaging and a more extensive range. While the same account managers are responsible for selling private labels and brands to distributors, to keep the focus on the brands, the incentives are based mainly on the branded products.

Today, private label manufacturing accounts for about a quarter of the total volume. The operating margins for the Apli brand are 40 percent, while for private label manufacturing they hover around 10 percent. The difference in operating margins demonstrates the dilemma that Apli faces. It is hard to give up 25 percent of the sales volume, but the operating margins are too low to be satisfactory.

When we asked Apli CEO Jaume Puigbo whether, if he had the choice now, he would enter the private label business, he observed, "It used to be a high-volume, moderate-margin business. Now it is a very low-margin business, and when you take into account the transportation and sales costs, it is difficult to justify. At the present level of margins, we would not enter this market."

The Vicious Circle of Dual Strategy

The preceding experiences illustrate the real danger that brand manufacturers can get trapped in a vicious circle of private label manufacturing (see figure 8-2). It is likely to reduce the company's focus on its own brands. Much time will have to be devoted to renegotiating contracts, reducing conflict in the company between salespeople selling brands versus private labels, and managing conflict with the retailer that demands that the manufacturer give priority to (less profitable) private label shipments.

FIGURE 8-2

A vicious circle of private label manufacturing by brand manufacturers

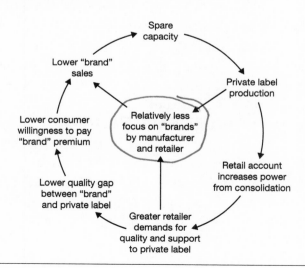

Moreover, private label production results in a reduction of the quality gap between manufacturer brand and private label because the retailer will pressure the manufacturer to share the latest technology. In fact, some leading manufacturers actually advertise this fact! For example, Swedish CPG giant SCA (2005 sales exceeded $13 billion) ran an ad in the German trade magazine *Lebensmittelzeitung* that featured its European account manager proclaiming: "We attach as much importance to the quality of our private labels as to the quality of our brands. Guaranteed! I and my team stand for this . . . because the private label division directly profits from the qualities and innovations of our own brands. This is exactly what makes SCA different from its competitors." While this may be true, it is less obvious whether it is desirable. SCA's operating margin is less than half that of its competitors such as Kimberly-Clark and Procter & Gamble. This is particularly worrisome, since we have seen in chapter 6 that a small quality gap is one of the key drivers of private label success.

A lower quality gap translates into a reduced willingness to pay the price premium that manufacturer brands command in the marketplace. Both the reduced focus on the company's own brands and the lower willingness of consumers to pay a premium price contribute to private label success. Increased private label share may provide a "rationale" to continue private label production. After all, this is what the market wants! In this way, private label production has become a self-fulfilling prophecy, creating a vicious circle of private label success.

Can Dual Strategy Succeed for Manufacturer Brands?

Should brand manufacturers conclude from this that it is always unwise to engage in private label production? That would be nearly as simplistic as supplying private labels because "otherwise, my competitor does it." The crucial question is, Under which conditions does private label production make sense? First of all, we believe that private label production does not make sense to fill up spare capacity. The understandable and economically profitable short-term decision nearly always leads to adverse long-term consequences. The long-term negative consequences far outweigh the short-term (modest) contribution to profits. Private label production is a strategic decision that should be made on sound, long-term considerations and involves evaluating production cost analysis, competitive considerations, and the stature of the brand.

The Crucial Role of Production Costs

The costs of production play a crucial role in the decision of whether or not to supply private label products. Three cost factors and price come into play:

- $VC_{\text{focal firm}}$, or the variable costs of producing private labels by "our firm," which refers to the costs of goods sold, which vary directly with production

- $TC_{\text{focal firm}}$, or the total costs of producing private labels by our firm, which includes variable as well as fixed costs

- $VC_{\text{competitor firm}}$, or the variable costs of producing private labels for a competitor firm, or the costs of goods sold as incurred by a competitor, which could be a dedicated private label manufacturer or another brand manufacturer

- Price, or procurement price for private label, which is the price the retailer pays the supplier for the private label

We assume that competitors engage in opportunistic behavior and have a short-term planning horizon. That is, they are willing to supply private labels if at least their variable costs of production are covered. Consistent with prevailing industry "wisdom" (e.g., figure 8-1) they will consider any price that is just above the variable costs of production worthwhile because it contributes to covering the fixed costs. Standard economic theory tells us that this will allow the retailer to drive its procurement price down to the variable cost of production of competitors: Price = $VC_{\text{competitor firm}}$. We can therefore distinguish between three scenarios (see figure 8-3).

FIGURE 8-3

When should brand manufacturers engage in private label production?

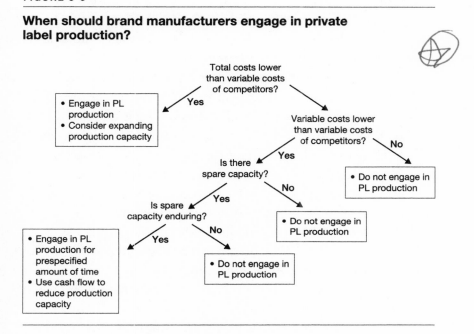

Three Scenarios

1. $TC_{focal\ firm} < VC_{competitor\ firm}$: *Supply private labels.* In this scenario, the total costs of our firm per unit of private label are lower than the variable unit costs of our competitors. In this case, the firm follows proper accounting rules and allocates fixed costs to different products, including private label, and still earns a profit on private label. In this scenario, private label production is economically sound. It contributes to the total profitability of the firm. It also enables the firm to accumulate a larger production volume and to reap the benefits of economies of scale. In this way, it becomes a tougher competitor. If the firm's production capacity is not sufficient to fulfill the demand for private labels, it may consider expanding production capacity, provided the investment meets standard ROI criteria.

Is this scenario realistic? Much of it depends on our firm's ability to realize lower variable costs than its competitors, since the variable costs of a typical S&P 1500 company are 3.5 times larger than fixed costs.[9] Thus, any gain in variable costs vis-à-vis competitors is weighing in heavily. The firm can realize lower variable costs by purchasing larger batches (size helps), by global sourcing, and through global production at low-cost sites. Working with different companies, we have been surprised at how vastly different their sourcing and production systems are. Some companies have an integrated global purchasing office and have rationalized production at a panregional, if not global, level, while other companies still organize procurement and production on a largely local basis. The cost advantages of the former type of organization are substantial. Rationalizing production into a few low-cost sites can also reduce *fixed* costs, and simple economies of scale help too. In sum, globally integrated, large companies stand the best chance of fulfilling the condition that total costs are lower than the variable costs of its competitors.

In this scenario, brand manufacturers supplying private labels must have strict rules to ensure that the integrity of their own brands is not compromised as they begin supplying private labels. Private label production by brand manufacturers should never (1) use copycat packaging, (2) incorporate the branded products' premium quality, (3) adopt the new innovations developed for the brands, and (4) require providing the retailers with significant marketing support, such as promotional materials, displays, advertising, and allowances.

2. $VC_{focal\ firm} > VC_{competitor\ firm}$: *Do not supply private labels.* This is a straightforward case. If the variable costs of private label production of the firm exceed the variable costs of private label production of its competitors, private label production is not recommended. The firm will not be able to command a price that covers the costs of goods sold.

3. $TC_{focal\ firm} > VC_{competitor\ firm} > VC_{focal\ firm}$: *It depends.* In this case, our firm will be able to command a price for its private label that exceeds its own variable costs of production (since the retail purchase price equals the variable costs of the competitor; see earlier). Hence, private label production makes a contribution to fixed costs. However, it does not fulfill its fair share. If the company does not have spare capacity, it should not engage in private label production, because it will reduce profitability.

If the company has spare production capacity, the firm should evaluate whether the overcapacity is temporary or structural. If it is temporary, we advise that the company not engage in private label production, since this will interfere with demand for its own brands when demand picks up, and it sets a precedent for the future. If the overcapacity is structural, the firm should do two things. First, develop a restructuring plan to bring production capacity in line with forecasted demand. Second, engage in private label production until the restructuring plan is completed, and use the contribution generated by this activity to cover restructuring charges. In this way, private label production is temporary and fits into the strategic vision of the company. Regardless of whether the overcapacity is temporary or structural, implementing our recommendations requires courage as the easy way out is to simply go for short-term gains. To help managers avoid "being led into temptation," this policy should be formulated at the board level.

Private Label Production as a Competitive Tool

Private label production by a brand manufacturer may also be used as a competitive tool. The firm can attempt to weaken a competitor by producing a private label whose quality characteristics imitate those of a leading competitive brand. Alternatively, the firm may offer an inferior-quality private label. In both cases, the manufacturer manages private label quality to ensure that it does not hurt its own brands. This may make strategic business sense, even if private label production per se is not profitable.

We are skeptical about the brand manufacturer's ability to use private label production as a competitive tool, unless the category is unimportant for the retailer. In that case, the retailer may simply buy on price rather than specifying detailed quality characteristics. An example is our work with a Dutch CPG company. Its main brand is the market leader in its category. This category is not important to Dutch retailers, which simply buy on price. Its economies of scale allow it to offer retailers a low-quality product at rock-bottom prices. In this way, the company achieves three purposes:

- It denies competitors the opportunity to hurt its main brand by offering a high-quality private label product.

- It denies competitors economies of scale in production.

- It caters to consumers who would never have bought its own (expensive) brand, since they do not care about quality in this category.

Secondary Brands

Private label production may also make sense for minor players in the marketplace. For companies that do not have leading brands, private label production may be the only way to survive. For example, the two leading chains in Australia, Coles Myer and Woolworths, began a push in 2004–2005 to cull the brands in a category from four or five to three, of which one is a private label. A retail observer remarked, "The smaller producers, especially those who are about to be delisted from the shelves of the big supermarkets, have very few choices. They can either provide private label produce to the supermarket, sell into smaller specialty retail outlets or, through consolidation, join a bigger food group that has greater bargaining power with the supermarkets."[10] Over time, some of these companies may migrate from brand manufacturers to dedicated private label suppliers, to which we turn next.

Dedicated Private Label Manufacturers

Companies can also decide to focus exclusively on the production of private labels. Such companies can be found in Asia, the Americas, Europe, and elsewhere, in a variety of industries ranging from food, beverages, household care, health and beauty, to home furnishing, do-it-yourself, footwear, clothing, and general merchandise. No precise estimate of the number of dedicated private label manufacturers is available, but it is sure to run in the thousands.

Dedicated private label manufacturers have several characteristics in common.[11] Most of these companies are small to medium-sized enterprises, specializing in a few product categories. They are high volume–low margin producers. Low cost is a mind-set: they pursue volume at almost any cost in order to fill capacity. Business processes are often highly flexible to cope with a wide variety of products and short runs. Growing the category and creating demand is left to manufacturer brands. Their own research and development is mostly on spotting, copying, and anticipating new product introductions by brand manufacturers, be it a household product or a new fashion design. They openly boast how easy it is to copy innovations introduced by manufacturer brands.

Nevertheless, significant challenges remain. A recent study carried out by the Private Label Manufacturers Association (PLMA) among retailers around the world identified the following important problems:[12]

- Lack of flexibility and ideas among private label manufacturers

- Lack of marketing support offered by private label manufacturers

- Inadequate quality control and product development

Of course, one can argue that these problems are inherent in the concept of dedicated private label manufacturers. Retailers want to have the best of both worlds: the innovative capacity and the marketing support of the manufacturer brands, and the high retail margins offered by private label manufacturers. Nevertheless, in the same PLMA study, over half of the retailers indicated that they were actively looking for private label suppliers that can address these problems. Two of the most successful companies in this respect are Canada's Cott and U.K.-based McBride.

Cott Corporation

Cott Corporation is the largest supplier of private label carbonated soft drinks in the world and the fourth-largest soft drinks maker in the world, after Coca-Cola, PepsiCo, and Cadbury Schweppes.[13] In addition to soda, Cott makes and distributes bottled water, juices, ice teas, and sports drinks. In the period 2000–2005, sales grew by 80 percent from $990 million to $1.8 billion. Operating income nearly doubled from $76 million to $145 million in the period 2000–2004, but fell to $73 million in 2005. Although it sells some products under own brand names (e.g., Cott, RC), it is primarily a private label supplier, in that private labels account for 93 percent of sales volume. Cott supplies 74 percent of all private label carbonated soft drinks sold in North America and 44 percent of those sold in the U.K. It produces private label brands for various retailers, including Sainsbury Classic, Sam's Choice and Great Value for Wal-Mart, and Safeway Select.

Cott's Strategy

Cott's strategy consists of several interlocking components. First, it has fully integrated operations extending from product development through concentrate manufacturing, to bottling and warehousing. This allows Cott to add value through the supply chain and optimize responsiveness to customers.

A second component is the role Cott's own brands and products play in the product development process for its customers. It offers its own brands to retailers, which can try them out before they commit their store brand to the product. An example is Cott's Vintage Fruit Refreshers, a line of noncarbonated, zero-calorie, fruit-flavored beverages. Various U.S. retailers tested these products in their stores before introducing them under their own store brand label.

A third component is Cott's customercentric focus. It is increasingly organizing itself around retailers, developing cross-functional teams aligned with a specific retailer. For five consecutive years, Cott was named "Category Colonel" for retailer brand soft drinks by *PL Buyers Magazine*. The award recognizes manufacturers who "are committed to quality and the establishment of true partnerships with retailers." Its willingness to share technology and products creates value for retailers. In 2004, it won the Beverage Forum Company of the Year award. As the award committee wrote, "With Cott's guidance, retailers have managed to shift store brands from a commodity position based solely on price to a value proposition associated with quality, innovations, and brand equity. By changing the private label category into the retailer category—in both name and spirit—Cott has helped its retailer customers to enhance their larger brand image and forge new connections with consumers."

Cott's Challenges

Notwithstanding Cott's success, it faces some serious challenges too. It is very dependent on its top customers, most notably Wal-Mart, which accounts for approximately 40 percent of total sales. The loss of any key customer will significantly affect the profitability of the company. Moreover, it depends on its customers to market its product successfully. A sobering lesson is provided by the cola war in the U.K. in the mid-1990s. In 1994, the British retail giant J. Sainsbury introduced Sainsbury's Classic Cola, supplied by Cott. Sainsbury's Classic Cola rapidly achieved a 60 percent share in-store and 17 percent of the total cola market in the U.K. Cott's share price soared. The sky was the limit. If Coke and Pepsi could be defeated, any brand was prey.

However, the two cola giants fought back. They retaliated with massive marketing investments: packaging innovation, price promotions, and advertising. Coca-Cola launched an advertising campaign capitalizing on its famous "Always" slogan. It showed a bottle of Coke, with "Always" as the heading and the payoff: "We only make the real thing. We always will." Next to the Coke bottle were a bunch of other cola bottles, with the heading "Never" and the payoff "We don't make colas for other companies." Over time, Pepsi and Coca-Cola regained most of their market share, and Cott's share price collapsed from a high of around \$35 in 1994 to a low of \$7 in 1996.

In 2004, the introduction of too many new products and increased manufacturing complexity contributed to a significant decline in operating cash flow. A significant downside of Cott's willingness to let retailers try out new products before adopting them is that Cott effectively absorbs the high risks associated with new product introductions.

In 2005, downward adjustments to the value of customer relationships, restructuring charges, and a decline in gross margins due to its inability to recover its increased costs through price increases contributed to a decline in operating income by over 50 percent, a profit warning, and a decline of its stock price by 50 percent.[14] Indeed, its net profit margin of 1.4 percent pales in comparison to its branded goods competitors Coca Cola (21 percent), PepsiCo (14 percent), and Cadbury Schweppes (17 percent). Cott is not a stock for the faint hearted. Its limited market power, vis-à-vis its customers, contributes to the considerable volatility of its stock price.

McBride Group — similar to Zara's strategy copy + infer quickly

While Cott Corporation is primarily active in North America, Britain's McBride Group is focused on Europe.[15] It is the largest supplier of private label household and personal care products in Europe. Sales in the last four years increased from \$871 million in 2000–2001 to \$967 million in 2004–2005. In the same period, operating profit increased from \$43 million to \$63 million, and return on sales grew from 5.2 percent to 6.5 percent. The U.K. is McBride's most important market, accounting for over 40 percent of sales. Continental Europe accounts for nearly all other sales.

McBride's Strategy

One element of McBride's strategy is to be extremely fast in *copying* new products launched by brand manufacturers. McBride positions itself as a follower in the marketplace. It is not in the position to develop innovations first. Rather, retailers expect McBride to be able to supply innovations at about the same time as they are introduced by brand manufacturers. In fact, it was able to supply an innovative detergent (liquitabs) to Co-op in the U.K. before this innovation was introduced by P&G's Ariel and Unilever's Persil. This means that McBride's substantial R&D department is focused not on developing truly new ideas but on spotting and forecasting the R&D activities of brand manufacturers. To achieve this, they visit trade shows, conduct desk research, and investigate patterns and trends in the marketplace.

A second component of McBride's strategy is unrivaled *flexibility* in the production lines. Its production lines are set up around delivery of flexible products that can be requested at very short notice by retailers. In effect, the machines are programmed to recognize a basic set of product attributes—for example, height of product or size of base—and they are able to add flexibility to the process by changing the mold. Basically, the same machine can make many different-looking products in rapid succession at a cost-efficient price. McBride makes its products using its own raw materials—for example, it doesn't buy its plastic bottles. As a result, it has a time advantage to respond to retailers' needs, and has control over the production process in terms of costs, planning, and just-in-time (JIT) delivery.

Third, McBride has strong *operating excellence*, including detailed knowledge of its production costs and production capabilities. This gives it an edge in tough Internet bidding auctions, which are becoming more common. Internet bidding allows a group of selected manufacturers to bid for large cross-European contracts. These bids can be for European consortia of retailers and are for very large volumes. Internet bidding takes place under heavy time pressures: the "bidders" may have only one to two hours to submit a bid. This is only possible if the company has detailed knowledge of its cost structure and production capabilities on a day-to-day basis. If McBride wins the bid, it adapts the product (marginally) to the requirements of local markets and formats.

Fourth, McBride further tries to build *long-term relationships* with retailers based on trust. To achieve this, account managers stay on the same account much longer than is usual for brand manufacturers. Moreover, compared with the salespeople of a brand manufacturer, McBride's salespeople have broader knowledge, including current technology, production, legislation, and cost structure of their products.

It is interesting to note that McBride recognizes the important and beneficial role that brand manufacturers play. It believes that manufacturer brands create and expand markets through advertising and innovations. This is a "luxury" that brand manufacturers—but not McBride—can afford since they are not selling at submarket prices.

McBride's Challenges

McBride faces important challenges, too. Profitability has been flat in the last years. At first sight, this is remarkable because private labels are enjoying healthy growth in various European markets. However, McBride faces a double pincer: higher input costs and "price deflation"—a nice term to indicate that the retailers are wringing price concessions out of McBride.[16] It is able to offset these negative effects through volume growth, reduced overheads, and increased operational efficiencies, but these have their limits, too.

McBride's sales are predominantly in household private labels (laundry detergents, cleaning products, aerosols, etc.). These markets are characterized by increased commoditization and price competition, which makes it difficult for McBride to command higher prices. Personal care markets are less price sensitive and offer more potential to avoid price competition.

McBride's model critically depends on market intelligence to spot innovations early—preferably before they are launched—and on its ability to copycat these products. Manufacturer brands are becoming increasingly aware of the threat private label manufacturers pose, and are increasingly taking precautions to keep innovations secret as long as possible and to protect them with patents.

It is difficult for McBride to generate high profits without strong own brands. Its operating margin of 6.5 percent pales compared with the operating margin of about 15 to 20 percent commanded by branded goods competitors such as Procter & Gamble, Unilever, Colgate-Palmolive, and Reckitt Benckiser. Reflecting its weak competitive position, its stock price performance in the last decade (+19 percent) has lagged aggregate indices such as the FTSE 250 and the index for personal care and household products, both of which more than doubled over the same period.

Key Success Factors for Dedicated Manufacturers (Zara)

These company examples reveal that key success factors of dedicated private label manufacturers are a ruthless focus on:

- Low costs

- Unsurpassed flexibility in the production lines

- Market intelligence focused on identifying and copying innovations by the time they appear in the marketplace

To the extent that these criteria—the first two in particular—are met, dedicated private label manufacturing can be a profitable business. The developed markets of North America and Europe are still the most important in the world. Hence, companies located in these markets have a natural advantage in market intelligence. However, companies located in emerging markets like India and China have a clear cost advantage and may not be worse, if not better, on flexibility in production.

Given that sophisticated retailers like Wal-Mart, Tesco, Home Depot, IKEA, H&M, and Carrefour are able to conduct their own market intelligence, the cost advantage of emerging markets' companies is weighing more heavily in today's marketplace. These companies can supply products at low prices while still making a profit on production.

Chapter Takeaways

Successful Dual Strategies

- Consider the *total* costs of engaging in private label production. The only exceptions are:
  - If producing private labels takes place on a strictly occasional and short-term basis, in which case income above the variable costs of producing private labels is a contribution to profits.
  - If there is hard evidence that supplying private labels leads to preferential treatment by the retailer of the manufacturer's own brands.
- Are profitable, usually because the company enjoys a great cost advantage over its competitors.
- Do not:
  - Reduce the brand manufacturer's ability to justify a price premium to the retailers for the company's own brands because of cost transparency.
  - Dilute the focus on manufacturer's own brands.
  - Borrow the latest innovations developed for the manufacturer's own brands.
- Have evaluated the alternative of reducing production capacity.

Successful Dedicated Private Label Manufacturers

- Have a ruthless focus on low costs, unsurpassed flexibility in the production lines, and market intelligence focused on identifying and copying manufacturer brand innovations by the time they appear in the marketplace.
- Tend to be small and medium-sized businesses, increasingly located in low-cost countries like India and China rather than in the industrialized West.

NINE

Partner Effectively
to Craft
Win-Win Relationships

Procter & Gamble's annual sales to Wal-Mart:
$10 billion

To VISUALIZE the power of retailers, it is interesting to consider the percentage of a manufacturer's global sales that Wal-Mart, the world's largest retailer, accounts for. For example, Wal-Mart is responsible for 28 percent of Dial's sales, 25 percent of Clorox's revenues, and 16 percent of Procter & Gamble's turnover (see table 9-1). These numbers have huge implications. It means that Wal-Mart bought products worth $9 billion and $4.5 billion from Procter & Gamble and Kraft, respectively. P&G has since acquired Gillette, and Wal-Mart now accounts for more than $10 billion of P&G sales—exceeding the GDP of Jamaica. In addition, Wal-Mart purchased more than a billion dollars' worth from Clorox, General Mills, Sara Lee, and Kellogg.

As retailers have consolidated, the share of a brand manufacturer's sales that flow through its largest retail accounts has grown

TABLE 9-1

Wal-Mart's share of CPG companies' sales

Company	Global sales ($ millions)	% Sales to Wal-Mart	$ Sales to to Wal-Mart ($ millions)
Dial	1,345	28*	377
Clorox	4,324	25**	1,081
Sara Lee (branded apparel segment)	6,426	22	1,414
Revlon	1,297	21**	272
Energizer	2,813	17**	467
Procter & Gamble	56,741	16	9,079
General Mills	11,244	16	1,799
Kellogg	9,614	14**	1,346
Kraft	32,168	14**	4,504
Gillette	10,477	13**	1,362

*2003
**2004—otherwise 2005
Source: Company annual reports.

and will continue to grow. The top ten retailers now typically account for 30 to 45 percent of a consumer packaged goods company's worldwide sales, a number that manufacturers rarely like to divulge because it reveals their vulnerability. However, in 2003, Dial reported that the top ten retail customers accounted for 57 percent of its sales! Brand manufacturers must learn to partner effectively with these large retailers and move their relationships with them from adversarial to win-win.[1]

Efficient Retailers Are Not the Enemy

Fast-growing retailers like Amazon.com, Best Buy, Costco, Lidl, Save-A-Lot, and Wal-Mart are often seen by manufacturer brands as destroying value because these retailers sell manufacturer-branded products at very low prices. This generates conflict for manufacturers vis-à-vis their traditional, and often inefficient, channels. But these retailers are growing precisely for this reason: they are extremely efficient in getting branded products from manufacturers to end consumers. The lower distribution costs means they are taking the branded products to the customer at a lower price and thereby expanding the market. Brand manufacturers have to follow and distribute their products where consumers want to shop, or they will be stuck in dying channels.[2] As Brenda Barnes, chief executive of Sara Lee, put it, "Where the customer buys our type of product, we should be there."[3] Sara Lee now sells pies at Save-A-Lot.

All of this does not mean that efficient retailers do not face their own challenges. There are three areas where even these retailers can benefit from effective partnering with brand manufacturers.

- Retailers need high-quality private labels.

- Retailers need to differentiate themselves from other retailers.

- Hard discounters need manufacturer brands in their assortment.

In the previous chapter, we already discussed private label production by brand manufacturers. Let us now turn to the other two areas.

Retailers' Need for Differentiation

Retailers want brand manufacturers to help them differentiate through exclusive brands and products. Historically, most brand manufacturers could not customize their offers for individual retailers without compromising their cost structures. Today the situation is a little different, with the large volume that mega-retailers are able to individually deliver. Brand manufacturers can cater to retailers' need for differentiation through developing exclusive brands, exclusive SKUs, and exclusive one-time-offers on a win-win basis.

Exclusive Brands

Estée Lauder has recently created four brands (American Beauty, Flirt, Good Skin, and Grassroots) that are, for now at least, available exclusively at the midpriced department store chain Kohl's. Kohl's cannot compete against Wal-Mart and Target on the mass-market brands, available from companies such as Procter & Gamble and Unilever. And it makes no sense for Estée Lauder to move its prestige brands Lauder or Clinique from traditional department stores to Kohl's. The exclusive brands may allow a mutually successful partnership if Kohl's is able to deliver the volume and Estée Lauder is able to keep its costs for these new brands under control.

Yet, in the long run, exclusive brands for individual retailers seem, to us at least, a costly strategy. If these brands become big hits, it is impossible to see the logic of restricting them to a single retailer. Restricting them to a single type of channel, in contrast to a single retailer—referred to as channel brands—is more viable. However, for many mass-market manufacturer brands, even this may not be appropriate. Instead, the manufacturer brands need to be present wherever target customers shop. After all, a key strength of manufacturer brands vis-à-vis private labels is their greater availability.

Custom SKUs

Rather than developing exclusive brands, we believe it is preferable for manufacturers to offer a dedicated SKU consistent with the individual retailer's strategy. Nestlé, for example, designed a unique two-liter container of Vittel mineral water with a slim middle section to make it easier to hold. This bottle was made exclusively for Lidl in Europe. Each week, fifty-four trains loaded with the bottles leave a Vittel plant in France bound for Lidl's European distribution centers. Peter Brabeck, Nestlé's chairman and CEO, says it is "getting into a very good partnership."[4]

As the result of such initiatives, about 5 percent of Nestlé grocery sales in Europe are through discounters. If managed well, such sales can be highly profitable for the manufacturer. In spite of the lower retail price, the margin on the sales of Vittel through Lidl is as high as Nestlé achieves through other outlets. Having such a large order for one item gives it economies of scale in production and distribution. For example, Nestlé can devote a manufacturing line to Lidl's Vittel bottle.[5]

It is such experiences that have led Peter Brabeck to observe, "Ten years ago we were in a cockfight with the retailers. But we must not forget that they invested in very, very expensive distribution systems that brought prices down and contributed to our volume growth. So now we want to be a partner, not a supplier."[6]

Macy's is an example of a department store that is increasingly relying on exclusive merchandise to differentiate itself from competitors. Collaborating with brand manufacturers like Tommy Hilfiger, it now sells $2 billion of SKUs sold only in Macy's stores.[7]

Exclusive One-Time Offers

Retailers can also help brand manufacturers reach a new segment, and if it is executed carefully, manufacturers can exploit this opportunity without compromising their brand positioning. Consider H&M's retail coup in the fall of 2004 through its collaboration with Chanel design chief Karl Lagerfeld. Recognizing that the closest most women got to Chanel was owning a bottle of the perfume, H&M persuaded Lagerfeld to design a limited edition collection exclusively for H&M. Specifically, Lagerfeld was instructed that H&M did not want haute couture, but that the line had to be commercially viable.[8]

On the day that the Lagerfeld collection hit the shops, hordes of bargain-conscious fashion consumers flocked to H&M stores. Many items, such as a $99 black Chanel-inspired cocktail dress, sold out within hours. Lagerfeld himself was amazed by the response: "Everything sold in three days, even the most expensive items."[9] For H&M, same-store sales soared by 12 percent the month the collection launched. And the one-time, limited-range and limited-time offer also helped create buzz for Chanel without any downside to the prestige of the brand. In 2005, Stella McCartney designed a forty-item exclusive line for H&M with similar success.

The limited-time exclusive-line strategy works because the manufacturing in this industry is outsourced to low-cost countries like China. Thus the cost of flexibility is borne by a large third-party network rather than by the designer, and the production is batch type. There is no limited-capacity production facility that is owned by the brand, and therefore such single orders do not have to be optimized and balanced against the normal production schedule.

Hard Discounters' Need for Manufacturer Brands

Increasingly, hard discounters—which traditionally had an overwhelming focus on private labels—are developing an interest in adding manufacturer brands. At present, price tends to be the dominant determinant of store choice for discount shoppers. This makes incumbent discounters' market position vulnerable if (even) more efficient discount competitors enter the market. Because of the success of hard discounters, their density increases—for example, over 80 percent of German households live within a fifteen-minute drive to an Aldi and a Lidl store. Consequently, discounters are looking for opportunities to differentiate themselves from one another through their assortment strategy, thereby moving beyond pure price-based competition. Having a balanced offering of both store and manufacturer brands may enhance that discounter's performance, since manufacturer brands are known to be major traffic builders. In addition, in many categories, there is a segment of consumers who prefer manufacturer brands.

In fact, manufacturer brands are currently a major engine of Lidl's continued growth. In 2004–2005, brand sales grew by 16 percent, versus 9 percent growth in Lidl's private labels. In contrast, overall sales of rival German discounter Penny declined because it deemphasized manufacturer brands, leading to a drop in brand sales of 7 percent, which could not be compensated by the increase in its private label sales (+1 percent).

Even mighty Aldi appears to be no longer immune to the lure of manufacturer brands as Lidl outpaces Aldi in some markets because of its larger share of manufacturer brands. According to reports in Lebensmittel Zeitung, Aldi is in talks with Ferrero and other brand manufacturers to sell their brands at its stores to win over customers from its biggest rival, Lidl.[10]

Figure 9-1 provides examples of some brand successes at Lidl in Germany.[11] In a number of categories, Lidl has increased its market share by adding major manufacturer brands, while simultaneously manufacturer brands have also increased their market

FIGURE 9-1

Examples of successful brands at Lidl

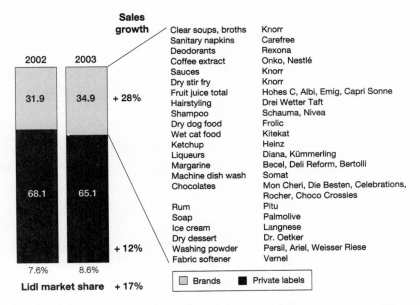

Category	Brands
Clear soups, broths	Knorr
Sanitary napkins	Carefree
Deodorants	Rexona
Coffee extract	Onko, Nestlé
Sauces	Knorr
Dry stir fry	Knorr
Fruit juice total	Hohes C, Albi, Emig, Capri Sonne
Hairstyling	Drei Wetter Taft
Shampoo	Schauma, Nivea
Dry dog food	Frolic
Wet cat food	Kitekat
Ketchup	Heinz
Liqueurs	Diana, Kümmerling
Margarine	Becel, Deli Reform, Bertolli
Machine dish wash	Somat
Chocolates	Mon Cheri, Die Besten, Celebrations, Rocher, Choco Crossies
Rum	Pitu
Soap	Palmolive
Ice cream	Langnese
Dry dessert	Dr. Oetker
Washing powder	Persil, Ariel, Weisser Riese
Fabric softener	Vernel

Sales growth: 2002: 31.9 / 68.1 / 7.6%; 2003: 34.9 / 65.1 / 8.6%
+ 28% / + 12%
Lidl market share + 17%

☐ Brands   ■ Private labels

Source: Thomas Bachl, "Big Splurge or Piggy Bank: Where Are the Markets Heading For?" (presentation given at the annual GfK Kronberg meeting, Kronberg, Germany, January 27, 2004). Reproduced with permission.

share within Lidl. This creates a stable win-win situation: both Lidl and manufacturer brands have profited from each other.

Drivers of Win-Win Situations at Hard Discounters

When are win-win situations more likely to occur? With our colleagues, we examined key success factors driving win-win situations for over four hundred brands at six discounters across three major European countries (U.K., Germany, and Spain).[12] All three countries have strong discounters and a vigorous private label landscape. We found that almost one-quarter of all branded goods in the sample were considered successful for both partners. Discounters and manufacturers both benefit from a large price difference between the manufacturer brand and the discounter's private label variant. A large price gap signals that they are not mere substitutes, but rather that the manufacturer brand and the private label are targeted at different consumer segments or purchase occasions. Of course, the optimal price gap will differ across categories, but we found that the optimal price gap is in the range of the manufacturer brand being between 75 percent and 150 percent more expensive than the private label. Above the 150 percent range, chances of a win-win decline significantly.

Our research demonstrated the striking finding that win-win situations occurred significantly more often when the brand was presented in a nice outer case. To save costs, discounters usually do not unpack the outer-case boxes when displaying the products in their stores. Forty-one percent of manufacturer brands were packed in an outer-case box. Thus far, few manufacturers implement this box as a marketing tool: only 14 percent of the outer cases presented in the shops were nicely decorated and designed attractively. We recommend that manufacturers invest in creating attractive, nicely designed outer-case boxes for their brands shipped to discounters, and simultaneously we advise discounters to present these manufacturer brands in their stores in these well-designed outer cases.

Finally, manufacturers are advised to use innovative, dynamic brands—that is, brands that are regularly updated with new characteristics rather than tired, old brands—for their offerings at the discounter. Innovative brands not only stand out more in a discounter's low-innovative assortment, they can also enhance the attractiveness of the entire category.

In our work with companies, executives frequently mention their concern that brand sales at discounters will cannibalize—allegedly more profitable—sales at higher-priced traditional retailers. This is a valid concern. However, it overestimates the actual or realized price—as opposed to the list price—consumers pay for brands in the traditional channel. In fact, our research showed that the actual price paid for manufacturer brands did not differ much between traditional retailers and discounters. How is that possible? This is because discounters often employ an EDLP (everyday low prices) strategy, while many traditional retailers employ a Hi-Lo (high-low prices) strategy, running frequent price promotions. Brand-loyal consumers stock up when a price promotion is run, resulting in a much lower realized price for the manufacturer. Further, our research shows that in many cases there was no appreciable cannibalization of sales at traditional retailers. Introducing the brand at discounters often results in incremental brand sales volume, drawing customers of rival brands and of the discounter's private label, and increasing the purchasing intensity of heavy buyers. The manufacturer might consider offering a different package size, though, to reduce the potential for channel conflict with its mainstream retail customers.

Maintaining the Balance Between Channels

Recognizing the new reality, Nestlé's top brass recently told investors they would fight back by negotiating deals with discount retailers to put more Nestlé products on their shelves.[13] But it is not that simple. It is not a question of just taking one's existing products and selling them through hard discounters. The question is how best to partner with hard discounters without destroying one's business with the traditional channels. In the U.S., P&G

realized that it would have to work with growing and efficient dollar stores. In 2004, P&G worked with Save-A-Lot to get its Folgers coffee in the stores by creating a lower-priced variety called Folgers Country Roast.[14]

In new product development, one must consider more than consumer needs. Brands also have to consider how the manufacturer's product meets the needs of different types of retailers—how the new product will help differentiate the retailer, generate higher revenues per square foot, increase store traffic, improve stock turnover, and lower the cost of capital for the retailer. These are the metrics by which retailers evaluate manufacturer brands. Above all, retailers want help in drawing other retailers' consumers, but this is where manufacturers have to tread carefully.

In sum, there is little doubt that manufacturers have to learn to partner effectively with precisely those retailers they hate or fear the most—the large and growing ones. While these retailers are always pushing back on manufacturers their challenge of differentiation with shoppers, this is a sensitive issue since most manufacturers have to partner effectively with competing retailers. In some cases, it is possible to have a dedicated brand by the type of channel. Customization at the SKU level—for example, offering the product in different sizes—is preferable. But even here, there are limitations. Most frequently, the partnership is instead going to have to be driven by working together to reduce joint distribution costs and developing a select portfolio of the manufacturer's product line that is consistent with the individual retailer's strategy.

Finally, it should be remembered that it is not the manufacturer's responsibility to make any individual retailer more competitive against other retailers. Brand manufacturers get into trouble when they attempt to favor existing channels at the expense of newer, faster-growing, more efficient distribution formats. Similarly, it must be noted that it is not the retailer's responsibility to favor any individual manufacturer over other manufacturers. Both do best when they follow the ultimate consumer's preferences and learn to work with the consumer's favorite brands or channels, as the case may be.

Chapter Takeaways

Successful Brand Manufacturers Craft Win-Win Relationships

- With fast-growing and superefficient retailers that see the need for manufacturer brands.

- By catering to the retailer's need for differentiation through:

  - Exclusive brands, if the retailer provides adequate scale.

  - Exclusive SKUs, if the brand manufacturer has flexible operations.

  - Exclusive one-time offers, if spare capacity can be contracted on a short-term basis.

- With hard discounters when:

  - There is a large price difference (75 to 150 percent) between the private label and the manufacturer brand.

  - The brand is displayed in an attractive outer case.

  - The brand brings innovative qualities to the hard discounter's category.

- By offering different sizes at hard discounters to reduce channel conflict.

- When they are seen as following the market trends with respect to consumer distribution preferences rather than steering distribution to their own preferences.

TEN

Innovate
Brilliantly to Beat
Private Labels

Private label success in categories with low innovation
versus those with high innovation:
56 percent higher

MANAGERS, ACADEMICS, and consultants all agree that the single best approach to combating private labels is to offer innovative new products. As an industry observer noted about managing relationships with Wal-Mart, "You need to bring Wal-Mart new products—products consumers need. Because with those, Wal-Mart doesn't have the benchmarks to drive you down in price. They don't have the historical data, you don't have competitors, they haven't bid the products out to private-label makers. That's how you can have higher prices and higher margins."[1] This could be said about relationships with all large retailers that have an active private label program.[2]

New Products as a Barrier
to Private Label

Academic studies and business experience support the fact that as the number of new product launches in an industry increase, the share of private labels in the category declines. The recent burst of new products by manufacturer brands in toothbrushes and yogurt saw private label shares dip in both these categories. Industries with a consistent history of new technology and brilliant innovation by brand manufacturers have powerful brands and relatively weak retailers.

In the sports shoe category, for example, adidas, Nike, and Reebok create the latest innovations and technological advancements. They set the competitive agenda and use top sport stars to drive the demand. Furthermore, this category happens to be one of extremely visible consumption. This has resulted in a brand-conscious, brand-driven market where buyers come asking for a Nike or an adidas shoe. If the retailer does not stock it, they quickly go out of the door. In 2005, JD Sports, a U.K. high-street retail chain, was acquired by Pentaland. Pentaland is the owner of sports brands such as Speedo, Kickers, and Ellesse. It is hard to imagine a major retail chain being acquired by a brand manufacturer in consumer packaged goods.

The most compelling evidence of the effectiveness of innovation activity in battling private labels comes from a study we conducted in twenty-three countries around the world in many CPG categories. In each country, private label success is greater in categories with low innovation activity. When the study data is aggregated across categories and countries, we find that private label share is 56 percent higher in categories with low innovation activity than in categories with high innovation activity.

Incremental and Radical Innovation

Almost every consumer packaged goods company has innovation and new products at the top of its corporate agenda, but the challenge is to develop innovative products with a distinctive point of difference. In the food industry, where retailer private labels are especially aggressive competitors, innovation is largely me-too in a relatively low-tech business where true differentiation is hard.

Firms therefore should have a two-pronged innovation attack strategy. The strategy with respect to incremental innovation is to have a constant stream of new products so that retailers and competitors are shooting at a moving target. In some sense this is close to improving quality constantly (see chapter 12). The continual incremental innovation strategy has to be combined with the search for more radical innovation, sustainable either through new technology or by creating new business models.

Industry leader Campbell Soup, for example, is attempting to generate a stream of incremental innovations. Twenty percent of the company's sales comes from new products. For example, in recent years, it introduced microwaveable bowls of soup and a range of chilled soups packaged in sterile cartons more commonly used for fruit juice. Douglas Conant, the chief executive of Campbell Soup, noted, "Private label is less of a threat because we're pioneering all new technology. It's an expensive proposition for someone to contemplate. Even the microwaveable platform people are having trouble following because once they make the capital investment then they have to compete with us."[3] As a consequence, Campbell Soup enjoys a strong position in its core markets and commands an operating margin of 16 percent.[4]

So we have seen that innovation is the most effective counterstrategy against private label success. But this is easier said than done. It is a very *risky* strategy in that the overwhelming majority of new products fail in the marketplace. Our consulting experience has revealed three important obstacles to successful new products:

- The *new product development process*, because the product developed by R&D did not appeal to the marketplace

- The *new product launch process*, because the strategy associated with the new product launch was ineffective

- The *intellectual property protection process*, because the new product was rapidly imitated by retailers

We take up each of these processes, focusing on what brand manufacturers should do to increase the odds for new product success.

New Product Development Process

An effective new product development process introduces new products with the appropriate amount of novelty and focuses on the right customers in initial testing of new product concepts.

The Crucial Role of Product Novelty

A key parameter of the new product's attractiveness is its degree of novelty. Our own research, involving hundreds of new product introductions in various countries, consistently reveals that a U-shaped relationship exists between newness and market success. Products of either incremental or radical novelty are more successful than products of intermediate newness. Products of intermediate newness appear to be stuck in the middle: too high in complexity, compared with products of incremental newness, and too low in relative advantage, compared with radical new products. This effect persists over time. Within this general rule, we find that in the longer run, radically new products offer the best platform for growth.

To assess the novelty of a new product concept before launch, using consumers and/or outside experts is superior to using managers from the company. In our experience, the company's executives are prone to overestimating the degree of novelty of their new products. Products that rate as intermediate on newness by outsiders may be identified before launch and subject to close scrutiny in order to assess whether certain features can be modified to enhance the novelty of the products. Measurement of novelty does not have to be complex. In our work, we have successfully used items like the extent to which the respondent (consumer, outside expert) judged the product to be new and unique, measured on straightforward 5- and 7-point scales.

One approach that combines both ends of the U is a *pulse strategy*, in which really new innovations are introduced from time to time. This is followed by incremental product improvements and line extensions, to fine-tune the product based on market feedback and to fill additional niches until the next really new innovation. Such a strategy is likely to be more successful than continual intermediate-level innovations. P&G's Swiffer cleaning system has followed this strategy to build a billion-dollar brand in a relatively short time. The original Swiffer was a major innovation. Subsequent incremental innovations include, for example, Swiffer Wet, Swiffer Dusters, Swiffer WetJet, Swiffer Mitts, and Swiffer Max.

Talk to the Right Consumers

While incremental new products are often relatively easy to achieve in the R&D process, radical new products are more problematic. It is well known that the generation of major new product ideas is the critical bottleneck for growth.[5] Consumers are a crucial source for new product ideas. Unfortunately, in the new product development process, many interesting ideas are killed because focus groups of consumers reject a radical concept. That is a basic psychological tendency. Many people routinely reject things they are not familiar with. Illustrative is the Dutch saying *"onbekend maakt onbemind"* (unfamiliar makes unloved). Unfortunately, most companies talk to the wrong people in the new product development process. They should not canvass for the opinions of a "representative" sample, but instead test radical concepts on a purposefully chosen segment of the population, consumers who are high in a personality trait called *dispositional innovativeness*.

Dispositional innovativeness is defined as the predisposition to buy new products and brands at an early stage, rather than to remain with previous choices and consumption patterns across a variety of goods and services. It is a basic personality trait. Consumers high in this trait have a higher tolerance for ambiguity, are more open to change, are curious and creative, and have a lower need for clarity and structure. This personality profile indicates that these people are less prone to reject really new ideas while being more likely to come up with less conventional ideas themselves. In short, these are exactly the kind of people whom a company wants to canvass for their opinion in developing radical new products.

We have developed the following set of eight items to measure this trait at the individual level.

- When I see a new product on the shelf, I'm reluctant to give it a try. (*)

- In general, I am among the first to buy new products when they appear on the market.

- If I like a brand, I rarely switch from it just to try something new. (*)

- I am very cautious in trying new and different products. (*)

- I am usually among the first to try new brands.

- I rarely buy brands about which I am uncertain how they will perform. (*)

- I enjoy taking chances in buying new products.

- I do not like to buy a new product before other people do. (*)

Items are measured on a 5-point completely disagree–completely agree scale. A person's dispositional innovativeness score is computed by adding their scores on the eight items, after reversing the scores on the items indicated by an asterisk (*). Figure 10-1 shows the typical distribution of dispositional innovativeness in society.

In sum, in order to increase the chances of coming up with major new product ideas, we recommend that in the R&D process, companies listen to "the voice of the customer," but to a specific

FIGURE 10-1

Distribution of dispositional innovativeness in society

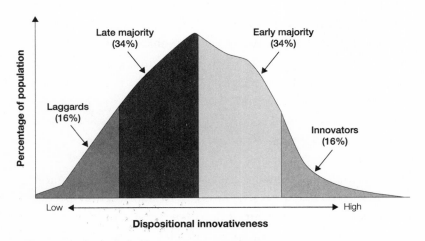

Source: AiMark, 2006; http://www.aimark.org/. Reproduced with permission.

type of customer only. One large U.S. CPG company has put this into practice, using a short form of the dispositional innovativeness scale as a screener (e.g., in mall intercepts) for recruitment for their concept testing.

Moreover, as we shall see later in the chapter, in this way, the company gets input from those consumers who have considerably higher purchase intensity with respect to the new product in the crucial first year after launch. After all, when a new product does not make it in the first year, it is likely to be delisted by today's demanding retailers.

New Product Launch Process

Even if R&D develops a new product that appeals to the marketplace, it may still fail because of an ineffective new product launch process. We identify three factors that impact new product launch success: initial target, international rollout strategy, and marketing resources.

Initial Target

New product adoption varies systematically and predictably across consumers, calling for a targeted marketing strategy emphasizing specific consumer segments. Buying intensity with respect to the new product over the first year is highest in the segment of innovators and lowest in the segment of laggards, with the other two segments in between. Figure 10-2 illustrates this for Unilever's laundry detergent innovation Skip Tablets, in France. After one year, nearly four times as many innovators (22 percent) as laggards (6 percent) had adopted Skip Tablets.

Note that this segmentation scheme is highly actionable because dispositional innovativeness can be measured beforehand—since it is a personality trait, it does not depend on the innovation in question. Thus, consumers can be classified according to their score on the innovativeness instrument before product introduction. This offers the firm the opportunity to develop targeted strategies beforehand rather than after the critical first months following introduction.

FIGURE 10-2

Adoption of Skip Tablets by dispositional innovativeness segments

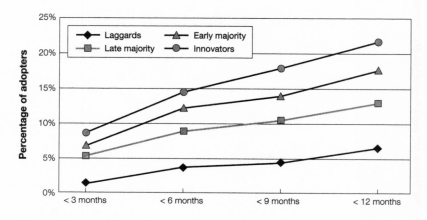

Source: AiMark, 2006; http://www.aimark.org/. Reproduced with permission.

One large CPG firm uses the dispositional innovativeness items on simulated test markets. It has started to build purchase intent benchmarks for consumers who rate high in dispositional innovativeness to decide on new product launches. Another large CPG firm uses the dispositional innovativeness items on its direct marketing databases in several European countries and the U.S.— for example, for targeting coupons at the innovator and early-majority segments.

International Rollout Strategy

With rapidly increasing R&D costs, falling trade boundaries (EU, NAFTA, ASEAN, Mercosur), and growing globalization of the world, new products are increasingly being introduced in multiple countries, rather than being a purely local affair as was common one or two decades ago. The firm can follow a *waterfall strategy* in that the new product is sequentially introduced in one country after another. Alternatively, the firm can introduce the new product in multiple markets simultaneously—called a *sprinkler strategy*.

Our work shows that a sequential, waterfall rollout strategy is most effective for *radical* new products, while the simultaneous, sprinkler strategy is most effective for *incremental* new products. For radical new products, getting the marketing strategy right is difficult, and the brand manufacturer learns from failures in getting it right in subsequent countries. On the other hand, it is much less challenging to develop an effective marketing strategy for incremental innovations, while there is a greater danger that success in other countries will be preempted by fast imitation by other brand manufacturers or retailers. As we have seen, spotting developments in the market and quickly copying innovations is a specialty of dedicated private label suppliers and copycat store brands.

If a waterfall strategy is more effective for radical innovations, with which country should we start? Economic (game) theory, as well as our empirical research, demonstrates that radical innovations should be introduced in countries with a relatively high proportion of innovative consumers.[6] Within Europe, this means that of the major countries, the U.K. is the most suitable country in which to commence a sequential rollout strategy for major new product introductions. In the U.K., the segment of innovators is 24 percent, compared with only 15 percent in France and 9 percent in Spain. In fact, our work shows that among all large European countries, the U.K. is the only country that is not hurt by the fact that the product has not been introduced elsewhere. From a global point of view, the U.S. is a prime candidate in which to introduce radical new products. On average, its population is among the most responsive to innovations in the world.

Marketing Resources

It may sound boring, but good old-fashioned marketing still matters. New product introductions supported by a well-known brand name, price promotions, feature and display activities, and advertising achieve much more success in the market. This may not be glamorous but is nevertheless still very true, even in the twenty-first century. And some recent insights, based on work with colleagues, can help brand manufacturers make more effective and efficient use of their advertising weapon.

The combination of advertising and new products is especially powerful. A dollar spent on advertising for new products is, on average, five times more effective in boosting sales than a dollar spent on ongoing, maintenance advertising. And if a new product is supported by heavy advertising, it is 70 percent more likely to be bought by consumers. Last but not least, advertising for a new product introduced by a well-known brand name increases the effectiveness of the ad spend because the consumer can draw on existing associations with the brand stored in memory.

Not only advertising *expenditure* but also advertising *content* matters. More specifically, in categories where functional performance plays a role (i.e., the product is not all about image, like perfume), ads using distinctive functional benefits generate stronger sales. Worrying, though, is the trend to deemphasize distinctive functional benefits in many categories. Such ads may be more enjoyable but generally turn out to be less effective.

Intellectual Property Protection Process

While one can exhort brand manufacturers to innovate and launch new products, brilliant innovation is wasted if retailers constantly copy successful products. Innovations, especially in the food industry, are difficult to patent protect because tastes, ingredients, and packaging designs are relatively easily, and in many countries legally, copied. But it is nevertheless possible to strike back with lawsuits, if necessary.

The Brand Manufacturer Strikes Back: Lawsuits

Lawsuits can be effective in the fight against the retailers, as Britain's United Biscuits, manufacturer of Penguin chocolate biscuits, proved by its lawsuit against the blatantly obvious Asda copy called Puffin. Penguin is a leading brand, selling 400 million biscuits and generating about $55 million in annual revenues. Almost all major supermarkets sell own-label chocolate sandwich biscuits, or "Penguin-type" biscuits. But none of these biscuits have on their packaging a brand name other than the name of the supermarket. Asda had its own-label biscuit, Take a Break, but decided on a revamp. The written design brief for the Asda product was to be a Penguin "brand beater" that must "clearly match . . . Penguin using cues [such as] color, typography."[7] A list of twenty-four possible names were considered, most of which were birds and animals.

Puffin was finally selected, with a similar package design and bird cartoon as Penguin. A seven-pack Penguin cost 67P, while a seven-pack Puffin cost 59P. Penguin sued and won. It is important to note that in the judgment, it was not merely the name and bird cartoon per se that created the problem, but rather it was these choices in the context of the overall package design that were problematic. The name and cartoon on their own, or the package design on its own without the name and bird cartoon, would not likely have been an issue. Put the name, cartoon, and package design together and, in this case, that became the recipe for legal liability.[8]

Other companies have also engaged in lawsuits. Recently, Unilever sued Dutch retailer Albert Heijn. Given Albert Heijn's market share of 25 to 30 percent, that was not a trivial thing to do. Unilever demanded that Albert Heijn change the packaging of thirteen of its store brand items because they resembled Unilever's brands too much. Unilever has registered the packaging of its brands. However, the court ruled in favor of Unilever in only two cases. Some have argued that this was a big defeat for Unilever. Others are not so sure, since the case got a lot of publicity and may render Albert Heijn more cautious in the future. This may have been evident in another case, involving Albert Heijn and Verkade (a Dutch subsidiary of United Biscuits). Verkade complained that the packaging of Albert Heijn's fruit biscuits was too similar to the packaging of its own Sultana fruit biscuits. Albert Heijn gave in and changed its packaging, and hence avoided a lawsuit.[9]

Procter & Gamble has successfully sued a number of private label manufacturers, rather than retailers, over private label products that it considered to be too similar to some of P&G's best-known brands, such as Charmin (bathroom paper), Crest (oral care), NyQuil (medicine), and Tampax (feminine protection). Diane Dietz, general manager of P&G North America oral care, explains: "Conduct from private label manufacturers that can mislead consumers cannot be tolerated. P&G invests heavily in research, development, and intellectual property and design, and must protect that investment."[10]

In most countries, to stand a chance in the court of law, companies need to prove that consumers are confused by the copycat imitation into thinking that they are dealing with a particular manufacturer brand. This is not easy to prove, because any extended exposure to a copycat brand will reveal that it is not the "real thing." However, on shopping trips, consumers are exposed to a stimulus for a few seconds at most, in which they make their decisions. HEC professor Jean-Noel Kapferer has developed a technique to mimic actual visual decoding processes in shopping situations. Using this technique, he demonstrated that a considerable group of people are indeed confused by copycat private labels, with percentages up to 80 percent! This technique can be used in settling legal disputes in court or as evidence to be presented to the retailer to reach an out-of-court settlement.[11]

Developing a Tough Enforcement Reputation

The Penguin, Unilever, and Verkade cases are exceptions rather than the rule. Historically, manufacturers have been reluctant to sue retailers on trademark infringement for two reasons: How do you sue your own customers? And will this not result in being removed from the shelves of the retailer in question? But this situation is untenable. Brand manufacturers have to be more proactive, like United Biscuits, in protecting their intellectual property at both the design and the enforcement stages.

Retailers' packaging often copies the packaging of the national brands, blurring distinctions for the customers. But the retailers cannot legally mimic the logo. Therefore, the red Kellogg logo on the new Frosted Bran cereal takes up over three-fourths of the box, both front and back, leaving little room for mimicking.

With respect to enforcement, brand manufacturers need to develop a reputation for aggressively pursuing retail copycat violators. The London-based sugar and sweetener producer Tate Lyle obtains some 20 percent of its profits from its zero-calorie, sucralose sweetener called Splenda. In 2005, Tate found that Wal-Mart was selling its own brand, Altern, at a 30 percent discount to Splenda. On investigation, Tate discovered that Wal-Mart had obtained its private label supply from a Tate customer that was supposed to use the Splenda for manufacturing food products. Tate enforced its contract requirement that the customer could not sell the product to third parties such as Wal-Mart, forcing Wal-Mart to drop Altern.

When manufacturers develop a tough enforcement reputation, it becomes more likely that the retailer will copy other manufacturers, which do not have such an aggressive patent protection history. No wonder Kraft has recently doubled the number of its patent lawyers to ensure that its innovations are adequately protected.[12]

Radical New Business Models

Branded goods manufacturers can push the innovation envelope further by working on radical new business models. The kind of innovation that is considered nirvana in consumer packaged goods companies is a change in business model that reduces their reliance on large retailers either through alternative channels or through enhanced consumer loyalty. What are characteristics of such radical new business models?

First, the brand manufacturer moves from a focus on its products to a focus on experiences. The success story is Starbucks selling a café experience. Second, it transfers its communication efforts from media such as television to *nontraditional* means of communication such as buzz marketing and Internet communities. The prototypical story is Red Bull, with its buzz marketing undercover creation of the new energy drinks category. Third, the brand manufacturer releases its focus on standalone products to *interlocking product bundles*. Gillette's success with almost giving away the razor to lock in a lifetime of proprietary blade sales is the example to emulate. These three examples have really captured the imagination of CEOs—they come up repeatedly in conversations. Numerous companies are trying to reproduce these successes. Unilever's Soup Factory and Bertolli restaurants, P&G's Swiffer system, and Marlboro's highly successful buzz marketing campaign are just a few examples.

Creating Product Experiences: P&G

P&G has devoted considerable thought to moving from selling products to selling experiences by elaborating on the concept of "moments of truth." P&G believes that there are two moments of truth that have to be won. First, at the retail shelf, the consumer has to be persuaded to choose P&G products. Second, at home, the consumer has to be delighted by the consumption experience in order to trigger repurchase.

P&G has changed its structure to be leaner and more responsive to these two moments of truth. National fiefdoms have been swept away.[13] Instead, complementing the customer development teams (dedicated to individual retailers) are a matrix of regional market development organizations (dedicated to countries) focused on winning the first moment of truth. The global business units (dedicated to product categories) focus on developing products that will win the second moment of truth.

To win the second moment of truth at home, P&G has concentrated on products that deliver an experience and leverage its existing product and brand competences. For example, a car-washing system, Mr. Clean Autodry, has water streaming out of a spray gun that is attached to the end of a hose and does not leave the normal beads of water. Mr. Clean Magic Eraser removes crayon from painted walls and ink from tables. Kandoo Toddler Care Wipes, Crest SpinBrush battery-powered toothbrush, and Swiffer electrostatic cleaning mops and dusters are some other new products in a similar vein. Crest Whitestrips tooth-whitening strips created and now dominate a new segment of the oral care market.

Branded Brands

As companies have realized that creating uniquely new experiences may require widely disparate skills, a new development is "branded brands": two brands combining their core competencies to deliver one truly new product or service.[14]

Heineken consumers who dream about being able to drink draft beer at home can now do so. Heineken and small domestic appliances giant Groupe SEB from France codeveloped the Beertender, an at-home tap that accepts special 4-liter kegs of Heineken. The refrigerated unit will keep the beer fresh for up to three weeks. Although the Beertender costs $349 and the price per liter is about twice as high as bottled Heineken, it has been a great success since its introduction in the Netherlands in 2005. Since then, it has been rolled out in other countries too. Even if private label beer were to be sold in kegs that would work with the Beertender, the experience simply would not be the same.

The packaged coffee brands, such as Sara Lee's Douwe Egberts, Folgers by Procter & Gamble, Kraft's Maxwell House, and Nescafé from Nestlé, were taken aback by the Starbucks phenomenon. Here in the store aisles, they were fighting for pennies in negotiations with retailers while consumers were jumping ship from one brand to another for a 25¢ coupon. There on the main street, Starbucks was on its way to becoming an icon by charging $3 for a cup of coffee, with the loyal Starbucks customer visiting the café twenty times a month!

Noting the success of Starbucks and Nespresso (discussed in the next section), the trend toward smaller households, and the yearning for a unique coffee experience, Netherlands' Philips Electronics and America's Sara Lee introduced a home concept for coffee, including a special machine (which works not unlike an espresso machine)—marketed by Philips—and special coffee pods—sold by Sara Lee. Since its introduction in 2001, Philips has sold millions of Senseo machines, priced at about $70. The machine allows people to brew single servings of café-style coffee from specially designed pods. This means better quality, less brewing time, and, since the pods come in various flavors, more choice for individuals and entire households. The coffee pods are sold through mass retailers and have been copied by private labels. Nevertheless, Sara Lee has been able to decommoditize the coffee category, upgrade the coffee experience, and earn substantial profits from this innovation.

Kraft Foods and Procter & Gamble only entered the market for single-serving coffee in 2004. In a bid to outdo Senseo and Nespresso, Kraft developed Tassimo, a dedicated appliance made by espresso machine manufacturer Saeco, claimed to be the first machine that can brew coffee, tea, and hot chocolate for home consumption.

Radical New Business Model: Nespresso

Nespresso is the type of brilliant innovation that is few and far between by the packaged goods companies. With Nespresso,

Nestlé managed to develop an innovative offering that combined the sought-after characteristics of selling an experience, avoiding the mass retailers, and creating a new category through buzz marketing with a business model based on proprietary supplies. In 1988, after ten years of research, Nestlé developed Nespresso as a system that consisted of a coffee machine and a coffee capsule hermetically sealed in aluminum. It enabled a no-mess, fast, and convenient way to make a cup of high-quality espresso coffee.

After initially trying to sell the machines and capsules primarily to offices and restaurants, Nestlé decided to change tack. It outsourced the Nespresso machine to select manufacturers, which in turn sold it to prestigious retailers like Bloomingdale's and Harrods. Nestlé focused its attention instead on the coffee capsules. It targeted households and organized distribution through the Nespresso Club.

The stylishly designed Nespresso machines are reasonably priced relative to espresso machines, though they are expensive when compared with the Senseo. They cost anywhere from $200 for a basic model to around $800 for a luxury model. A consumer who buys a machine is automatically enrolled in the Nespresso Club and receives a "starter set," made up of the range of Nespresso capsules and information brochures.

The capsules are sold in sleeves of ten, exclusively by phone, fax, or Internet (and shipped within twenty-four hours) or in forty-two worldwide Nespresso boutiques. The capsules are color-coded according to flavor and do not fit any other machine. Nor can regular ground coffee be used in the machine. In this way, Nespresso has 250,000 captive customers who are locked into the system, having bought a machine. Sales have risen consistently at 30 percent a year to reach $600 million, despite stagnant worldwide sales in the ground coffee market.

The Nespresso business model meant that retailers were completely circumvented, and private labels are no part of the equation anymore. However, the price of both the machine and the pads is such that the customer base will be modest—compared with, for example, Senseo—but nevertheless highly lucrative.

Chapter Takeaways

Brilliant Innovation to Beat Private Labels

- Develop new products of either incremental or radical novelty while avoiding new products of intermediate levels of novelty.

- Listen selectively to the voice of those customers who are high in dispositional innovativeness.

- Initially target innovators and the early majority rather than the general population.

- Adopt a waterfall (sequential) rollout strategy for radical new products and a sprinkler (simultaneous) launch strategy for incremental new products.

- In Europe, radical new products are best introduced first in the U.K., before rolling them out into other countries. From a global point of view, the U.S. is a prime candidate in which to introduce radical new products first.

- Support the new product with a strong brand name, high advertising levels, and ads that communicate distinctive functional benefits.

- Defend new products through lawsuits against copycatting by retailers and by developing a reputation for aggressively pursuing retail copycat violators.

- Pursue radical new business models that focus on experiences, branded brands, nontraditional communication, and interlocking product bundles.

ELEVEN

Fight Selectively to Marshal Resources Against Private Labels

Germany 1999–2005 share: private labels, up 50 percent; brand leaders, down 8 percent; second brands, down 15 percent; other brands, down 30 percent

WITH THEIR ACTIVE private label programs, retailers today are explicit about which manufacturer brands they see as adding value. Manufacturers with new innovative products are important to retailers because they ensure that retailers' shelves are stocked with the most attractive and high-margin products. For the rest, they have their own private labels. Therefore, retailers wish to deal only with those manufacturer brands that have a capability for successful product innovation and are able to command a price premium in the category. Given that many categories are mature, both factors are a challenge for brand manufacturers.

The Squeeze on Weak
Manufacturer Brands

The rise of private labels has put a squeeze on manufacturer brands. But the impact has been asymmetric. It is the weaker manufacturer brands—those that do not occupy the number-one or number-two market positions—that have borne the brunt of the negative impact. The assortment strategy at many retailers with active private label programs is to accept only the top two or three manufacturer brands. They delist the rest of the weaker brands, replacing them with their own private labels. Even if weaker brands are able to get on retailer shelves, the manufacturers have to pay disproportionate amounts in terms of retailer margins and support to persuade the retailers to stock them.

Furthermore, companies find it uneconomical to devote the minimum resources necessary for innovation and advertising to smaller brands. As a result, the smaller market share brands in a category suffer from poor profitability and have few prospects unless they are niche, premium brands. Germany is a useful case that demonstrates this squeeze phenomenon rather well against the backdrop of increasing private label success, as shown in figure 11-1.

When the data in figure 11-1 was examined in greater depth, a GfK study isolated those cases where a particular manufacturer brand had increased its market share in a category. Several such examples were found between the years 1999 and 2002, but what was remarkable was the fact that the share gains for the manufacturer brand had come from other manufacturer brands rather than from private labels. Table 11-1 has the data for four of these brands.

The four brands followed different strategies to grow their market share. Langnese Cremissimo ice cream upgraded itself through a newly designed transparent packaging that showcased novel exotic flavors with gourmet fruits. Rotkäppchen (translates into Little Red Riding Hood) champagne increased advertising intensity to claim a larger share of voice and thereby increase familiarity and penetration in households in those parts of the country where it was relatively unknown. Lenor fabric softener

FIGURE 11-1

Brands versus private labels in Germany

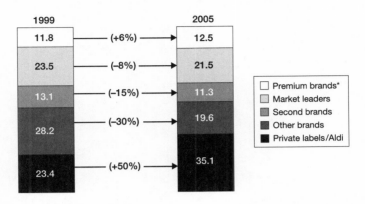

*Average price ≥ price market leader (brands)

Source: Adapted from "Consumption with Pleasure Instead of Frustration" (presentation given at the annual GfK Kronberg meeting, Kronberg, Germany, January 26, 2006).

and Rexona cream lowered prices by 17 percent and 7 percent, respectively, in order to become more competitive against the private labels. What is interesting in table 11-1 is that in each case, it was other manufacturer brands that lost share, while private labels actually gained share in those categories.

According to us, this scenario is not unique to Germany but rather applies to other countries as well. As a result, there are three valuable but sobering lessons for manufacturer brands:

1. Manufacturer brands' share of the category is declining over time relative to retailer brands.

2. Manufacturer brands are fighting to gain share from each other, mostly from weaker brands rather than from private labels. Sales growth for manufacturer brands will come primarily either from growth of the category or from other, weaker manufacturer brands.

3. It is difficult to see how a small share brand in the category is going to achieve success unless it is a premium niche brand.

TABLE 11-1

Growing manufacturer brands in Germany, 1999–2002

Category (annual growth)	Focus brand	MANUFACTURER BRANDS		PRIVATE LABELS	
		Focus brand share increase	Change in other manufacturer brands	Change in Aldi	Change in other private labels
Premium ice cream (7%)	Langnese Cremissimo (Unilever)	18.1% → 29.2%	47.3% → 33.3%	19.3% → 18.9%	9.6% → 18.3%
Champagne (–1%)	Rotkäppchen	11.3% → 13.8%	75.8% → 67.4%	10.8% → 13.1%	2.1% → 5.7%
Fabric softener (2%)	Lenor (P&G)	25.3% → 28.8%	59.0% → 51.4%	6.7% → 8.6%	9.0% → 11.2%
Body cream (3%)	Rexona (Unilever)	12.5% → 17.2%	64.9% → 53.2%	3.8% → 5.4%	4.5% → 11.6%

Source: Adapted from "Is There a Way Back for the Brand?" (presentation given at the annual GfK Kronberg meeting, Kronberg, Germany, March 27, 2003).

Focus the Brand and Product Portfolio

Over the past decade, the preceding lessons have become rather clear for manufacturer brands. It is now impossible to support brands that do not have a strong position. Given the amount of innovation and advertising required to keep a brand alive and fit to fight against private labels, a manufacturer can support only a limited number of brands.[1] In the face of large and powerful retailers with quality private label programs, one must choose one's battles where there is a reasonable chance of winning. Each company must have a clear vision with respect to the categories it desires to compete in and with what brands and SKUs. The answer is to fight selectively rather than on all fronts.

Category Portfolio Reconfiguration

The result of much soul searching on this topic has led firms down the path of acquisitions and divestments in order to construct their ideal portfolio. Which categories are critical for us? Where do our competences lie? Where can we fight and win against the private labels by adding value for consumers through innovation and advertising? In which categories is it easier to demonstrate added value to consumers? The result is that most companies have gone though a reexamination of the product categories they wish to operate in.

For example, Kraft Foods between 2000 and 2004 gobbled up ten rivals, including Nabisco Holdings Corporation for $19 billion. Kraft is now phasing out businesses that account for less than 5 percent of total revenues and concentrating on four core areas: coffee, cheese and dairy, biscuits (such as Oreos and Ritz), and specialty refreshment beverages (such as Kool-Aid).[2] Kraft wants to divest laggard and peripheral product lines to concentrate on the blockbuster brands that can be tops in their categories worldwide. As a result, in 2004, Kraft sold Life Savers and Altoids candies to Wrigley. The reason, according to CEO Roger Deromedi: "We want the products that consumers and retailers are more excited about."[3]

Brand Rationalization

Electrolux, Unilever, and Procter & Gamble are some of the many companies that have reconstructed their brand portfolios. Often, these firms were selling multiple brands within the same category. It only makes sense to have multiple brands within a category if each of them can be positioned against a unique segment. The larger the number of brands, the less likely this is possible since the brands start overlapping each other.

Unilever, for example, has taken its number of brands from 1,600 to 400, by selling, delisting, or merging 1,200 brands. One of the criteria in deciding between brands that would remain versus brands that would be deleted was *brand power*. Brand power was defined as the potential to be number one or two in its market and to be a must-carry brand to drive retailers' store traffic.[4] Brands with these characteristics were dubbed "core brands" and given disproportionate resources.

SKU Rationalization

Beyond category and brand focus, SKU rationalization programs have been big, from Heinz to Hershey.[5] Most firms have weeded out and are continuing to shed slow sellers. Increasingly, companies are taking orders from Wal-Mart and other large retailers, which only want products that fly off their shelves. The enormous amount of data available helps these retailers identify those SKUs that are not earning their shelf space. At the same time, at retailers like Tesco, manufacturer brands are being crowded out by the retailer's own labels. In 2004, General Mills (Cheerios cereal, Progresso soups, Green Giant frozen vegetables) announced it would trim 20 percent of the products it sells within a year.[6]

Portfolio Rationalization at P&G

Procter & Gamble has done a remarkable job in turning around its brand and product portfolio. Under CEO A. G. Lafley, P&G

has shed Punica and Sunny Delight juice brands, Jif peanut butter, and Crisco pastry shortening. The company has also gotten rid of Biz, Milton, Sanso, Rei, and Oxydol detergent brands. In turn, P&G has acquired Clairol, a hair-coloring firm; Wella, a German beauty products company; and Gillette.

The result has been a lower exposure to foods, where sustainable innovation against private labels is more difficult. Instead, the portfolio has a much sharper focus on health, beauty, and personal care products that tend to have higher margins and lower private label competition.

P&G also realized that the pharmaceutical business is becoming more brand driven, an area of P&G competence. After the Gillette acquisition, health and beauty care now account for more than half of P&G's portfolio. In general, relative to food categories, consumers are more easily convinced of the emotional benefits in the health and beauty categories.

In 2000, P&G owned ten brands with annual sales of more than $1 billion. Five years later, it had sixteen brands that together generated $30 billion, 60 percent of P&G's total revenues.[7] The acquisition of Gillette has added five more billion-dollar brands. By shedding product categories and brands, P&G is able to reinvest the sales proceeds into fewer brands (e.g., Pantene, Lenor, Pampers, Crest, Ariel) where the firm has the best chance of winning. Rather than having the innovation effort spread over many small brands, R&D can now work on the most promising brands and products, while marketing can concentrate on exploiting their maximum potential. The latter includes increased penetration of the large brands in developing countries, where the trade is less consolidated.

The Challenge of Greater Focus

The question with respect to category and brand rationalization is whether firms focused on a few core brands will inevitably lose out to cross-category giants with diversified portfolios, like

Nestlé. Those who advocate size think a larger company can leverage scale to cut costs. These savings can then be invested in more advertising and innovation, thereby helping gain even more scale.

On the other hand, there are diseconomies since larger companies find it hard to move quickly, and costs balloon. Perhaps stronger brands are more important than the overall scale of operations achieved through multiple category presence and mushrooming brand portfolios. For example, Beiersdorf, Reckitt Benckiser, L'Oréal, and Danone are all thriving despite being focused on a few categories. Danone operates in just three categories and is a world leader in all three: biscuits, water, and yogurt.[8]

The challenge is to capture the benefits of both focus and scale. Despite having an enormous product portfolio with 8,000 products and up to 20,000 variants, Nestlé achieves focus through six umbrella brands that it uses to cover most of its activities. These are Nestlé, which accounts for 40 percent of the business, Purina pet foods, Maggi, Nescafé, Nestea, and Buitoni.[9]

We are believers in portfolio rationalization because it makes no sense to support brands by which the manufacturer is not differentiated from a consumer perspective and cannot earn its shelf space from a retailer perspective. The lessons from our brand portfolio rationalization research and consulting projects are now clear. Rationalization does help cut costs and focus on the better-selling items. As a result, the boost to company profits is immediate. However, it does not ensure sales growth. For example, Heinz cut 40 percent of its items between 2001 and 2003 to concentrate on fast-moving items such as ketchup in easy-to-pour upside-down bottles. It wanted to focus on products that are number one or two in their categories. While operating profits rose 17.5 percent in 2003, sales were flat at 0.4 percent.[10] Ultimately, one has to grow the brands and SKUs that remain. The challenge of growing individual brands against rising private label share we take up in the next chapter.

Chapter Takeaways

Fight Selectively to Marshal Resources Against Private Labels

- Support only market leaders or premium niche brands since secondary manufacturer brands bear the brunt of the private label onslaught.

- Reorient the portfolio toward categories where innovation and brands have greater potential to add value.

- Delete (sell, merge, or delist) brands that:

  - Do not have adequate scale

  - Lack brand power

  - Are not must-haves for the retailer

- Rationalize SKUs to weed out slow sellers.

- Recognize that these actions help improve profitability but fail to generate needed sales growth unless the resources freed up from portfolio rationalization (categories, brands, and SKUs) are invested in acquiring complementary brand leaders and growing the sales of remaining brands.

TWELVE

Create Winning Value Propositions for Manufacturer Brands

Price premium for brand image: 23 percent

I N T H E E N D, the battle against private labels must be fought at the level of each individual manufacturer brand. There must be a compelling value proposition for consumers to buy the manufacturer brand instead of the private label. Part of this battle is of course won through innovation, having products that are not comparable to private labels. But if reasonably similar choices are available, then consumers make buying decisions by trading off price against the value provided. Value has both rational and emotional aspects to it. Rational reasons to purchase a particular brand or private label are all about functional benefits, performance, and quality. Emotional reasons are all about image and building close bonds with consumers. Great brands have both logic and magic.

Figure 12-1 demonstrates how consumers use information about image, prices, and quality in a reinforcing manner in their consumption decisions.[1] If the manufacturer brand does not have

FIGURE 12-1

Consumer decisions

Source: Derived from Jean-Philippe Deschamps and P. Ranganath Nayak, *Product Juggernauts: How Companies Mobilize to Generate a Stream of Market Winners* (Boston: Harvard Business School Press, 1995), 87.

the right image, the prospect is lost. If the brand passes the image test, then the consumer examines whether the price is competitive, compared with the private label. If the price gap is acceptable, then the consumer purchases the manufacturer brand. Then comes the quality test: does it deliver performance that satisfies the consumer enough to start a relationship with the brand?

Building a winning value proposition for manufacturer brands against private labels therefore raises three imperatives: manage the price gap to be competitive, improve quality constantly to enhance the rational logic, and build an emotional bond and enduring relationship with consumers. We take up each of these in turn.

Manage the Price Gap

Perhaps the most complex issue in managing manufacturer brands against retailer brands is pricing products competitively. If prices are too high compared with private labels, volume drops. On the other hand, while it is easy to drop prices, cutting prices disproportionately impacts the bottom line. Take the economics of the typical S&P 500 company.[2] Of total revenues, 19.2 percent is needed to cover fixed costs, while variable costs constitute 68.3 percent of revenues, which leaves an operating profit margin of 12.5 percent. Assuming that volumes are constant, these economics imply that a small 2 percent average drop in realized prices from retailers can reduce overall profits for the firm by 16 percent, while a 2 percent price rise can increase profits by 16 percent. Further, if prices drop 2 percent, volume would have to increase by 7.5 percent to merely keep profits constant. Such strong price elasticities are quite rare. In sum, given the sensitivity of profits to pricing for companies, being able to charge as much as possible while maintaining the appropriate price gap with private labels is crucial to success.

A keen understanding of price elasticity (what will happen to our volume when we change our prices) and cross-elasticity (what will happen to our volume as the gap between us and the competitors change) is necessary before adapting prices. For example, between 2000 and 2003, Kraft allowed the price gap between its brands and private labels to grow too large while failing to develop new products that private labels could not copy. The result was three successive years of share losses to private labels in its three largest categories. In 2003, this culminated in a series of sales and profit forecast reductions, and ultimately cost Betsy Holden her job as co-CEO.[3] Firms have to avoid the temptation of increasing prices beyond sustainable levels.

Category price elasticity, which varies widely across categories, drives the optimal price gap between manufacturer brands and private label brands. Unilever found that it lost market share to private labels in ice cream when trying to raise prices, and it was difficult to persuade consumers to pay extra for its branded margarine. However, the successful deodorant business demonstrated that if brands were able to endow the products with emotional qualities rather than pure functional qualities, they could command a premium price. For example, Axe deodorant (Lynx in the U.K.) promises teenage boys sexual success, and that is worth paying extra for.[4]

The Inability to Pass On Increased Costs

Some of the pressure to increase prices occurs because retailers are using their clout to squeeze more money from manufacturers. At many retailers, manufacturer brands have to pay for everything—for introducing new products, slotting allowances for existing products, for displays, in-store promotions, and eye-level shelf space. One study estimated that the sales of consumer packaged goods companies included in the S&P 500 index of big American companies have grown at a compound annual rate of just 4.7 percent. Meanwhile, their sales, general, and administrative expenses have been rising 5 percent a year.[5]

There was a time when consumer goods firms could pass on rising costs to their customers. But today this is difficult, if not impossible. Consolidation means that the spread of aggressive, big-box retail chains such as Wal-Mart, Carrefour, and Costco have destroyed much of the industry's pricing power. A Wal-Mart spokesperson observed, "When suppliers bring price increases to us, we don't just accept it. We ask them to show us that raw materials costs have actually gone up and that's the reason for the increase."[6] Wal-Mart only accepts price increases that are based on increases in raw material costs. Marketing cost increases are the supplier's problem.

Given the tough negotiating environment and competition from private labels, companies must focus on cost control. With their large global operations, complex organizations, premium prices, and high gross margins, consumer packaged goods companies have never been as cost conscious as retailers. Consider that most retailers are working off gross margins between 12 and 30 percent, while consumer packaged goods firms can comfortably average gross margins between 40 and 60 percent. Therefore, companies like

Unilever and Nestlé are restructuring their operations and redeploying the savings generated toward innovation and marketing.

Increase Realized Price, Not List Price

While it is increasingly difficult to pass on increased costs, there may be one way out for companies. At the end of the day, what matters are not the official prices but the actual or realized prices. The latter often are considerably lower than the former because of the numerous ways in which retailers can get discounts, ranging from standard discounts and on-invoice promotion to merchandising allowances and off-invoice special promotions. Illustrative is the case of a global lighting supplier, which found out that the realized price varied between 30 percent and 90 percent of the list price.

Management suggested a "rational" reason for such a large price band—namely, that larger accounts got bigger discounts. However, when price discounts were plotted against account size, no such relationship was found. In fact, many small customers received large discounts! As a result, the company developed clear guidelines about acceptable price ranges as a function of account size and took other steps to rein in the independence of the account managers. While it lost some customers in the process, the average realized price increased by 3.6 percent (the list price remained the same), and operating profits jumped 51 percent.[7]

Overuse of Consumer Promotions

As manufacturer brands lose sales to retailer private labels and it becomes clear to them that the price gap cannot be supported, some brands have started to schedule more frequent and deeper consumer promotions. These consumer promotions take a variety of forms, including coupons, temporary price reductions, free gifts, and two-for-one type of deals. The hope with such consumer promotions is that they will attract private label customers to try the manufacturer's brand. It is then expected that eventually some percentage of these trial customers will become loyal brand users, presumably because they will now see the extra value provided by the manufacturer.

Unfortunately, our research suggests that this happens rather infrequently and consumer promotions tend to deliver only short-term volume gains. In the long term, they typically backfire and may even help private labels. There are several reasons for this. First, a large proportion of the volume sold on promotion is purchased by brand loyals: consumers who would have purchased the manufacturer brand anyway at the higher, nonsale prices. U.S. data reveals that two-thirds of the sales promotion bump is due to brand loyals stocking up![8]

Second, frequent promotions reduce the integrity of nonsale, regular prices and teach consumers to wait for the sale periods. It becomes a cat and mouse game, converting manufacturer brand buyers into promotion buyers. And if they cannot find their favorite brand on sale, having become used to a lower price, they trade down to a private label. In other words, some of the promotion buyers turn into private label buyers over time because of excessive consumer promotions by manufacturer brands. Ultimately, a proportion of these buyers, as they become comfortable with buying store brands, even migrate to hard discounters where manufacturer brands are either shut out or have a minimal presence.

Effectiveness of Price Cuts

Figure 12-2 demonstrates the challenge of managing the price gap.

- Brand B provides a higher value but without a price penalty against private labels and clearly is a winning position for brands. However, brand position B is un-likely to be observed in reality. Retailers will not introduce a private label (PL) with such a poor value proposition against B.

- Brand C is unfortunately where manufacturer brands fre-quently find themselves as a result of upgrades in private

FIGURE 12-2

Price gap management

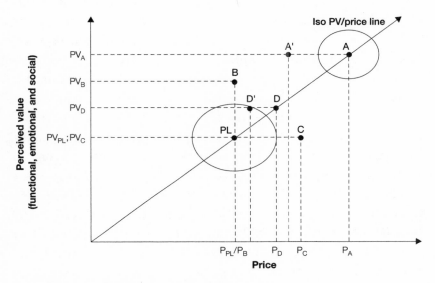

A, B, C, and D represent manufacturer brands; PL is for private label.

label quality and copycat packaging, and increased private label advertising. Consumers see no additional (functional, emotional, or social) value for the higher price paid for brand C. This situation is not sustainable.

- Brands A and D offer the classic brand proposition, with higher prices and also higher value. While customers agree that A and D provide greater value than the private label, the critical question is, How many customers believe it is worth paying extra for the greater value? One can be at position A, a lot more value for a much higher price, or at D, a little bit more value at a somewhat higher price. This becomes a segmentation game.

Managing the price gap through reactions to price cuts is different if the manufacturer brand occupies position A versus position D.

Consider Procter & Gamble in Germany in its battle against private labels, particularly Aldi. In diapers, P&G's Pampers brand was priced at a 31 percent premium, while in feminine care, P&G's Always brand had a price premium of 140 percent over the Aldi store brand. In terms of figure 12-2, one could view Pampers as occupying position D, while Always was at A.

Frustrated at the success of private labels that had a market share of 53.9 percent in diapers and 45.9 percent in feminine care, P&G decided to cut the prices of Pampers by 11 percent and of Always by 18 percent. The impact of the price cut was dramatic for diapers, where the Pampers market share climbed from 31 percent to 42 percent, but quite tepid for Always, where share increased by only 3 percentage points.[9]

Figure 12-2 can help explain why the results were so different for the two price cuts. For Pampers, the segment buying private labels was relatively close by in figure 12-2. Lowering the price on Pampers put the brand within the price-value preferences of some private labels customers (it moved from D to D' in figure 12-2). In contrast, even a larger price cut on Always, which was serving a very different segment, did not bring it close enough to the price-value preferences of the private label buyers. In terms of figure 12-2, it moved from A to A', both positions being far removed from the preferences of the private label buyers.

The point is that managing the price gap is a complex process, as research has demonstrated:[10]

1. If the manufacturer brand is positioned very far away in terms of price from the private label, even a substantial price cut will not have a significant impact.

2. On the other hand, if the manufacturer brand is positioned near the private label, a relatively small price cut can result in significant sales gains.

3. A price cut by the private label will not have much impact on the manufacturer brands, especially when the price differences are large.

Maintain a Quality Edge

As we saw earlier, the optimal price gap depends partially on the quality of the product, or its functional performance. Historically, consumers preferred brands for the reassurance on quality that they provided. Unfortunately, for many brands, over time this quality difference has disappeared, and thus they end up at point C in figure 12-2, especially if one considers only functional performance.

Transparency and Commoditization of Quality

Today consumers are much better informed about product quality as various independent rating and testing agencies, such as Consumers Union, help make the "objective" quality of brands more transparent. For example, Consumers Union recently tested products across those six categories that *Consumer Reports* readers reported as the categories where they most frequently purchase store brands.[11] Table 12-1 presents the results for three categories, and they are not flattering to manufacturer brands.

Ziploc storage bags (14¢ per bag) were easy to open and close, and they were puncture resistant, but so were Wal-Mart's Great Value Slider food storage bags (8¢ per bag). Hefty, another manufacturer brand, was so variable in strength, from spectacular to acceptable, that *Consumer Reports* could not rate it!

In yogurt, store brands from A&P (10¢ per ounce) and Stop & Shop (8¢), rated "very good," were the clear winners. There was little to choose from the others that were rated "good," including Dannon (11¢; Dannon is called Danone in Europe) and Yoplait (12¢) as well as the many store brands, like Kroger (8¢), Publix (6¢), Albertsons (6¢), and Winn-Dixie (5¢). This is bad news for manufacturer brands.

Only in facial tissues was there a clear winner: Puffs ($1 for 100 sheets) from Procter & Gamble. It turned out that many store brands (usually at 60¢) were as soft as Puffs, but when it came to

TABLE 12-1

Consumer Reports results on quality

Category	Excellent	Very good	Good	Fair or poor
Facial tissues (price per 100 tissues)	*Puffs ($1)	Safeway Select ($0.80) Stop & Shop ($0.60)	*Kleenex ($1) Albertsons ($0.80) America's Choice ($0.70) Great Value (Wal-Mart) ($0.60) Kirkland Signature (Costco) ($1.10) Kroger ($0.60) Trader Joe's ($0.60) Winn-Dixie ($0.80)	Publix ($0.70)
Yogurt (price per ounce)		America's Choice Fruit on the Bottom ($0.10) Stop & Shop Fruit on the Bottom ($.0.08)	*Dannon Fruit on the Bottom ($0.11) *Yoplait Original ($0.12) Albertsons Fruit on the Bottom ($0.06) Great Value (Wal-Mart) blended ($0.06) Kirkland Signature Swiss Style ($0.06) Kroger Fruit on the Bottom ($0.08) Lucerne (Safeway) Fruit on the Bottom ($0.08) Publix Fruit on the Bottom ($0.06) Trader Joe's Pre-Stirred ($0.10) Winn-Dixie ($0.05)	Kirkland Signature Swiss Style (Costco) ($0.06)
Plastic bags (price per bag)	*Ziploc ($0.14) Great Value (Wal-Mart) ($0.08)	America's Choice (A&P) ($0.14) Kroger Slider ($0.13)	Albertsons ($0.15) Stop & Shop ($0.13)	

*Manufacturer brands

Source: Derived from "Battle of the Brands," *Consumer Reports,* August 2005, 12–15.

strength, none of the tissues were as strong—but then, neither was Kleenex ($1).

As a result of its testing, Consumers Union had the following three conclusions from its study, all damning for brand manufacturers:

1. Many store brands are at least as good as national brands.

2. Switching to a store brand can cut the cost of a product by as much as 50 percent.

3. The companies that make store brands are often household names.

Price and Quality

A study using data from various Consumers Union investigations found:

1. In twenty-two out of seventy-eight product categories, the average store brand was higher in quality than the average manufacturer brand.[12] In these categories, manufacturer brands cost 30 percent more.

2. In the remaining fifty-six categories, when manufacturer brands were higher in quality, they cost 50 percent more.

The point is that quality differences between private labels and manufacturer brands are constantly declining. And even if there is a difference, as the results from table 12-1 indicate, it is not always clear that manufacturer brands are better than store brands. It is almost as if quality has now become a commodity. When this is combined with the fact that quality today is a lot more transparent, the job of the manufacturer brands becomes very difficult. The transparency of quality reduces the importance of emotional benefits imbued in the brands, especially in categories that are not socially visible (e.g., detergents versus cars).

The paper towels category demonstrates this challenge in figure 12-3. The two manufacturer brands, Bounty and Brawny, are,

FIGURE 12-3

Price and quality of paper towels

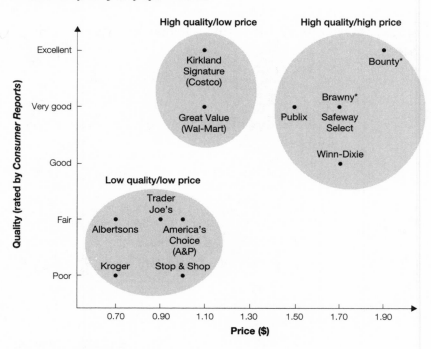

*Denotes manufacturer brand.

Source: Derived from "Battle of the Brands," *Consumer Reports*, August 2005, 12–15.

on average, of higher quality than the store brands and offer the value proposition "high quality/high price." The traditional trade-off between price and quality can be made between these two manufacturer brands and the group of store brands under the value proposition "low quality/low price." But then there are at least four store brands—Kirkland from Costco, Great Value from Wal-Mart, Safeway Select, and Publix—that are rated as "very good" or "excellent." And the Costco and Wal-Mart paper towels are much cheaper, though, in fairness, one has to buy them in multiple-unit packs.

In such an environment, the question becomes, Why does any-body buy manufacturer brands? It turns out that manufacturer brands can sell only to those customers to whom at least one of the following conditions apply:

1. *Emotional/social benefit seekers.* Consumers who perceive emotional (e.g., love Bounty or Brawny for the years, perhaps generations, of service and good performance) or social benefits (visitors may think I am using cheap towels if I have the store brands) from the manufacturer brands beyond those available from the retailer brands (and thus makes them analogous to A or D in figure 12-2) and see the resultant higher value worth the price premium.

2. *Customer ignorance.* Consumers who are unaware of the true functional benefits of the store brands versus manufacturer brands and instead perceive that manufacturer brands have higher functional quality, compared with store brands, and value these differences enough to pay the price premium.

3. *Risk avoidance.* Consumers who know that no retailer brand is the best in all categories (see table 12-1) and time-harassed shoppers who engage in one-stop shopping and believe that purchasing manufacturer brands ensures one will obtain good quality consistently. This is reinforced because the top manufacturer brands in a category are available in most retail chains, which makes it easier for customers to purchase regardless of which retailer they frequent.

4. *Store accessibility.* The store (e.g., Wal-Mart and Costco) with the best private label may be so far away that it negates the price advantage. In contrast, manufacturer brands are widely available. Of course, with the aggressive expansion plans of retailers like Wal-Mart and Costco, the stores are getting closer to the consumers. For example, now 85 percent of German households are within a fifteen-minute drive of an Aldi store.

Constantly Seeking the Quality Edge

The alternative to reducing prices is for manufacturer brands to rediscover the quality edge. To us, it seems imperative that this is where manufacturer brands must put their resources. A product should not be allowed out of the factory if it cannot prove that its functional quality is better than that of the private labels. No wonder, on the day that Patrick Cescau was named the sole CEO of Unilever, he remarked, "We need to spend more time and money differentiating ourselves from private label."[13]

Functional quality means that there has to be a real performance difference. Historically, this is what the pharmaceutical industry has pursued. As GlaxoSmithKline argues, "Customers are looking for the best scientific differentiation," and this is what it attempts to build into its products. Thus, it has launched Nicorette for those seeking to quit smoking, Flixonase for hay fever, and Poligrip dental strips, which have been judged more effective and cleaner than the existing adhesives on the market for denture users.[14]

Brand manufacturers have to ensure that the fight against private labels takes place on the grounds of quality and they are superior on quality and features. This can be a goal in any industry, even those that are traditionally considered emotional industries. For example, one explanation given for the low market share of retailer brands in France, compared with Germany, in the cosmetics industry is that L'Oréal has dragged the competition into a war fought on scientifically proven performance, supported by massive advertising budgets to communicate this as well as emotional benefits.[15] In Germany, the leading brand Nivea relies more on soft emotional differentiators like empathy and softness.

Ultimately, there will almost always be a price gap between (leading) manufacturer brands and store brands. Thus, manufacturer brands will have to prove to price-conscious consumers that their brands are worth that extra amount. This requires brand manufacturers to invest in communicating their product advantages. Early in CEO A. G. Lafley's tenure, when he was engineering the turnaround of P&G and profit pressure was severe, he faced the dilemma of whether to go with strong marketing support for the launch of several new brands, such as Actonel and Toregonos in the U.S. and Iams in Europe. Because the businesses believed in these products, all of which tested better than those of competitors, the company went ahead. As is often said, advertising is the final coat of paint, but it can only work if what lies behind it has been thoroughly prepared. Nothing kills a bad product faster than lots of advertising.

Create Consumer Bonds

Beyond functional performance, manufacturer brands can add emotional benefits to the products—making them cool, hip, lovable, prestigious, socially desirable, emotionally satisfying, and so on. It helps create consumer bonding with the brand. To achieve this requires marketing and communication investments vis-à-vis consumers.

From Advertising to Trade

Manufacturer brands seem to be moving in the wrong direction. While industries with higher advertising intensity tend to have lower private label share, companies are increasingly diverting money away from advertising to promotions. With the growing power of retailers, their ability to extract money for promotions, gondola displays, floor graphics, shelf advertising, coupons, merchandising, and listing fees also increases. Nowadays, trade spending is second only to the cost of goods sold and can amount to 30 percent of sales revenue.

For example, Heinz global marketing spend is up 8 percent in 2004. But this increase is mostly accounted for by a rise in its trade expenditure with customers such as Tesco, Carrefour, and Wal-Mart. Traditional above-the-line advertising is flat. As the director of the Heinz brand in U.K. observed, "It's a case of consumer versus trade. Inevitably the pot of money is broadly fixed and the trade environment is more of a battleground every year."[16]

Diverting money from communicating with customers to retailer support is the beginning of a vicious cycle for manufacturer brands. As manufacturer brands spend less building their brands with end consumers, they lose brand equity with the ultimate arbiter in the marketplace. This increases the relative power of retailers and their negotiating power. As a result, manufacturer brands are subject to even greater concessions by retailers. In order to fund these concessions to retailers, manufacturer brands divert more money from consumer communications to retailers. It is to counter this trend that companies such as Unilever and Colgate-Palmolive are now spending more on communicating the benefits of their brands to shoppers amid pricing pressure from retailers. As reseller equity goes up, to maintain balance, manufacturer brands have to spend more rather than less money communicating with customers.

Moving Beyond Traditional Advertising

Traditional media has become less effective because proliferation in television channels has led to an increasingly fragmented audience. This makes it more difficult and more expensive to reach the same numbers of customers. Moreover, there is competition from other media, such as computer games and the Internet, for the attention of younger viewers. Finally, digital recording technologies such as TiVo now enable a growing number of viewers to ignore advertisements when watching television.

Buzz marketing, also known as "word-of-mouth marketing," "guerrilla marketing," or "stealth marketing," has emerged as a way for companies to get on the right side of consumers in the battle for sales. Buzz marketing involves getting the trendsetters in any community to carry the brand's message, thus creating interest in the brand with no overt advertising or promotion. The brand message can be transmitted physically (for example, people may be seen with the brand), verbally (the brand can crop up in conversation), or virtually (via the Internet). With the proliferation of e-mail and mobile phones, word of mouth spreads faster than ever.

Red Bull is the master of buzz marketing. It has created an edgy, slightly dangerous image for its drink. The company keeps tight control on how it markets itself to clubs and bars. In its eight U.S. sales areas, representatives scout out hot spots—the bars and clubs frequented by trendsetters. Once they have identified five key venues, they offer them branded refrigerators and other freebies along with their first order. If other, more conventional establishments ask to stock Red Bull, the company refuses, reinforcing its underground association and street credibility. To cultivate its link with the club crowd, Red Bull set up the Red Bull Music Academy, a two-week annual event that brings together aspiring DJs and their idols.

Consumer education teams also help generate buzz. One of the first marketing techniques Red Bull employed was to hire student brand managers at university campuses, giving them each a case of Red Bull and encouraging them to throw a party. It hired hip locals to drive around in cars emblazoned with the logo and decorated with a four-foot model of the trademark blue and silver can. The cars carry fridges stocked with more than 250 cans of Red Bull, which they distribute to "those in need of energy": shift workers, truck drivers, university students, executives, clubbers, and athletes.

Red Bull sponsors a number of extreme sports events, including cliff diving, kite boarding, snowboarding, motocross, mountain biking, paragliding, street luge, ice cross downhill, skateboarding, and surfing. By allying itself with those who push the boundaries in these extreme sports, Red Bull has become an extreme drink by association. Dangerous and not supported by the establishment, extreme sports events and their related social circles are ideal for word-of-mouth marketing.

Brand Turnarounds

Encouragingly, there are instances where manufacturer brands and companies have achieved a successful turnaround in the battle against private labels by creating winning value propositions.

In the mid-1990s, private label accounted for 60 percent of the "plant" bread category in the U.K. Plant bread is mass-produced bread, as opposed to bread produced by specialist bakeries. Brand manufacturers such as Allied Bakeries and Warburtons fought back with new product development and marketing, adding benefits like high-fiber, low-salt, 100 percent whole grain and added calcium, and the launch of superpremium brands such as Kingsmill Gold. Ten years later, private label share is down to 36 percent.[17]

In Europe, as we have seen earlier, Procter & Gamble had been forced to cut prices selectively, in categories like diapers, detergents, and shampoo, to counter private labels. However, it is not enough to just change the price gap with private labels; one can surround the private labels with product and brand extensions. When Procter & Gamble reduced prices on its basic Pampers, it also introduced the new Pampers Contour disposable diaper. Similarly, to sell more toilet paper, it created a more expensive version of Charmin, along with an advertising campaign reassuring consumers: "Don't you deserve a bit of luxury?"[18] On the other hand, to avoid slashing Ariel's price, the company introduced Mr. Clean as a cheaper detergent in Germany to compete with the hard discounters.

We will discuss now two brand turnaround examples in more detail, one from the U.S. (Heinz ketchup) and one from Europe (Danone La Copa).

Heinz Ketchup

Prior to 1998, Heinz ketchup was premium priced but supported by little advertising. As a result, it was losing market share to private labels and lower-priced second- and third-tier brands.[19]

Between 1999 and 2002, Heinz launched several enhancements to the product and packaging, including EZ Squirt bottles, spicy flavors, a "trap cap" that eliminates watery ooze, and "mystery colors" to appeal to kids.[20] For example, one of its packaging enhancements was easy-squeeze ketchup in an ergonomically designed upside-down bottle with no mess and no waiting. This was a major mind shift for Heinz, which for years had extolled the virtues of the "anticipation" of a slow pour.

It also supported these introductions with a major ad campaign. The profits generated from these new flavors were then employed to close the price gap between Heinz and private label by 17 percent. As a result of these moves, Heinz managed to grow its share by six points. Most of this gain was wrested from second- and third-tier brands as well as leaving private labels little room to grow.[21] Having turned around its ketchup business, the company then overhauled its portfolio in 2002 by selling businesses in seafood, pet food, baby food, and private label soup to Del Monte.[22] Since then, Heinz has been less successful. The value of its brand name declined from its peak in 2002 of $7.35 billion to $6.22 billion in 2006.[23] Analysts have been wary of Heinz's continuous ability to create value in foods like ketchup and beans, and to keep store brands at bay.

Danone La Copa

La Copa, a creamy chocolate yogurt dessert sold by Danone (Dannon in the U.S.), was a traditional favorite in Spain, positioned as a luxury treat for children and adults. Despite its rich heritage, over the years it had lost share to competitors, especially private labels. By 2004, while La Copa was still the category leader with 30 percent market share, private labels had captured 45 percent, with Nestlé accounting for the remaining 25 percent of the category. An analysis of the category revealed that La Copa, which had always been premium priced, did not currently offer any noticeable difference in product experience to justify its price premium. Determined to capture share back from competitors, especially private labels, Danone decided to relaunch the product.

The product formulation was changed to more cream (18 to 22 percent) and less chocolate (82 to 78 percent) in order to give it a creamier and lighter feel. This was supported with a new message: "cream until the last spoon." In addition, to increase value, Danone increased the container size from 100 grams per pot to

115 grams per pot. The pot itself was given a more modern, rounded shape and was made from a transparent plastic so that the product was visible to the consumer instead of packaged in an out-of-date brown container. To compensate for the enhanced value, the company raised the price from €1.02 to €1.13. These changes, implemented at the end of 2004, generated a dramatic turnaround in fortunes for La Copa. Its market share increased from 30 percent to over 50 percent, while private label share declined from 44 percent to 30 percent. Nestlé's market share also declined.

Unfortunately, too often, manufacturer brands do not invest in continuously improving their value proposition. This allows competitors, and especially private labels, to shoot at a target that is standing still.

Chapter Takeaways

Creating Winning Value Propositions for Manufacturer Brands

- Actively manage the price gap, constantly improve quality, and build an emotional bond with the consumer.

- Resist the overuse of consumer promotions since it only makes consumers more price sensitive and leads to trading-down by a significant number of customers.

- Monitor realized prices carefully by controlling discounts rather than increasing list prices.

- Never trade off product performance in the face of price and cost pressures. The cost cuts must come elsewhere as quality becomes more transparent.

- Profit from the inability of any store brand to be a consistent quality winner across categories.

THIRTEEN

Are Brands Dead?

Private label share: Switzerland, 45 percent;
United States, 20 percent

THE *ECONOMIST* MAGAZINE observed that every industry has its golden age. For brand manufacturers, it was the middle of the twentieth century, when distribution channels were fragmented and the media was consolidated. Powerful brand manufacturers like Coca-Cola, General Mills, Nestlé, Procter & Gamble, and Unilever would delight their customers by launching one new product after another.[1]

We hope our book has demonstrated to the reader who has followed us until the last chapter that we are now in a new era, where the retailers have power and have used it to transform the competitive brand landscape. With the rise of giant retailers like Aldi, Carrefour, Costco, Gap, The Home Depot, IKEA, Staples, The Limited, Target, Tesco, Wal-Mart, and Zara, there has been a private label revolution over the past two decades. This revolution has important implications for consumers, retailers, and manufacturers.

The Consumer Is the Winner

An overlooked story in the private label revolution has been the impact on consumer welfare. The megaretailers have used their negotiating power to push brand manufacturers to reduce their prices. Rather than pocket all these negotiating gains, retailers have plowed a large part of them into price cuts for the consumer. There is little doubt that consumers have benefited from the price pressure that global retailers like Costco, H&M, Lidl, and Metro have put on other retailers as well as brand manufacturers. A McKinsey study estimated that over the second half of the 1990s, Wal-Mart accounted for 12 percent of the productivity gains in the U.S. economy!

The private label revolution can also claim credit for the increased quality, product choice, and price-value combinations available to consumers. As we recommend in chapters 10 and 12, the only way for manufacturer brands to compete against private labels is by launching innovative products and constantly improving quality. In the attempt to beat private labels, brand manufacturers have had to invest more time and money in doing so than they otherwise would have. Today, there are more products, and of better quality, because of the private label revolution.

To tempt consumers to try new products as well as store brands, most manufacturers and retailers now offer a money-back guarantee, with no questions asked. This has considerably reduced the risk for consumers to adopt new products and brands, thereby enhancing real choice. The private label revolution has helped empower the consumer.

The Private Label Revolution Marches On

Unlike what is sometimes believed, the increase in private label share in industries ranging from consumer packaged goods and apparel to home furnishings, office supplies, and do-it-yourself is not a pendulum that will swing back and forth. In every annual survey since 1999 by *Progressive Grocer*, the U.S. industry trade magazine, supermarket executives have ranked "Stress Private-Label" first out of the twenty-six priorities as being the most important to them. Figure 13-1 captures the vicious circle that brand manufacturers are caught in.

Similarly, in the consumer packaged goods industry, the world-wide share of private labels is expected to increase to 22 percent by 2010 (see table 1-2). Taking 2020 as the time frame, we do not see any reason, with increasing globalization and consolidation of retail, that private label share would not be in the 25 to 30 percent

FIGURE 13-1

The vicious circle for manufacturer brands

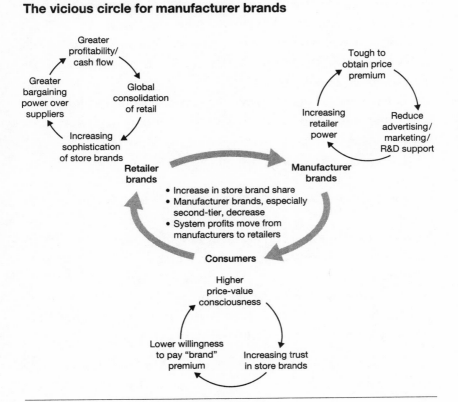

range. In fact, western Europe is already expected to reach the 30 percent mark by 2010 (see table 1-2). And this development is not restricted to packaged goods, as witnessed in the success of private labels in other industries. For example, the U.S. share of private labels in apparel is predicted to increase from around 40 percent today to 60 percent in 2020. We estimate that by 2010, an additional $100 billion to $200 billion per year will be lost that otherwise would have gone into the pockets of brand manufacturers.

In the United Kingdom, private labels now represent about 40 percent of sales in supermarkets. One could argue that the United Kingdom will no longer be an anomaly in private label development.[2] Indeed, private label share at Wal-Mart is estimated at 40 percent (see table 1-1), compared with less than 10 percent two decades ago. By 2020, private labels in the U.S. could approach U.K. levels of share and profitability. If that happens, all of the preceding projections will turn out to be conservative.

In conclusion, within any particular category over some period of time, one may see brand manufacturers win battles against private labels and increase their share. But it is hard for us to imagine any scenario in the war between manufacturer brands and private labels that could lead to a decline in the overall private label share between now and 2020.

The Limits of Private Labels for Retailers

While all of this will seem like great news to retailers, and for the most part it is, there are some pitfalls along the way that retailers must tread around carefully. To be successful with private labels, retailers must remember when private labels add value—they should "fill a void in the category" either in price or in value.[3] Private labels add real value in three situations.

    1. In a category that is dominated by one or perhaps two brands, with little price competition. Here a copycat

brand (see chapter 2) can give consumers a real choice where there was previously none.

2. By reengineering the value chain and product, the retailer creates a dramatically lower-priced private label à la Aldi (see chapter 4). This helps expand the market by providing good quality at low prices for the masses.

3. By introducing new products and concepts that are not offered by brand manufacturers (see chapter 3). As a Wal-Mart executive remarked, "If we can come up with private label items that can bring something different, unique, or new to a category, that allows us to be a better agent for our consumers."

But retailers, especially mainstream retailers, can overstress private labels from the consumer's perspective. In this respect, Sainsbury cola was a watershed for Sainsbury. It did significantly bite into Coke's market share, but Sainsbury lost share of the total cola market. Now Sainsbury realizes that it needs to sit down with Coca-Cola and design its cola so that it is complementary, not cannibalistic, to leading brands. It took years for Sainsbury to learn that the role of private label is not just to offer the same quality at a lower price, but to give a choice of different qualities at different prices.[4] Too much emphasis on private labels at mainstream retailers, where consumers expect to see choice, can turn shoppers away.

In conclusion, retailers should stress private labels that add real value. Since manufacturer brands from a retailer's perspective are commodities, available everywhere, it is understandable that retailers wish to emphasize their own private labels. But retailers need to be careful that this does not deflect them from their real mission, which is to sell what the consumer wants, rather than what a retailer would wish to sell. In other words, we believe that there is an upper limit to private labels for mainstream mass retailers like Albert Heijn, Carrefour, Metro, Tesco, and Wal-Mart. In our estimate, this is around 40 to 50 percent. However, have manufacturer brands planned for a future when this is true?

The Brand Manufacturers' Challenge

In this new retail environment, to meet the challenge of private labels, brand manufacturers must have realistic expectations, focus on innovation, and seek growth through acquisitions and penetration of emerging markets.

Realistic Expectations

In such a tough environment, brand manufacturers need to have realistic expectations about growth in sales and profitability. It is easy to promise but difficult to deliver. Coca-Cola learned this the hard way after having to change three CEOs in rapid succession for overpromising at a time when the U.S. carbonated beverage market shrank 7 percent between 1999 and 2004. Finally, in 2004, when Neville Isdell took over as CEO, one of his first steps was to lower the company's growth targets by a third. He remarked, "That was part of the problem I inherited—trying to meet the numbers that could not be met over the near term."[5] The revised projections called for annual income growth of 6 to 8 percent and volume growth of 3 to 4 percent.

Similarly, when asked what the most important lesson from the turnaround of Procter & Gamble was, A. G. Lafley, the CEO, mentioned facing up to reality and seeing things as they are.[6] One of his first actions was to reduce previous CEO Durk Jager's over-ambitious targets of 7 to 9 percent annual sales growth to a more realistic 4 to 6 percent, while reducing the 13 to 15 percent earnings per share annual growth target to at least 10 percent.[7]

Most companies aspire to increasing both profitability and market share, but there are trade-offs to be made between the two objectives in the new retail environment. While companies may have different preferences, these should be clearly articulated at the top of the organization. As Manfred Wennemer, chief executive of Continental Tires, noted, "We have the objective of being one of the most profitable suppliers to the auto industry but we don't have to be the biggest."[8]

The financial community, of course, presses companies to be specific on the anticipated numbers because it makes the work of the analysts easier. But it may not be wise to play along with this game. For example, Nestlé has a policy of not promising specific financial targets but instead articulating its strategy and letting analysts do the work of computing the expected numbers.

Of course, we realize that it is easy for us, as academics, to ask firms to have lower expectations for growth and market share in the new private label world. But CEOs of brand manufacturers cannot simply hold up the white flag and surrender in front of retailer brands. To motivate their people, stretch them to achieve their best, and energize the organization, they must have as their goal to grow and beat retailer brands. Only with that attitude can they win.

While we recognize this, our point is that one needs to be realistic in promises of top-line growth to the external community between what is achievable and what motivates the organization. We believe that brand manufacturer firms can grow despite the increasing share of private labels. But the growth will be hard fought and come from new products, acquisitions, and increased penetration of new markets. For manufacturer brands, the easy days are behind them. No wonder, as table 13-1 demonstrates, even many top brands have faced stagnant valuations over this decade.[9]

Innovation

Our view is that as private label share grows, the competitive landscape requires a new approach by manufacturer brands. Growth in the developed markets will be hard and depends primarily on the ability to launch successful new innovative products and concepts, as articulated in chapter 10. Given the resources needed to support ambitious new product programs, only brands with adequate size and share can be supported. As in chapter 11,

TABLE 13-1

Brand valuations, 2000–2006

2006 rank	Brand name	2006 brand value ($ billions)	2000 brand value ($ billions)	Change in value 2000 to 2006
1	Coca-Cola	67.00	72.54	−7.6%
12	Marlboro	21.35	22.11	−3.4%
16	Gillette	19.60	17.36	+12.9%
22	Pepsi**	12.69	11.14	+13.9%
23	Nescafé	12.51	13.68	−8.6%
27	Budweiser	11.66	10.69	+9.1%
40	Kellogg's	8.78	7.36	+19.3%
53	L'Oréal***	6.39	5.08	+25.8%
54	Heinz*	6.22	7.06	−11.9%
58	Colgate	5.63	4.42	+27.4%
59	Wrigley's	5.45	4.32	+26.2%
64	Kleenex	4.84	5.14	−5.8%
79	Kraft*	3.94	4.03	−2.2%
87	Moet & Chandon	3.26	2.80	+16.4%
88	Johnson & Johnson***	3.19	2.51	+27.1%
93	Smirnoff	3.03	2.44	+24.2%
99	Nivea*	2.69	1.78	+51.1%
	Total	198.23	194.46	+1.9%

*2001, because the 2000 figures were unavailable.
**2002, because brand-value data was revised upward due to new data.
***2002, because 2000-2001 figures were unavailable.

Source: Derived from BusinessWeek, "The 100 Top Brands," 2001, 2002, 2003, and 2006.

the rationale to keep weak brands, those not occupying share positions 1 or 2, is hard to see in most categories.

Continually finding new products is a challenge for the best of companies. Traditional models of innovation have limitations in producing the required number of new products, and in any case, large companies have never been great at innovation. In 1970, 5 percent of global patents were issued to small entrepreneurs, while today the number is around one-third and rising.[10] When P&G realized this, it saw that its old model of purely internal innovation was suboptimal. Why not tap these entrepreneurs and scientists? Therefore, P&G launched the "connect and develop" model of open innovation.

With the open innovation model, P&G recognized that it was competing to pick up these ideas for ready-made global distribution with other brand manufacturers as well as retailers. Nabil Sakkab, head of R&D at P&G, observed, "My biggest competitor is a person with an idea . . . I have to find them before Wal-Mart does." To succeed, P&G had to offer inventors the ability to develop and market their products quickly and better. As Lafley noted, "Anyone in a garage anywhere in the world can come up with an idea that could be important to one of our businesses. We want them to bring it to us."[11] The resulting change in the P&G attitude toward intellectual property was described as moving from the Kremlin to the Acropolis.[12]

Acquisitions and Penetration of New Markets

Beyond innovation, top-line growth will have to come from either acquisitions or growth in emerging markets. In general, large acquisitions do not lead to the desired results for the shareholders of the acquiring firm. And the acquisition may even deflect the acquirer from focusing on the challenges faced by its existing brands and businesses. As Neville Isdell, CEO of Coca-Cola, observed, "People tell me we should make an acquisition and I say, 'Fine, but you're telling me that we're not running our own business very well. What makes you think we can run someone else's business better than they can?"[13]

The best growth opportunity for brand manufacturers is the emerging markets in Asia, eastern Europe, Latin America, and Africa. Population growth and economic growth are typically much higher than in Western countries, while the retail trade is fragmented. In these markets, brand manufacturers face challenges at which they have typically excelled, such as brand building, advertising, and sales management. Although private labels are also slated to grow in these markets, they will remain a minor presence for the foreseeable future (see table 1-2). Increasingly, aspiring managers will seek to work in these countries to make their mark. Illustrative is the reaction of a South African manager of a large CPG company when he was invited to run operations in Europe. He preferred to continue working in emerging markets. That was where the "action" was.

Are Brands Dead?

The preceding changes may lead brand manufacturers to become pessimistic about their future. But while second-tier brands may be on life support, strong manufacturer brands have a promising future. Today, despite the growth in private labels and the ubiquity of premium private labels, consumers are still passionate about manufacturer brands. In contrast, few private labels from mass retailers elicit the same strong feelings.

Even in the U.K., the most advanced country with respect to private label development, when homemakers were asked to name their most desired supermarket brands—the ones they would miss the most if they were not available on the shelves—the top forty-nine spots were taken by manufacturer brands, such as Heinz baked beans, Kellogg's cereals, Nescafé coffee, Colgate toothpaste, and Walker's snacks.[14] Only in the fiftieth place, with Tesco cheese, did a store brand make an appearance. Clearly, brands have built their relationships with consumers over many decades and still have a reservoir of goodwill to draw on. Yet, Tesco, with eight products, had the fifth-largest number of brands in the top one hundred after Unilever, Procter & Gamble, Heinz, and PepsiCo, indicating that private labels are making steady progress vis-à-vis consumer affections.

In many categories, the multibrand strategies of leading retailers like Tesco and Wal-Mart have put a pincerlike grip on the manufacturer brands and turned them into fighter brands. By having economy and premium lines, the retailer can say with its premium brand, "Oh, look at my private label! It is so much better than the manufacturer brands, but it only costs you a few cents more." And the retailer is also credible in saying, "Here is my cheap, generic, private label. It is almost as good as the manufacturer brand, but it costs much less."

No wonder brand manufacturers are paranoid. They feel there is a gang of interlopers who are sneaking behind them hoping to infiltrate the elite club of "brands" consumers know, love, and buy. And it is true that retailers covet the brand status that manufacturer brands have. As Paul Polman, the previous head of P&G Europe, noted about Aldi, "These people are using brands just as much as we use brands. They believe in brands. Don't be fooled."[15]

The two main sources of competitive advantage that manufacturer brands have against private labels—universal availability and innovation—are now both under fire. David McNair, director of brand marketing for Sainsbury, on whether Sainsbury brands could be sold outside the store, noted, "We have built brands that do not need to be confined to the four walls of a piece of property with the same name." Somerfield Chocolate chip cookies are now sold in Amsterdam. Tesco peanut butter is available in the Costa del Sol.[16] Staples is planning to open a Staples-branded section in 550 Stop & Shop supermarkets, and in Giant Food stores throughout the Northeast, 40-by-80-foot Staples sections will feature 500 to 1,200 Staples and nationally branded products.[17]

It is not that brands are dead. As Colgate-Palmolive, Procter & Gamble, and Unilever are discovering, they are alive and kicking. But some of them are now owned by retailers.[18] Consider this: what single name does the homeowner think of when they want to replace a leaky faucet—Delta, Kohler, or Home Depot? Retailers have succeeded in building themselves up as trusted brands in the mind of the customers. Overall, manufacturer brands still have an edge on this, but the gap has substantially reduced over the years. As a result, the manufacturer brands on the retail shelves have become less important.

Manufacturer brands will always be there, but they have already lost some of their significance. Only when they respond aggressively to the threat from store brands, will manufacturer brands be able to recapture their luster.

Retailer Facts

Retailer	2005 sales in US$ billion	Headquarters—operating continents	Primary format
AEON	34	Japan-Asia, U.S., Europe	Multiformat
Albertsons	41	U.S.	Supermarket
Aldi	43	Germany—Europe, North America	Hard discounter
Amazon.com	9	U.S.—Europe, Asia	Online retailer
A&P	11	U.S.	Supermarket
Auchan	38	France—Europe, Asia, Africa, South America	Hypermarket
Barnes & Noble	5	U.S.	Book retailer
Benetton	2*	Italy—Asia, North America South America, Europe, Africa	Speciality apparel
Best Buy	27	U.S.—North America	Category killer electronics
Bloomingdale's	2*	U.S.	Department store
Boots	10	U.K.—Asia, Europe, U.S., South Africa	Pharmacy
Brooks	2	U.S.	Pharmacy
C1000	5	Netherlands	Supermarket
Cape Union Mart	NA	South Africa	Outdoor equipment retailer

(continued)

Retailer	2005 sales in US$ billion	Headquarters— operating continents	Primary format
Carrefour	94	France—North America, South America, Asia, Europe, Africa	Hypermarket
Circuit City	10	U.S.—North America	Category killer electronics
Coles Myer	28	Australia—New Zealand	Supermarket
Costco	53	U.S.—Europe, Asia	Cash and carry
CVS	37	U.S.	Pharmacy
De Bijenkorf	0.5	Netherlands	Department store
Decathlon	3	Germany—Europe, U.S., Asia, South America	Sports equipment retailer
Delhaize	23	Belgium—Europe, Asia, U.S.	Supermarket
Dollar General	7	U.S.	Soft discounter
Dollar Tree	3	U.S.	Soft discounter
Dominick's	2	U.S.	Supermarket
Duane Read	2	U.S.	Pharmacy
eBay	5	U.S.—Asia, Europe	Online auction
Edah	4*	Netherlands—Europe	Supermarket
Edeka	2	Germany—Europe, Asia	Supermarket
El Corte Inglés	16	Spain—Portugal	Department store
Family Dollar	6	U.S.	Soft discounter
Federated (Macy's and Bloomingdale's)	23	U.S.	Department store
Fidelity	10	U.S.	Financial supermarket
Fnac	3	France—Europe, Asia, South America	Category killer electronics
Fred Meyer	8	U.S.	Department store
Gap	16	U.S.—Europe	Specialty apparel
Giant Eagle	6	U.S.	Supermarket
Giant Food	3	U.S.	Supermarket
H&M	8	Sweden—Europe, North America	Specialty apparel
H-E-B	12	U.S.	Supermarket
Home Depot	82	U.S.—North America	Category killer DIY
IKEA	18	Sweden—Europe, North America, Asia	Category killer furniture

Retailer	2005 sales in US$ billion	Headquarters—operating continents	Primary format
Intermarché	42	Europe	Supermarket
Intersport	10	Switzerland—Europe, North America	Sports retailer
Ito-Yokado	28	Japan—North America, Europe, Asia	Supermarket
JCPenney	17	U.S.—South America	Department store
JD Sports	1	U.K.	Sports retailer
Kmart	19	U.S.	Mass merchandiser
Kohl's	13	U.S.	Department store
Kroger	61	U.S.—North America	Supermarket
Kruidvat	3	Netherlands—Europe	Drugstore
Lidl	38*	Germany—Europe	Hard discounter
Limited Brands	10	U.S.	Mainly apparel
Loblaws	25	Canada	Supermarket
Lowe's	44	U.S.	Category killer DIY
Makro	2*	England—Europe	Cash and carry
Marks & Spencer	13	U.K.—Asia, U.S.	Supermarket
Metro	73	Germany—Europe, Asia, Africa	Multiformat
Migros	17	Switzerland—Europe	Supermarket
Neiman Marcus	4	U.S.	Department store
Netto	1	Denmark—Europe	Hard discounter
Office Depot	15	U.S.—Europe, Asia	Category killer office supplies
Old Navy	6	U.S.	Specialty apparel
Pick 'n Pay	5	Cape Town, South Africa—Australia	Supermarket
Publix	17	U.S.	Supermarket
Quill	1	U.S.	Catalog retailer
Rewe	51	Germany—Europe	Supermarket
Rite-Aid	17	U.S.	Pharmacy
Royal Ahold (Albert Heijn)	56	Netherlands—Europe, North America	Supermarket
Safeway	40	U.S.—Europe	Supermarket
Sainsbury	28	U.K.	Supermarket
Saks	6	U.S.	Department store

(continued)

Retailer	2005 sales in US$ billion	Headquarters—operating continents	Primary format
Save-A-Lot	4*	U.S.	Soft discounter
Sears	36*	U.S.—North America	Mass merchandiser
7-Eleven	12*	U.S.—North America	Convenience store
Shaw's	25	U.S.	Supermarket
Somerfield	5	U.K.	Supermarket
Staples	16	U.S.—Europe, Canada	Category killer office products
Starbucks	6	U.S.—Asia, Europe, Australia, North America, South America	Coffee chain
Stop & Shop	11	U.S.	Supermarket
Supervalu	18	U.S.	Discount store
Target	53	U.S.	Mass merchandiser
Tchibo	10	Europe	Coffee chain
Tesco	71	U.K.—Europe, Asia	Superstore
Toys "R" Us	11	U.S.—Asia, Europe, Africa	Category killer toys
Trader Joe's	4	U.S.	Specialty grocery
Ukrop's	1	U.S.	Supermarket
Victoria's Secret	4	U.S.	Specialty apparel
Virgin Superstores	NA	U.K.—Europe, U.S., Asia	Specialty electronics
Walgreens	42	U.S.	Pharmacy
Wal-Mart	316	U.S.—North America, South America, Asia, Europe	Supercenter
Whole Foods	5	U.S.	Supermarket
Winn-Dixie Stores	11	U.S.	Supermarket
Woolworths Australia	24	Australia—Australasia	Supermarket
Woolworths South Africa	2	South Africa	Supermarket
Zara	5	Spain—Europe, North America, South America, Africa, Asia	Specialty apparel

*2004 sales figure.

NOTES

Chapter 1

1. Nirmalya Kumar, *Marketing as Strategy: Understanding the CEO's Agenda for Driving Growth and Innovation* (Boston: Harvard Business School Press, 2004), chapter 5.

2. M+M Planet Retail, 2005, www.planetretail.net, and "Fortune Global 500," *Fortune*, July 24, 2006, 113–120.

3. Data based on Planet Retail, *Global Retail Concentration 2004* (London: M+M Planet Retail, 2005).

4. Toys "R" Us Corporate Page, http://www2.toysrus.com/index.cfm ?lb=1.

5. ACNielsen, "ACNielsen Research Finds U.S. Sales of Private Label Consumer Packaged Goods Growing Much Faster Than Branded Products," news release, September 18, 2003, http://www.acnielsen.com/news/american/us/2003/20030918.htm.

6. Simon Lloyd, "Retail: Bye-Bye Brands," *BRW Magazine*, April 14, 2005, http:// www.brw.com.au/freearticle.aspx?re1Id=13067.

7. "The Cheap Gourmet," *Forbes*, April 10, 2006, 76–77.

8. ACNielsen, "Consumer Attitudes Toward Private Label: A 38-Country Online Consumer Opinion Survey," http://www2.acnielsen.com/press/documents/ACNielsen_PrivateLabel_GlobalSummary.pdf (presentation, 2005).

9. "Retailers Push Private Labels," Beverage Industry, http://www.bevindustry.com/content,php?s=BI/2004/06&p=6.

10. Carol Matlack and Rachael Tiplady, "The Big Brands Go Begging," *BusinessWeek*, March 21, 2005, 18–19.

11. "Measuring Brand Premium," *Textile Consumer*, vol. 31, Winter 2003, http://www.cottoninc.com/TextileConsumer/TextileConsumer Volume31/1203TC.pdf.

12. Robert Spector, "Category Killers—Private Labels," http://www .800ceoread.com/excerpts/archives/000841.html.

13. "Make It Your Own," *The Economist*, March 4, 1995, 8.

14. Reported in Jean-Noel Kapferer, *The New Strategic Brand Management* (London: Kogan Page, 2004), 137.

15. Shelly Branch, "Going Private (Label)—Store Brands Go Way Upscale as Designer Items Lose Cachet; $675 for Macy's Own Sheet," *Wall Street Journal*, June 12, 2003.

16. Robert Berner, "Race You to the Top of the Market," *BusinessWeek*, December 8, 2003, 98.

17. Mathew Boyle, "Brand Killers: Store Brands Aren't for Losers Anymore," *Fortune*, August 11, 2003.

18. To enhance readability, all amounts in this book have been converted into dollars, using the exchange rate of 1.8 dollars to a British pound and 1.2 dollars to a euro.

19. Kapferer, *The New Strategic Brand Management*, chapter 6.

20. Kerry Capell, "Ikea: How the Swedish Retailer Became a Global Cult Brand," *BusinessWeek*, November 14, 2005, 44–54.

21. Personal communication to the authors, August 23, 2005.

22. ACNielsen, "Consumer Attitudes Toward Private Label."

23. "Retail Reshaped," Ketchum, http://www.ketchum.com/ DisplayWebPage/0,1003,2802,00.html.

24. "By George," *The Economist*, September 25, 2004, 39.

25. Stuart Elliot, "Breaching the Barriers Between Name Brands and Private Labels," *New York Times*, October 20, 2004.

26. Based on Jan-Benedict E. M. Steenkamp et al., *Fighting Private Label: Growth Drivers, Brand Defense Strategies, and Market Opportunities* (London: Business Insights, 2005).

27. Thomas Bachl, "Big Splurge or Piggy Bank: Where Are the Markets Heading For?" (presentation given at the annual GfK Kronberg meeting, Kronberg, Germany, January 27, 2004).

28. Google search, April 17, 2006.

29. Josh Sims, "A Style of Their Own," *Financial Times*, August 9, 2003.

30. Lorrie Grant, "Wal-Mart Sets Sight on Target While Keeping Core Customers," *USA Today*, August 5, 2005.

31. Kusum L. Ailawadi, Scott A. Neslin, and Karen Gedenk, "Pursuing the Value-Conscious Consumer: Store Brands Versus National Brand Promotions," *Journal of Marketing* 65 (January 2001): 71–89; Scott Burton, Donald R. Lichtenstein, Richard G. Netemeyer, and Judith A. Garretson, "A Scale for Measuring Attitude Toward Private Label Products and an Examination of Its Psychological and Behavioral Correlates," *Journal of the Academy of Marketing Science* 26 (1998): 293–306; Alan Dick, Arun K. Jain, and Paul S. Richardson, "Correlates of Brand Proneness: Some Empirical Observations," *Journal of Product & Brand Management* 4 (1995): 15–22; Judith A. Garretson, Dan Fisher, and Scott Burton, "Antecedents of Private Label Attitude and National Brand Promotion Attitude: Similarities and Differences," *Journal of Retailing* 78 (2002): 91–99; and Paul S. Richardson, Arun K. Jain, and Alan Dick, "Household Store Brand Proneness: A Framework," *Journal of Retailing* 72 (1996): 159–185.

32. John Quelch and David Harding, "Brands Versus Private Labels: Fighting to Win," *Harvard Business Review*, January–February 1996, 99–109.

33. "Make It Your Own."

34. Cited in GfK, "Markets, Discounters, Private Labels: The German Marketplace" (presentation given at the annual GfK Kronberg meeting, Kronberg, Germany, March 27, 2003).

35. Lien Lamey, Barbara Deleersnyder, Marnik G. Dekimpe, and Jan-Benedict E. M. Steenkamp, "How Business Cycles Contribute to Private Label Success: Evidence from the U.S. and Europe," *Journal of Marketing* 71 (January 2007). The four countries span a wide range of private label settings. While the U.K. is generally regarded as the most sophisticated private label market, the German market is dominated by "no frills" private labels, with the United States and Belgium in between.

36. "Who's Wearing the Trousers?" *The Economist*, September 6, 2001.

37. Debbie Howell, "Today's Consumers More Open to Try New Brands," *DSN Retailing Today*, October 25, 2004.

38. Based on Steenkamp et al., *Fighting Private Label*.

39. ACNielsen, "Consumer Attitudes Toward Private Label."

40. Lucy Brady, Aaron Brown, and Barbara Hulit, "Private Label: Threat to Manufacturers, Opportunity for Retailers," Boston Consulting Group Publications 2003 (available at http://www.bcg.com/publications/files/PrivLabel.pdf). http://www.bcg.com/publications/publication_view.jsp?pubID=885&language=English.

41. "Towards Retail Private Label Success," Coriolis Research, February 2002, http://www.coriolisresearch.com/pdfs/coriolis_towards_private_label_success.pdf.

42. We used a statistical technique called regression analysis to relate aggregate country private label shares to three sets of country drivers—namely, culture (power distance, uncertainty avoidance), socioeconomics (country competitiveness, socioeconomic modernity), and retail environment (concentration, number of international retailers, presence of hard discounters)—as well as the number of years private labels are present in the country. Our model explained a high 77% of the variance in country private label shares.

43. Stephen J. Hoch, "How Should National Brands Think About Private Labels?" *Sloan Management Review* 37 (Winter 1996): 89–102; and Jan-Benedict E. M. Steenkamp and Marnik G. Dekimpe, "The Increasing Power of Store Brands: Building Loyalty and Market Share," *Long Range Planning* 6 (1997): 917–930.

44. "In Search of the Ideal Employer," *The Economist*, August 20, 2005, 45.

45. Queena Sook Kim, "Hot Wheels Chases Extreme Look," *Wall Street Journal*, June 8, 2004.

46. "Private Label Corners Real Juice Trend," Beveragedaily.com, http://www.beveragedaily.com/news/printNewsBis.asp?id=60950.

47. Constance L. Hays, "What's Behind the Procter Deal? Wal-Mart," *New York Times*, January 29, 2005.

48. Susan Chandler and John Schmeltzer, "Sandwiched, and in a Pickle," *Chicago Tribune*, February 7, 2006.

49. Shuba Srinivasan, Koen Pauwels, Dominique M. Hanssens, and Marnik G. Dekimpe, "Do Promotions Benefit Manufacturers, Retailers, or Both?" *Management Science* 50 (2004): 617–629; Shuba Srinivasan, Koen Pauwels, Dominique M. Hanssens, and Marnik G. Dekimpe, "Who Benefits from Price Promotions?" *Harvard Business Review*, September 2002, 22–23.

50. "Kraft Profit Is Hurt by Private Labels," *Wall Street Journal*, July 18, 2003; "Consumers Snub General Mills Price Rise," Bakery and Snacks.com, March 29, 2005, http://www.bakeryandsnacks.com/news/news-ng.asp?n=59033-consumers-snub-general; Boyle, "Brand Killers"; Lloyd, "Retail"; and Matlack and Tiplady, "The Big Brands Go Begging."

51. Helen Wellings, "Store Brand Takeover," Today Tonight on Seven, April 13, 2005, http://seven.com.au/todaytonight/story/?id=19990.

Chapter 2

1. Carol Matlack and Rachael Tiplady, "The Big Brands Go Begging," *BusinessWeek*, March 21, 2005, 18–19.

2. Thomas Stockwell, "Resellers Private Label for Differentiation," http://www.os-od.com/stories/print.php?Story_ID=171.

3. Constance L. Hays, "More Gloom on the Island of Lost Toy Makers," *New York Times*, February 23, 2005.

4. Molly Prior, "Offering Unrivaled Convenience to Every Customer, Every Time," *Drug Store News*, March 22, 2004.

5. The Zara story is extracted from Nirmalya Kumar and Sophie Linguri, "Zara: Responsive, High Speed, Affordable Fashion," July 2005, available from European Case Clearing House (http://www.ecch.cranfield .ac.uk).

Chapter 3

1. Robin Rusch, "Private Labels: Does Branding Matter?" brandchannel.com, http://www.brandchannel.com/features_effect.asp?pf _id=94.

2. Lisa B. Fasig, "Kroger Muscles Up Store Brands," *Cincinnati Business Courier*, January 23, 2006.

3. Laurie Sullivan, "Retailers Ply Their Own Brands," *Information Week*, April 18, 2005, http://www.informationweek.com/shared/ printableArticleSrc.jhtml?articleID=160901292.

4. Rusch, "Private Labels."

5. Ibid.

6. Ibid.

7. Woolworths annual report, 2005.

8. David Dunne and Chakravarthi Narasimhan, "The New Appeal of Private Labels," *Harvard Business Review*, May–June 1999, 41–52.

9. Mathew Boyle, "Brand Killers: Store Brands Aren't for Losers Anymore," *Fortune*, August 11, 2003.

10. Ibid.

11. Dunne and Narasimhan, "The New Appeal of Private Labels."

12. Ibid.

13. ACNielsen, "Europe, US Still Largest Private Label Markets, But Other Regions Seeing Huge Growth Fueled by Retailer Expansion," news release, September 16, 2003.

14. L. Hamson, "Mark's Quality Is Its Key Advantage," *Grocer*, November 6, 2004, 28–29.

15. Mike Duff, "Private Label Hits Its Stride," *DSN Retailing Today*, October 25, 2004.

16. Rusch, "Private Labels."

17. Shelly Branch, "Going Private (Label)—Store Brands Go Way

Upscale as Designer Items Lose Cachet; $675 for Macy's Own Sheet," *Wall Street Journal*, June 12, 2003.

18. John J. Pierce, Sean Ryan, and Peter Berlinski, "Premium Private Label Stars in All Channels of Trade, Large and Small Retailers," *Private Label Magazine*, September–October 2002, http://www.privatelabelmag .com/pdf/september _2002/cover.cfm.

19. Ibid.

20. Elaine Walker, "Private Brands Boost Department Store Sales," *Miami Herald*, May 8, 2005, http://www.miami.com/mld/miamiherald/ 11586218.htm?template=contentModules.

21. Lucy Brady, Aaron Brown, and Barbara Hulit, "Private Label: Threat to Manufacturers, Opportunity for Retailers," Boston Consulting Group Publications, 2003 (available at http://www.bcg.com/publications/ files/PrivLabel.pdf).

22. Terilyn A. Henderson and Elizabeth A. Mihas, "Building Retail Brands," *McKinsey Quarterly*, 2000, 3.

23. Sullivan, "Retailers Ply Their Own Brands."

24. Thomas Lee, "Supervalu's Carlita Brand Says 'Hola!' to Hispanic Market," *Star Tribune*, May 6, 2005.

25. Brady, Brown, and Hulit, "Private Label."

26. Jan-Willem Grievink, "Retailers and Their Private Label Policy" (presentation given at the 4th AIM Workshop, June 29, 2004).

Chapter 4

1. Karsten Knothe and Anna Wynnyczuk, "PL Outshines Brands in Category," *Private Label Magazine*, Summer 2005, http://www .privatelabelmag.com/pdf/pli_summer2005/print/6.cfm.

2. See the Aldi U.K. Web site, "What the Papers Say," http://www .aldi-stores.co.uk.

3. "Aldi: The Next Wal-Mart," *BusinessWeek*, April 26, 2004, 20–23.

4. For what is probably the best description available of Aldi, see Dieter Brandes, *Bare Essentials: The Aldi Way to Retail Success* (London: Cyan Campus Books, 2004).

5. John Gapper, "Brands Get the Worst of a Hard Bargain," *Financial Times*, March 17, 2005.

6. Ann Zimmerman, "The Almighty Dollar Store," March 2005, http://www.wsjclassroomedition.com/archive/05mar/econ_dollarstore.htm.

7. Janet Adamy, "Bare Essentials," *Wall Street Journal*, August 30, 2005.

8. Ibid.

9. The H&M story is extracted from Nirmalya Kumar and Sophie Linguri, "Zara: Responsive, High Speed, Affordable Fashion," July 2005, available from European Case Clearing House (http://www.ecch.cranfield .ac.uk).

10. Lisa Margonelli, "How Ikea Designs Its Sexy Price Tags," Business 2.0, October 1, 2002, http://www.business2.com/b2/web/articles/ 0,17863,515048,00.html.

11. The IKEA example is from Nirmalya Kumar, *Marketing as Strategy: Understanding the CEO's Agenda for Driving Growth and Innovation* (Boston: Harvard Business School Press, 2004), chapter 7.

Chapter 5

1. Jean-Noel Kapferer, *The New Strategic Brand Management* (London: Kogan Page, 2004).

2. Jean-Claude Alpi, "Intermarché Adopts 3-Tier PL Strategy," *Private Label International*, Fall 2004, http://www.privatelabelmag.com/pdf/ pli_fall2004/print/4.cfm.

3. "Be Good to Yourself," Food Forum, http://www.foodforum.org.uk.

4. "Wal-Mart Wins Retailer of the Year Award," *Private Label Magazine*, June–July 2004.

5. Lucy Brady, Aaron Brown, and Barbara Hulit, "Private Label: Threat to Manufacturers, Opportunity for Retailers," Boston Consulting Group Publications, 2003 (available at: http://www.bcg.com/publications/ files/PrivLabel.pdf).

6. Ibid.

7. Sophie Buckley, "The Brand Is Dead; Long Live the Brand," *Financial Times*, September 25, 2005.

8. E. Rigby, "Tesco and Asda Cut Prices Again," *Financial Times*, April 4, 2005.

9. Louise Lee, "Thinking Small at the Mall," *BusinessWeek*, May 26, 2003, 94.

10. John Stanley, "Brands Versus Private Labels," About.com, http:// retailindustry.about.com/library/uc/02/uc_stanley2.htm.

Chapter 6

1. Google search, April 15, 2006.

2. ACNielsen, *The Power of Private Label 2005* (ACNielsen Global Services, 2005). Classification into high versus low based on median split.

3. Valarie A. Zeithaml, "Consumer Perceptions of Price, Quality, and

Value: A Means-End Model and Synthesis of Evidence," *Journal of Marketing* 52 (July 1988): 2–22.

4. Susan Fournier, "Consumers and Their Brands: Developing Relationship Theory in Consumer Research," *Journal of Consumer Research* 24 (March 1998): 343–373.

5. Jan-Benedict E. M. Steenkamp and Marnik G. Dekimpe, "The Increasing Power of Store Brands: Building Loyalty and Market Share," *Long Range Planning* 6 (1997): 917–930.

6. Jan-Benedict E. M. Steenkamp, *Product Quality* (Assen, Netherlands: Van Gorcum, 1989).

7. Data on the perceived quality gap between manufacturer and store brands in a category was collected among a representative sample of 4,300 U.S. consumers, using the following items: "In the category *(X)*, the quality of brands is very high" and "In the category *(X)*, the quality of shops' own labels is very high." Items were pretested and measured on 5-point disagree–agree scales. The score on the second item was subtracted from the score of the first item, and the resulting difference score was averaged across respondents within a category to arrive at the market's perception of the quality gap between manufacturer and store brands. Although, *theoretically*, the perceived quality gap can range from –4 to +4, this is unlikely to occur in the real world, because private labels and manufacturer brands are not that dissimilar in perceived quality. Practically, given that for many consumers perceived quality is much more important than price, a perceived quality gap of 0.5 or higher is managerially meaningful. In table 6-1, "store brand better" refers to a perceived quality gap less than –0.1; "quality equivalent" is a gap between –0.1 and 0.1; "small quality gap" is between 0.11 and 0.49; "large quality gap" is between 0.5 and 1; and "very large quality gap" refers to a perceived quality gap exceeding 1.

8. See Patrick Barwise and Sean Meehan, *Simply Better: Winning and Keeping Customers by Delivering What Matters Most* (Boston: Harvard Business School Press, 2004).

9. Steenkamp, *Product Quality*.

10. See note 7 for the data collection procedure. Items were presented in French (after back translation), and the total sample was 3,929 consumers.

11. Eidan Apelbaum, Eitan Gerstner, and Prasad A. Naik, "Do Quality Improvements Enable Store Brands to Charge Price Premiums?" (working paper, University of California at Davis, 2002); and Raj Sethuraman, *What Makes Consumers Pay More for National Brands Than for Store Brands: Image or Quality?* (Cambridge, MA: Marketing Science Institute, 2000), Report 00-110.

12. Fournier, "Consumers and Their Brands."

13. Jennifer L. Aaker, "Dimensions of Brand Personality," *Journal of Marketing Research* 34 (August 1997): 347–356.

14. We measured image utility with three items: "You can tell a lot about a person from the brand in category *(X)* he or she buys"; "The brand in the category *(X)* a person buys, says something about who they are"; and "The brand in the category *(X)* I buy reflects the sort of person I am."

15. Fournier, "Consumers and Their Brands."

16. Sethuraman, *What Makes Consumers Pay More for National Brands?*

17. Fiona S. Morton and Florian Zettelmeyer, "The Strategic Positioning of Store Brands in Retailer-Manufacturer Bargaining" (working paper 7712, National Bureau of Economic Research, Cambridge, MA, 2000).

18. Sergio Meza and K. Sudhir, "The Role of Strategic Pricing by Retailers in the Success of Store Brands" (working paper, New York University, 2003).

19. Package similarity in a category was based on consumer perceptions, using the item "In the category *(X)*, shops' own labels and brands look very similar."

20. Susan Zimmerman, "A Rosy Future," *Progressive Grocer*, November 1998, 45–52.

21. Meza and Sudhir, "The Role of Strategic Pricing by Retailers in the Success of Store Brands."

22. Stephen J. Hoch and Leonard M. Lodish, "Store Brands and Category Management" (working paper, Wharton School, Philadelphia, PA, 1998).

23. Hoch and Lodish, "Store Brands and Category Management"; and Sethuraman, *What Makes Consumers Pay More for National Brands?*

24. To maintain confidentiality, the results are expressed relative to the price gap of 15% in table 6-2.

Chapter 7

1. Kusum L. Ailawadi and Bari A. Harlam, "An Empirical Analysis of the Determinants of Retail Margins: The Role of Store Brand Share," *Journal of Marketing* (January 2004): 147–165.

2. Kusum L. Ailawadi, "The Retail Power-Performance Conundrum: What Have We Learned?" *Journal of Retailing* (2001): 299–318.

3. A&P annual report, 2001.

4. Marcel Corstjens and Rajiv Lal, "Building Store Loyalty Through Store Brands," *Journal of Marketing Research* (August 2000): 281–291.

5. Ibid.

6. Francois Glemet et al., "How Profitable Are Own Brand Products?" *McKinsey Quarterly* 4, 1995, 173–175.

7. Lucy Brady, Aaron Brown, and Barbara Hulit, "Private Label: Threat to Manufacturers, Opportunity for Retailers" Boston Consulting Group, 2003) (available at: http://www.bcg.com/publications/files/PrivLabel.pdf)

8. The authors thank Professor Kusum Ailawadi of the Tuck School of Business at Dartmouth College for providing data on gross margins.

9. For example, Brady, Brown, and Hulit, "Private Label: Threat to Manufacturers, Opportunity for Retailers," report velocity data for two products (diapers and cereals). In their data, the velocity of the leading brand is about 50% higher than the velocity of the private label.

10. Chakravarti Narasimhan and Ronald T. Wilcox, "Private Labels and the Channel Relationship: A Cross-Category Analysis," *Journal of Business* 4 (1996): 573–600.

11. This issue has been studied in several analytical papers, including David E. Mills, "Why Retailers Sell Private Labels," *Journal of Economics and Management Strategy* (Fall 1995): 509–528; Narasimhan and Wilcox, "Private Labels and the Channel Relationship"; Fiona S. Morton and Florian Zettelmeyer, "The Strategic Positioning of Store Brands in Retailer-Manufacturer Bargaining" (working paper 7712, National Bureau of Economic Research, Cambridge, MA, 2000); Jorge Tarzijan, "Strategic Effects of Private Labels and Horizontal Integration," *International Review of Retail, Distribution, and Consumer Research* (July 2004): 321–335.

12. Morton and Zettelmeyer, "The Strategic Positioning of Store Brands in Retailer-Manufacturer Bargaining."

13. Pradeep K. Chintagunta, Andre Bonfrer, and Inseong Song, "Investigating the Effects of Store Brand Introduction on Retailing Demand and Pricing Behavior," *Management Science* (October 2002).

14. Ailawadi and Harlam, "An Empirical Analysis of the Determinants of Retail Margins."

15. Morton and Zettelmeyer, "The Strategic Positioning of Store Brands in Retailer-Manufacturer Bargaining."

16. Jan-Benedict E. M. Steenkamp and Marnik G. Dekimpe, "The Increasing Power of Store Brands: Building Loyalty and Market Share," *Long Range Planning* 6 (1997): 917–930.

17. Narasimhan and Wilcox, "Private Labels and the Channel Relationship," have developed an analytical model and provide empirical evidence that indeed manufacturers may not find it worthwhile to lower the wholesale price of their brands if the store brand share in their category is very high.

18. Corstjens and Lal, "Building Store Loyalty Through Store Brands."

19. Kusum L. Ailawadi, Scott A. Neslin, and Karen Gedenk, "Pursuing the Value-Conscious Consumer: Store Brands Versus National Brand Promotions," *Journal of Marketing* (January 2001): 71–89.

20. Jan-Benedict E. M. Steenkamp et al., *Fighting Private Label: Growth Drivers, Brand Defense Strategies, and Market Opportunities* (London: Business Insights, 2005).

21. Roland T. Rust, Valarie A. Zeithaml, and Katherine N. Lemon, *Driving Customer Equity* (New York: Free Press, 2000).

22. Ailawadi and Harlam, "An Empirical Analysis of the Determinants of Retail Margins." The authors thank Professor Ailawadi for providing additional data not reported in their paper to develop table 7-2.

Part II

1. Lucy Brady, Aaron Brown, and Barbara Hulit, "Private Label: Threat to Manufacturers, Opportunity for Retailers," Boston Consulting Group Publications, 2003 (available at: http://www.bcg.com/publications/files/PrivLabel.pdf).

Chapter 8

1. "Consumer Reports' Tests Find Quality of Store Brands' Products on Par with National Name Brands," *Kansas City infoZine*, August 2, 2005, http://www.infozine.com/news/stories/op/storiesView/sid/9281; and Andrew Wileman and Michael Jary, *Retail Power Plays* (London: McMillan Business, 1997).

2. John A. Quelch and David Harding, "Brands Versus Private Labels: Fighting to Win," *Harvard Business Review*, January–February 1996, 99–109.

3. Margaret Littman, "House Brands Hit Home: Growing Private Label Market," *Prepared Foods*, April 1992, http://www.findarticles.com/p/articles/mi_m3289/is_n5_v161/ai_12471761.

4. Quelch and Harding, "Brands Versus Private Labels."

5. Wileman and Jary, *Retail Power Plays*.

6. "Campina Profits from Added-Value, But Private Label Slips," Dairy Reporter.com, March 14, 2005, http://www.dairyreporter.com/news/ng.asp?id=58715.

7. Ibid.

8. Information for the United Biscuits example is from Wileman and Jary, *Retail Power Plays*; United Biscuits, http://www.unitedbiscuits.co.uk/80256C1A0047922E/vWeb/pcCHAS5DADU9; and "UB to Cut Biscuit

Capacity," Confectionary News.com, February 6, 2003, http://www
.confectionerynews.com/news/ng.asp?id=14206-ub-to-cut.

9. Michael V. Marn, Eric V. Roegner, and Craig C. Zawada, "The
Power of Pricing," *McKinsey Quarterly*, 2003, 27–36.

10. Stephen McMahon, "Smaller Producers Feel the Heat," *The Age*,
November 30, 2005, http://theage.com.au/news/business/smaller-producers
-feel-the-heat/2005/11/29/1133026467261.html.

11. Information collected in field interviews at the Private Label Manufacturers Association (PLMA) conference, Amsterdam, Netherlands, May
27–29, 2002.

12. Presentation given by PLMA at the annual PLMA trade fair,
"World of Private Label," Amsterdam, Netherlands, May 24–25, 2005;
and see http://www.expovisie.nl/site2/index.php?url=http://www.expovisie
.nl/site2/nieuws.php?content_id=3141&categoryid=1.

13. Information for the Cott example obtained from the 2004 and 2005
Annual Reports of Cott Corporation (available at http://www.cott.com/).

14. Cott Corporation, "Cott Corporation Expects 2005 Earnings to
Be Substantially Below Previously Announced Guidance," news release,
September 21, 2005, http://www.corporate-ir.net/ireye/ir_site.zhtml?ticker
=COT&script=410&layout=-6&item_id=759222.

15. Information for this example based on McBride's annual report,
Working Together, 2005, available at http://www.mcbride.co.uk, and field
interviews at the Private Label Manufacturers Association conference,
Amsterdam, Netherlands, May 27–29, 2002.

16. McBride's annual report, *Working Together*, 2005, available at
http://www.mcbride.co.uk, 20.

Chapter 9

1. Nirmalya Kumar, "Create Trust, Not Fear in Manufacturer-
Retailer Relationships," *Harvard Business Review*, November–December
1996, 96–106.

2. Nirmalya Kumar, *Marketing as Strategy: Understanding the
CEO's Agenda for Driving Growth and Innovation* (Boston: Harvard Business School Press, 2004).

3. Janet Adamy, "Bare Essentials," *Wall Street Journal*, August 30,
2005.

4. John Gapper, "Brands Get the Worst of a Hard Bargain," *Financial Times*, March 17, 2005.

5. Ibid.

6. Alex Benady, "Nestlé's New Flavour of Strategy," *Financial Times*,
February 22, 2005.

7. Lisa B. Fasig, "Federated Readying Millions for May Stores Overhaul," *Business First of Columbus*, February 13, 2006.

8. "H&M: Bringing Haute to the Hoi Polloi," *BusinessWeek Online*, May 30, 2005, http://www.businessweek.com/magazine/content/05_22/b3935090_mz054.htm.

9. Ibid.

10. M+M Planet Retail, "Daily News by Planet Retail," August 29, 2005.

11. Thomas Bachl, "Big Splurge or Piggy Bank: Where Are the Markets Heading For?" (presentation given at the annual GfK Kronberg meeting, Kronberg, Germany, January 27, 2004).

12. Barbara Deleersnyder, Marnik G. Dekimpe, Jan-Benedict E. M. Steenkamp, and Oliver Koll, "Win-Win Strategies at Discount Stores" (working paper, Marketing Science Institute, Cambridge, MA, 2006).

13. Carol Matlack and Rachael Tiplady, "The Big Brands Go Begging," *BusinessWeek*, March 21, 2005, 18–19.

14. Adamy, "Bare Essentials."

Chapter 10

1. Charles Fishman, "The Wal-Mart You Don't Know," *Fast Company*, December 2003, 68.

2. Various parts of this chapter draw on several projects with companies, conducted by the authors. See Katrijn Gielens and Jan-Benedict E. M. Steenkamp, "What Drives New Product Success? An Investigation Across Products and Countries" (working paper, Marketing Science Institute, Cambridge, MA, 2004); Jan-Benedict E. M. Steenkamp and Steven M. Burgess, "Optimum Stimulation Level and Exploratory Consumer Behavior in an Emerging Market," *International Journal of Research in Marketing* 19 (June 2002): 131–150; Jan-Benedict E. M. Steenkamp and Katrijn Gielens, "Consumer and Market Drivers of the Trial Probability of New Consumer Packaged Goods," *Journal of Consumer Research* 29 (December 2003): 368–384; and Jan-Benedict E. M. Steenkamp, Frenkel ter Hofstede, and Michel Wedel, "A Cross-National Investigation into the Individual and National Cultural Antecedents of Consumer Innovativeness," *Journal of Marketing* 63 (April 1999): 55–69.

3. Jeremy Grant, "An Own-Label Lesson for Bean-Counters," *Financial Times*, March 11, 2005.

4. Authors' calculations are based on Campbell Soup's 2005 Annual Report (available at http://www.campbellsoupcompany.com/index.asp?cpovisq=).

5. John D. Cook and Pantelis A. Georgiadis, "Packaged Goods: It's Time to Focus on Product Development," *McKinsey Quarterly* 2, 1997, 91–99.

6. Shlomo Kalish, Vijay Mahajan, and Eitan Muller, "Waterfall and Sprinkler New-Product Strategies in Competitive Global Markets," *International Journal of Research in Marketing* 12 (June 1995): 105–119.

7. Eric J. Swetsky, "The Dangers of Me-Tooism," FindLaw, http://library.findlaw.com/1997/Nov/1/131329.html.

8. Ibid.

9. "Albert Heijn Gives In," *Shield Mark Nieuwsbrief*, July 2005, 2.

10. Simon Pitman, "Procter & Gamble Files Lawsuit over Mouth Rinse," Cosmeticsdesign.com, February 17, 2006, http://www.cosmetics design.com/news/ng.asp?n=65915-p-g-vi-jon-oral-care-mouth-rinse -packaging.

11. Jean-Noel Kapferer, "Stealing Brand Equity: Measuring Perceptual Confusion Between National Brands and 'Copycat' Own-Label Products," *Marketing and Research Today*, May 1995, 96–103; Jean-Noel Kapferer, "Brand Confusion: Empirical Study of a Legal Concept," *Psychology & Marketing*, September 1995, 551–568.

12. Jeremy Grant, "Kraft Cooks Up Strategic Innovations," *Financial Times*, May 17, 2005, 21.

13. For more details, see Nirmalya Kumar, *Marketing as Strategy: Understanding the CEO's Agenda for Driving Growth and Innovation* (Boston: Harvard Business School Press, 2004), chapter 5.

14. For the concept of branded brands, see Trendwatching.com, http://www.trendwatching.com, a Web site on global consumer trends, ideas, and insights.

Chapter 11

1. Nirmalya Kumar, "Kill a Brand, Keep a Customer," *Harvard Business Review*, December 2003, 86–95.

2. Jeremy Grant, "Kraft Cooks Up Strategic Innovations," *Financial Times*, May 17, 2005.

3. Michael Arndt, "Why Kraft Is on a Crash Diet," *BusinessWeek*, November 29, 2004, 46.

4. Nirmalya Kumar, *Marketing as Strategy: Understanding the CEO's Agenda for Driving Growth and Innovation* (Boston: Harvard Business School Press, 2004).

5. Robert Berner, "There Goes the Rainbow Nut Crunch," *BusinessWeek*, July 19, 2004, 38.

6. Ibid.

7. "The Rise of the Superbrands," *The Economist*, February 5, 2005, 67–69.

8. Ibid.

9. Alex Benady, "Nestlé's New Flavour of Strategy," *Financial Times*, February 22, 2005.

10. Berner, "There Goes the Rainbow Nut Crunch."

Chapter 12

1. Jean-Philippe Deschamps and P. Ranganath Nayak, *Product Juggernauts: How Companies Mobilize to Generate a Stream of Market Winners* (Boston: Harvard Business School Press, 1995).

2. Michael V. Marn, Eric V. Roegner, and Craig C. Zawada, "The Power of Pricing," *McKinsey Quarterly*, 2003, 27–36.

3. Chris Hoyt, "Kraft's Private-Label Lesson," *Reveries Magazine*, February 2004, http://www.reveries.com/reverb/essays/outthere/hoyt20.html.

4. Adam Jones, "No Peace for the Market Behemoths as Unbranded Onslaught Continues," *Financial Times*, September 21, 2004.

5. "The Rise of the Superbrands," *The Economist*, February 5, 2005, 67–69.

6. "Fed Watches to See If Wal-Mart Accepts Higher Priced Huggies," Bloomberg.com, June 20, 2005.

7. Marn, Roegner, and Zawada, "The Power of Pricing."

8. Harald van Heerde, Sachin Gupta, and Dick R. Wittink, "Is 75% of the Sales Promotion Bump Due to Brand Switching? No, Only 33% Is," *Journal of Marketing Research* (November 2003): 481–491.

9. Data obtained from "Is There a Way Back for the Brand?" (presentation given at the annual GfK Kronberg meeting, Kronberg, Germany, March 27, 2003).

10. Raj Sethuraman, V. Srinivasan, and Doyle Kim, "Asymmetric and Neighborhood Cross-Price Effects: Some Empirical Generalizations," *Marketing Science* 18 (Winter 1999): 23–41; and Raj Sethuraman and V. Srinivasan, "The Asymmetric Share Effect: An Empirical Generalization on Cross-Price Effects," *Journal of Marketing Research* 39 (August 2002): 379–386.

11. "Battle of the Brands," *Consumer Reports*, August 2005, 12–15.

12. Eidan Apelbaum, Eitan Gerstner, and Prasad A. Naik, "The Effects of Expert Quality Evaluations Versus Brand Name on Price Premiums," *Journal of Product and Brand Management* 2–3 (2003): 154–165.

13. "Procter & Gamble's New, Improved European Strategy: Cut Prices," Bloomberg.com, April 6, 2005.

14. Andrew Jack, "GSK Puts Its Faith in Drinks and Toothpaste," *Financial Times*, September 17, 2005.

15. Jean-Noel Kapferer, *The New Strategic Brand Management* (London: Kogan-Page, 2004).

16. Sian Harrington, "Will Rising In-Store Activity Leave Traditional Advertising on the Shelf?" *Financial Times*, August 3, 2004.

17. Jane Bainbridge, "Sector Insight: Bread—Upper Crust," *Design Bulletin*, April 27, 2005.

18. "Procter & Gamble's New, Improved European Strategy."

19. Hoyt, "Kraft's Private-Label Lesson."

20. Ibid.

21. Ibid.

22. Jenny Wiggins, "Heinz to Sell Weak European Businesses," *Financial Times*, May 27, 2005.

23. Information taken from *BusinessWeek*'s article "The 100 Top Brands," published in *BusinessWeek*, August 6, 2001, 60–64; *BusinessWeek*, August 4, 2003, 72–78; *BusinessWeek*, August 2, 2004, 68–71; *BusinessWeek*, August 1, 2005, 90–94; *BusinessWeek*, August 7, 2006, 60–66.

Chapter 13

1. "The Rise of the Superbrands," *The Economist*, February 5, 2005, 67–69.

2. Lucy Brady, Aaron Brown, and Barbara Hulit, "Private Label: Threat to Manufacturers, Opportunity for Retailers," Boston Consulting Group Publications, 2003 (available at http://www.bcg.com/publications/files/PrivLabel.pdf).

3. Constance L. Hays, "More Gloom on the Island of Lost Toy Makers," *New York Times*, February 23, 2005.

4. Alan Mitchell, "Own Label Versus Brands War Moves to New Terrain," *Marketing Week*, October 15, 1998, 34–35.

5. Andrew Ward, "Coke Gets Real: The World's Most Valuable Brand Wakes Up to a Waning Thirst for Cola," *Financial Times*, September 22, 2005.

6. Ali Ashurov, "Focus on the Core," *Harbus Online*, News, April 22, 2003, http://www.harbus.org/media/storage/paper343/news/2003/04/22/News/Focus.On.The.Core-423008.shtml?norewrite200608071129 &sourcedomain=www.harbus.org.

7. Neil Buckley, "The Calm Reinventor," *Financial Times*, January 29, 2005.

8. Richard Milne, "Conti's Formula for Racing Ahead," *Financial Times*, March 30, 2005.

9. Table 13-1 was computed using the *BusinessWeek* surveys of the top 100 brands in 2001, 2002, 2003, and 2005.

10. Neil Buckley, "Procter's Gamble on Outside Ideas Has Paid Off," *Financial Times*, January 14, 2005.

11. Ibid.

12. Buckley, "The Calm Reinventor."

13. Ward, "Coke Gets Real."

14. See Grocery Brand Preference Study 2005, Geronimo, http://www .geronimo.co.uk/brands/.

15. "Procter & Gamble's New, Improved European Strategy: Cut Prices," Bloomberg.com, April 6, 2005.

16. Mitchell, "Own Label Versus Brands War Moves to New Terrain."

17. Laurie Sullivan, "Retailers Ply Their Own Brands," *Information Week*, April 18, 2005, http://www.informationweek.com/shared/ printableArticleSrc.jhtml?articleID=160901292.

18. Sophie Buckley, "The Brand Is Dead; Long Live the Brand," *Financial Times*, September 25, 2005.

INDEX

ABOUT THE AUTHORS

Nirmalya Kumar is Professor of Marketing, Faculty Director for Executive Education, Director of the Centre for Marketing, and Codirector of the Aditya Birla India Centre at the London Business School.

Kumar received his PhD in marketing from Northwestern University and has taught at Columbia University, Harvard Business School, IMD (Switzerland), and Northwestern University.

Kumar has been coach and consultant to more than fifty Fortune 500 companies in fifty different countries. He has served on the board of directors of ACC, Bata India, BP Ergo, Gujarat Ambuja Cements, and Zensar Technologies. He frequently appears in the press, including BBC, CNBC, CNN, and is a contributor to the *Financial Times*.

A prolific writer, he is the author of *Global Marketing* and *Marketing as Strategy: Understanding the CEO's Agenda for Driving Growth and Innovation* (translated into six languages). He is currently writing *Rare Commodity: Moving Business Markets Beyond Price to Value* and *Brand Turnarounds*. He has published four articles in the *Harvard Business Review*. More academic papers have appeared in *Academy of Management Journal, Journal of Marketing*, and the *Journal of Marketing Research*.

Winner of several teaching honors, he has written more than forty cases. These cases have won three *Business Week*/ECCH awards for adoption.

Jan-Benedict E. M. Steenkamp (BSc, MSc, and PhD summa cum laude, Wageningen University, the Netherlands) is one of the world's leading experts on global marketing, branding, and private labels. He is the C. Knox Massey Distinguished Professor of Marketing and Marketing Area Chair, University of North Carolina at Chapel Hill. He is also Executive Director of AiMark (www.aimark.org/), a global center studying key marketing strategy issues. AiMark involves leading U.S. and European researchers as well as two of the world's top five market research agencies, GfK and Taylor Nelson Sofres.

Steenkamp has written or edited five books and written more than a hundred scholarly articles for both management practice journals and academic journals. He is the highest ranked marketing scholar in the Global Top 100 most-cited scientists in economics and business, based on citations in the last decade.

The Royal Netherlands Academy of Sciences has awarded him the prestigious Hendrik Muller lifetime prize for "exceptional achievements in the area of the behavioral and social sciences." Individual articles on global marketing, branding, and marketing effectiveness have won numerous awards.

Steenkamp has chaired eight conferences for industry, and has contributed to more than a hundred conferences and executive seminars for marketing practitioners. He does executive teaching in the areas of global marketing, branding, private labels, innovation, and strategy. He has consulted with numerous companies on these topics, including Procter & Gamble, Kraft, Unilever, Reckitt Benckiser, Zurich Financial Services, KPMG, Sara Lee, Johnson & Johnson, and Campina.

Branded Mfct need to decide whether they want to focus on being marketers or manufacturers. That will help them decide whether or not a Dual strategy will support their strategic g